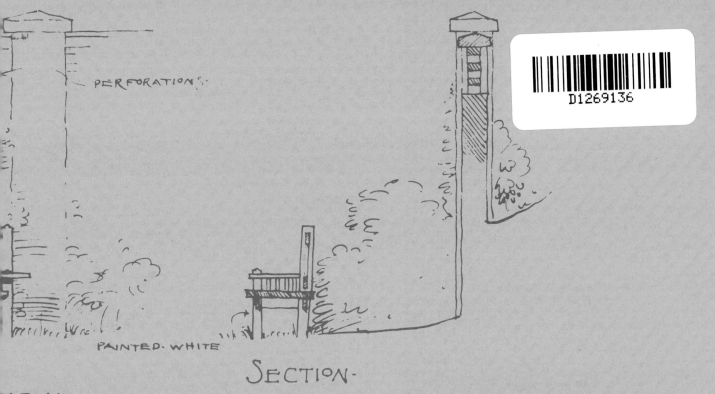

PERFORATION.

PAINTED· WHITE

·SECTION·

EEN·

NTAIN·COURT·

SKETCHES· of·
SPECIAL·FEATURES·
OF ·GARDENS·
Nº· 2988 ·8
NOV· 7· 1904·

THE
CHANGING
LANDSCAPE

Picture Editors
Carla Hirst Wiltenburg and Mary Alenstein

Published for the

BRIARCLIFF MANOR-SCARBOROUGH
HISTORICAL SOCIETY

by
PHOENIX PUBLISHING
West Kennebunk, Maine

The Hudson River looking north from Scarborough
Oil painting by David Patterson
Private collection

THE CHANGING LANDSCAPE

a history of Briarcliff Manor-Scarborough

Mary Cheever

P E R M I S S I O N S

Excerpts from *Maverick in Mauve: The Diary of a Romantic Age*, by Florence Adele Sloane with a commentary by Louis Auchincloss, and published by Doubleday & Company in 1983, which appear on pages 47, 48, 49, and 50, copyright 1963 by Louis Auchincloss and Shiela Burden Lawrence, are reprinted with the kind permission of DOUBLEDAY.

The excerpt from *The History of the New Croton Dam*, by Mary Josephine D'Alvia, which appears on page 114, printed by Caltone Litho, Inc., 1976, is reprinted with the kind permission of the author.

The excerpts from *Roughly Speaking, the Autobiography of Louise Randall Pierson*, which appear on pages 95, 96, and 97, are reproduced with the kind permission of Simon & Schuster, Inc.

The excerpts from *From Farm Boy to Financier*, by Frank A. Vanderlip, which appear on pages 93 and 111, are reproduced with the kind permission of Frank A. Vanderlip, Jr.

The excerpt from *The Incredible Detective*, by Gene Caesar, which appears on page 119 is reproduced with the kind permission of Elizabeth R. Colombo, Executor for the Estate of Gene Caesar.

The excerpt from *This Planted Vine*, by James Elliott Lindsley, which appears on page 22, is copyright ©1984 by the Episcopal Diocese of New York, and is reprinted with the kind permission of Harper & Row, Publishers, Inc.

The excerpt from *Our Crowd*, by Stephen Birmingham, which appears on pages 104 and 106 is copyright 1967 © by the author, and is reprinted with the kind permission of Harper & Row, Publishers, Inc.

The excerpt from *Edith Wharton*, by R. W. B. Lewis, which appears on page 88, is copyright 1975 © by Harper & Row, and is reprinted with the kind permission of Harper & Row, Publishers, Inc.

Library of Congress Cataloging-in-Publication Data

Cheever, Mary.
    The changing landscape : a history of Briarcliff Manor-Scarborough / by Mary Cheever; picture editors, Carla Hirst Wiltenburg and Mary Alenstein.
        p. cm.
    Includes bibliographical references and index.
    ISBN 0-914659-49-9 : $35.00
    1. Briarcliff Manor   (N.Y.)—History.   I. Briarcliff Manor-Scarborough Historical Society. II. Title.
F129.B48C48   1990
    974.7'277—dc20   90-45613
                                                       CIP

Printed in the United States of America

CONTENTS

PREFACE

WITH THE PASSING of each decade, it becomes more difficult to form an accurate assessment of events that help shape the life of a community. Just thirteen years ago, *A Village Between Two Rivers* was published to mark the 75th anniversary of Briarcliff Manor. In that short time, the landscape has gone through some remarkable changes.

The Historical Society would not have attempted to sponsor a new history of our village if that anniversary book were still available and could be reprinted. The plates disappeared when the publisher went out of business, and we were left with just two copies in the archives. Not a month went by without a request for the book, and it became obvious that we would have to do something about the situation.

Five years ago, Mary Cheever agreed to begin research for a new book, and the result of her countless working hours is a well-annotated, scholarly but highly readable history that we are certain will be a valuable research tool for future historians. Our founding fathers, mothers, brothers and sisters are brought to life on its pages (sometimes with comic results), illuminating the diverse backgrounds and many talents that give the village its unique character.

For the first time, Scarborough, which is not "just a state of mind," as some people call it, is defined and given its proper place in village history. In 1899 Walter Law attempted to incorporate the village under the name of Scarborough but failed because the area did not contain three hundred persons per square mile as required by state law. He solved the problem by building houses on Dalmeny Road and selling them to his employees (See Chapter 5). A favorable vote was held on September 12, 1902, and the village was officially incorporated as Briarcliff Manor.

The Historical Society is especially grateful to Mrs. Cheever for her dedication to the project and, also, to all the society members and friends whose varied contributions have helped to assure the publication of *The Changing Landscape*. We are confident that present and future residents will appreciate this history of their village now, and in the years to come.

Rosemary Bonnett Cook

Scarborough, New York
November 1, 1990

ACKNOWLEDGMENTS

FOR INFORMATION, anecdotes, pictures and other valuable material I am particularly indebted to: Myril Adler, Marie and Leonard Alpert, David Bogdanoff, Charles L. Brieant, Betsy Brown, Burnham Carter, Barrett Clark, Ruth Comfield of Faith Lutheran Brethren Church, Rosemary Bonnett Cook, Kay Courreges, Greta Cornell, Mary Douglas Dirks, Gerard Dorian, Alison Harden Dunscomb, Lisbe Elwyn, Marie Davis Evelyn, Margaret Pearson Finne, Carrie Wallach Garrison, Tom Glazer, Joan Borough Goldsborough, Audrey Graham, Shirley Hibbard, William C. Holden, Beatrice Hrubec, Carsten Johnson II, E.J. Kahn, Jr., Gerard LaCroix, Alice Low, Natalie Mackintosh, Kate Marden, Dan McBride, D. Williams McClurken, Ruth Oakley, David Patterson, Samuel Puner, Alexander Racolin, Ginger Reiman, Charlotte Ricks, Frances Rust, Jane Scheline, Nicholas A. Shoumatoff, Ruth Lichtenburg Simon, Marilyn Slater, Elizabeth Holden Smith, Sol Stein, Anthony Turiano, Frank Vanderlip, Jr., Eileen O'Connor Weber, Mary Laura Weigel, Carole Williams, and the late William Zuydhoek.

Thanks also to Harry Appel, Brooke Astor, Aline Benjamin, Lucy Blachman, Caroline Boute, George V. Comfort, Mayor Ed Dorsey, Peter Fazzolare, Murrie Marden Fitch, Alice and Stanley Goldstein, Allan Gowen, Michelle Grant, Jean Harper, Cheryl Klein, Patricia Knapp, Martin Low, Dutsa Maisel, Joseph P. McHenry, Charles Newman, Pamela O'Keefe, Martin Parker, Sidney Polivnik, Florence Radice, the late Dudley N. Schoales, Mrs. Dudley V. Schoales, Bill and Audrey Sharman, Tom and Pam Shearman, Edna Jane Ailes Sprague, Arthur P. Spear, Jr., Charlotte Tuckerman, Angelo Turco and William Wetzel.

Mary Cheever

Ossining, New York
June 15, 1990

Tiffany stained glass window in the Briarcliff Congregational Church

THE
CHANGING
LANDSCAPE

Public swimming pool, 1927

FOREWORD

Briarcliff in the hills of Westchester

"AN ALL YEAR HOME village . . . strictly residential . . . the conveniences of a city, the freedom and natural beauty of a charming country . . . people who are cultured, democratic and believers in progressive village government"—these phrases from a 1921 Briarcliff Realty booklet might have been written yesterday. There have been changes, chiefly the population increase from less than a thousand to well over seven thousand (in 1985). Neighboring farms no longer "supply poultry, milk, fresh butter and eggs," nor is "natural ice supplied from a spring-fed lake" (for home iceboxes). But the village is still 80 percent residential, and "acres of parklike building sites heretofore under control of large estates" is still appropriate. In 1985, Briarcliff Manor was commended by the Westchester Planning Federation for the adaptive reuse of estates, specifically Beechwood (formerly the Vanderlip estate), Rosecliff (formerly the Wilderness, estate of the Harden family), and F. B. Hall (formerly the O'Connor estate). Many of the fine houses pictured in the old Briarcliff Realty booklet still grace the village—Hillcrest, Mount Vernon, The Elms, the Richard Whitson house and others, as well as several west of Scarborough Ridge that are not mentioned in the booklet—Beechwood, Ashridge and Weskora, now renamed Holly Hill. The "Manor House" of Walter W. Law, founder of

Why Homeseekers Choose
BRIARCLIFF

All-Year Home Village, not a summer colony nor a typical New York suburb.

Educational Advantages, with the best of private and public schools, and live churches.

Healthful, with high elevation, good sanitary system, fine water and no mosquitoes. A modern hospital nearby, with an excellent staff of physicians.

All the Advantages of an independent community, with people who are cultured, democratic, and believers in progressive village government.

Modern Conveniences for home comfort. Gas, electricity, telephone, village water and sewage system. Good markets. Absolutely free from manufacturing interests.

Accessible to New York with transportation facilities on three railroads. Motor bus connections. Finest of motor roads. Riding school. Attractive walks and bridle paths. Appeals to the lover of outdoor sports. A favored centre of golf, tennis and country clubs. A section of great natural beauty and historic interests.

Reasonable Tax Rates. Nearby banking facilities. Good mail service with rural delivery.

Free from Inflated Values. Briarcliff is not an experimental development. The future character of the community is well established.

Home of Briarcliff Lodge—one of the finest big hotels near New York. Home of the National Girl Scouts with a camp site of one hundred and fifty-four acres. Home of Briarcliff Country Club with a new 18-hole golf links. Home of Mrs. Dow's School for Girls, a modern building with equipment accommodating one hundred and fifty pupils. Home of the Briarcliff Green Houses, famous for American Beauties. Home of Camp Fire Club of America, and Briarcliff Community Center. Home of many people of taste and refinement who find in Briarcliff, environments and conditions which satisfy their exacting demands.

1

the village, is now a part of the King's College, a Christian liberal arts college. King's College also owns and occupies Law's Briarcliff Lodge, built in 1902 and for more than twenty years "one of the best modern country hotels in existence," the resort and favored summer residence of the wealthy and prominent of New York and other cities. Along with all that could be offered to assure "a sense of comfort as in the best appointed home," the Lodge had fifteen tennis courts, an indoor swimming pool, croquet lawns, a nine-hole golf course, a riding school, stables, miles of bridle paths and a very large outdoor swimming pool converted from a pond in 1924 for the Olympic trials.

Then as now, Briarcliff had "a public park with bathing facilities." The present public swimming pool was the first in the county. The "bathing facilities" in the 1920s, as the writer John Hersey, who did lifeguard duty then, remembers, were a pond alive with interesting creatures like leeches, as well as little children who dove from his shoulders. The Community Club, "center of village social life, whose members represented almost every family," was discontinued to make way for the Briarcliff-Peekskill Parkway (Route 9A) in 1928.

The Briarcliff Realty Company's 1921 appeal to homeseekers marked a turning point in the history of the village, one of four major changes in the landscape: from the forest that grew for thousands of years beside the great tidal river that gave access to it, to the farms that felled the forest, to the estates of millionaires that absorbed the farms, to residential lots, of decreasing acreage and increasing value, connected by three state highways and a railroad.

Old Folks Concert, Briarcliff Community Club, 1909

PART I

THE FOREST

Robert Bolton's West Chester Indian Map, 1609 (printed 1881).

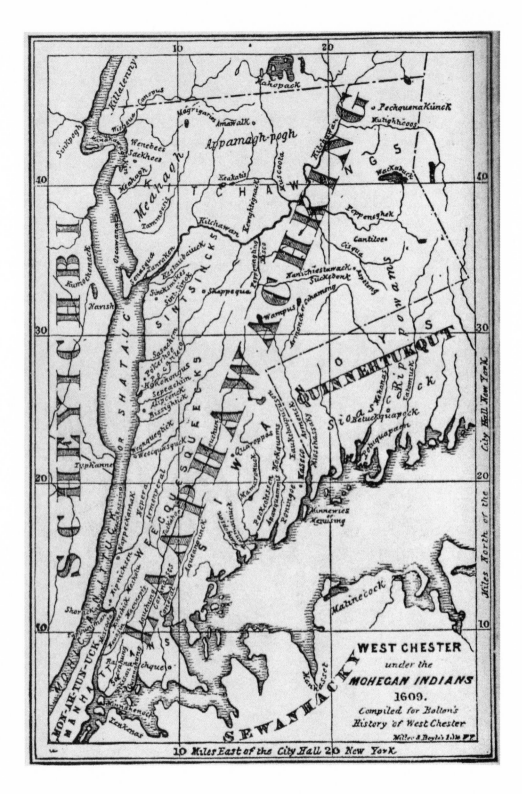

1

Indians and Europeans

WHEN THE ICE sheet had retreated, about twelve thousand years ago, and as the ground warmed, the forest changed gradually from tundra-spruce to pine to oak-chestnut to maple-hickory-hemlock. The first people of the forest, whose ancestors are believed to have travelled on foot from Asia, hunted the caribou and the woolly mastodon.

Archeologists, in the 1960s and 1970s, most notably the late Louis Brennan of Ossining, investigated three sites in Scarborough: at Kemeys Cove and on the Route 9 property now owned by Tetko, and on the River Road property of Dr. Carl Towbin. At these sites in the "middens," heaps of oyster shells, some carbon-dated at more than five thousand years, stone tools were found—knives, scrapers, spear points—and, at Kemeys Cove, bolas, stones wrapped in hide slings and probably used to bring down water birds. Most of these tools date from the Archaic Period, 8000 to 1000 B.C., preserved from the destructive acidity of the soil by the lime content of the shells. Later sites, particularly those on the cultivated uplands, have been mostly obliterated.

The first people of the forest, joined by others with varied skills, developed a complex culture over the centuries. When the first European explorers entered the river, the inhabitants were no longer wandering hunter-gatherers, surviving the cold in rock shelters, but citizens of an established social order rich in tradition and lore. They believed in a colorful hierarchy of spirits, from the powerful Creator to the smallest animals and plants. They were governed by councils on which women and youths might sometimes sit with the men. Their chiefs, sachems and sagamores were first among equals, distinguished for wisdom as well as leadership in war and the hunt. Local tribes—Wiechquaskeck, Sintsinck, Kitchawanck, Wappinger and others—united against more warlike tribes to the north in what came to be called the Wappinger Confederacy. They cultivated beans, squash, pumpkins, sunflowers and corn, from which they made bread. They stored quantities of provisions, dried and smoked venison, fish and shellfish, and vegetables, as well as grain for the winter months. In winter they gathered in houses built of hickory saplings and sheets of chestnut bark. Some of the lodges were communal "long houses" sixty to one hundred feet long, partitioned with hides and woven matting, in which as many as sixteen families might live, each around a small fire with a smoke hole in the roof above it. During the cold months, they fashioned tools and weapons, bowls and spoons of stone and wood, baskets and clay cooking pots.

The coming of a travelling storyteller to these winter villages, a "Grandfather" or "Grandmother" carrying a bag of "winter stories," was a great event. All the children crowded around to listen. The stories carried lessons about courage, kindness, moral purity and reverence for all the natural world. They went on for hours and included many songs which the listeners joined in singing. The storyteller started each one by opening his bag, saying, "I open this story . . . " and taking out an object: a reed for the story of the wily fellow who hid under water and sang a warning song, through a reed, to his unkind mother-in-law; a tooth or a scrap of scaly skin for the story of the water monster, in which some boys climbed the long shadows to the sky and asked the sun for some sun-dust to defeat the monster.[1]

Delaware Indian family

Some of these people lived in villages near the present hamlet of Sparta and Sing Sing Kill (Killbrook) in Ossining, a name derived from their words *asin* (stone) and *asinesing* (place of stones). These words were, by early accounts, even more descriptive then than now of the country, especially along the river shores. The tribe, or tribes, that sometimes lived here came to be called the Sint Sincks or Sing Sings—spelling varied, as spelling did in those times. They spoke coastal Munsee, a dialect of the Algonkian language, reported by William Penn and others to be beautifully musical. They believed their language was understood by plants, animals and deities. They called themselves "Lenape," the People.

These Lower River Indians were peaceable, perhaps because they believed the Creator intended his bounty for all his people equally, a belief easy to hold in this country, for here was God's plenty—the forest alive with game, with "fruits in great profusion," and nuts and berries. In his journal, Robert Juet wrote that the river teemed with fish—"Salmons, and Mullets, and Rayes very great."[2] There were also striped bass, shad, eel and sturgeon. More than two hundred years later William Verplanck wrote, "Sturgeon weighing 250 pounds would be seen leaping several feet into the air. . . . The catching and packing of these fish became an important industry, the product known as 'Albany Beef!'"[3]

The river, which the first people travelled in dugout canoes, was sighted by European explorers, including John Cabot in 1498, as they sailed along the coast in search of a northwest passage to the riches of India. The first recorded entrance of the river was in 1524 by Giovanni da Verrazano, a Florentine, who wrote to his patron, Francis I of France, that his ship "being anchored off the coast in good shelter," he and some of his crew entered the river in "the small boat. . . . The people, clothed with the feathers of birds of various colors, came toward us joyfully, uttering great exclamations of admiration, showing us where we could land with the boat more safely. . . . They exceeded us in size, and they were of a very fair complexion: some of them incline more to a white, others to a tawny color, their faces are sharp, their hair long and black. . . . Their expression [is] mild and pleasant. . . . Their women are of the same form and beauty, very graceful, of fine countenances and pleasing appearance in manners and modesty." A gale blew up and Verrazano and his sailors were forced to return to their ship.

The first recorded voyage up the river was Henry Hudson's, in 1609, in the *Half Moon*, a high-pooped Dutch yacht. Hudson was an English captain in the employ of the Dutch East India Company. Robert Juet, a member of Hudson's crew, wrote in his journal that they had found "a land as pleasant with flowers and goodly trees as ever they had seen," and described the several meetings of Hudson and his men with the people of the forest. These were at first very amiable, for the Indians were generous and kindly hosts, "a very good people," Hudson later called them. But before the *Half Moon* set sail again over the ocean one Englishman and at least ten Indians had been killed. This proportion of fatalities was prophetic.

The "Half Moon" on the Hudson River

Although Hudson failed in his purpose to find a northwest passage to the riches of India, Amsterdam merchants soon observed that there were riches to be had, specifically furs, along the river. In 1521, the Dutch West India Company was established and trading posts were set up from New Amsterdam (New York City) to Fort Orange (Albany). One of the earliest historians of the New World, Adrian Van der Donck, put at eighty thousand the number of beaver taken annually for their pelts. Otter, mink, bear, elk and deer also were taken. The region was largely trapped out by 1640.[4] The hunters, who were mostly Indian, were forced far afield, and many never returned.

From earliest times, farming was for export as well as subsistence, and along the river, trader's landings and hamlets to support them served the needs of the Dutch. Timber, grain, flax and flaxseed oil eventually followed furs into the sloops and schooners that plied the river. Scarborough, on the river near Sparta Landing, attracted settlers earlier than the inland part of the present village of Briarcliff Manor, but during the fifty-odd years of Dutch rule the region was largely unsettled and remained so until after the Revolution. The Dutch, although eager traders, were reluctant colonists. Unlike the English Puritans and Quakers, the French Huguenots and others, they had no pressing need to leave their home country. In an effort to promote settlement, the Dutch West India Company in 1629 granted members of the company the right to purchase from the Indians a tract of land above Manhattan extending sixteen miles on one side of the river or eight miles on both sides and "so far into the country as the situation of the Occupyers will permit," provided they plant on the tract a colony of fifty persons.[5] Within their domains these landlords, called patroons, had near-feudal powers. Even with these inducements, only one patroonship was established in the present county, that granted in 1646 to Adrian Van der Donck (known as *Jonckheer*, or young sir), in acknowledgment of his services as peacemaker between the Indians and Company Director Willem Kieft. This tract extended from Spuyten Duyvil sixteen miles north along the Hudson and east to the Bronx River. Donck's Colony, where that gentleman settled, was called Yonkers (*Jonckheer's*) after him.

Meanwhile, the Indian population, which had never been numerous—the entire Wappinger Confederacy has been estimated at less than five thousand in 1600—was much reduced. Contagious diseases brought from Europe (smallpox, cholera, malaria, measles, bubonic plague, alcoholism) against which the Indians had no immunity, wiped out whole villages. Settlers and Indians were soon at war. Dutch cows plundered Indian cornfields. An Indian picked peaches in a Dutchman's orchard. There were murders, raids, retaliations and massacres, particularly during the administration of Director Kieft. Within five years some sixteen hundred Indians were killed, and the fields of the Dutch, as one settler wrote, were laid waste "Our dwellings and other buildings are burnt, not a handful can be planted or sown this fall on all the abandoned places. All this through a foolish hankering after war, for it is known to all right-thinking men here that these Indians have lived as lambs among us until a few years ago, injuring no one and affording every assistance to our nation."[6]

Exhausted by the Indian wars and under pressure from expanding English settlements in Connecticut and Long Island, in 1664 the Dutch surrendered easily to an English squadron of four ships under the command of Richard Nicolls. New Amsterdam became the Province of New York and Nicolls its first governor.

The terms of the English takeover were liberal, and prominent Dutch citizens, particularly Vredryck Flypsen (his name anglicized to Frederick Philipse) and Stephanus Van Cortlandt, Philipse's future brother-in-law and neighbor in Westchester, retained their property and took places in the new colonial government. Philipse, who was not, as some histories have it, the grandson of a refugee Bohemian nobleman,[7] had emigrated from Friesland, in the Netherlands, probably with Peter Stuyvesant in 1647. Damage from a tidal wave that struck the northern coast of Europe in 1634 may have caused both these Friesians to emigrate. Philipse was a carpenter, and his skill in building during his first years in the colony earned him the name of Stuyvesant's "architect builder."[8] He became a merchant, trading with the Five Nations (Iroquoian Indian tribes), England, the East and West Indies and Africa, exchanging furs and timber for woven goods and slaves for sugar and rum. He also manufactured wampum. He married Margaret Hardenbroek, widow of the wealthy merchant Pieter R. DeVries, "a very desirable business partner as well as wife."[9] When she died, he married Catharine Van Cortlandt, widow of John Derval. Both marriages increased his already considerable wealth, and in 1674 he was rated the richest man in the Province.[10] Philipse kept his place on the governing council of the colony until 1698, when the English Lords of Trade found that his connection with Captain William Kidd's illegal commerce with pirates was clear enough to warrant his dismissal. Philipse, who was by this time more than seventy years old, retired. (Originally, Captain Kidd's enterprises were legitimate and Philipse was not the only leading citizen who cooperated with him.)

PART II

THE FARMS

*"Briarcliff Farm," property of
James Stillman on Pleasantville
Road circa 1886*

2

The Manor and the Revolution

IN 1672, FREDERICK Philipse added a portion of Donck's Colony to his property in Manhattan, and in a series of purchases through the 1680s, extended his holdings north to the Croton River and east to the sources of the Bronx River. The local Indians, in an attempt to preserve their way of life, had adopted a strategy of selling land in small parcels while retaining hunting, fishing and camping rights—"a skillful holding action in the face of impossible odds."[1] The eleventh and last Philipse purchase within the Manor was "that tract or parcel of land commonly called by the Indians Sinck Sinck,"[2] the site of Scarborough, Briarcliff Manor and Ossining. Local histories tell us this transaction took place in 1685 on a rise of land east of the present Scarborough railroad station, in the presence of eight Indian chiefs. The name of one of the chiefs has come down to us as "Weskora," and in 1867, Scarborough, and later one of its great houses, took that name for a time. "Weskora" was probably Wessecanow, "identified as Wiechquaskeck, Wappinger or Kitchawank, depending on where he happened to be living . . . the primary agent between his people and the English from 1676 to 1690."[3]

Besides wampum, which was common currency at the time, the Indians were paid in the imported goods they had come to covet and depend on: iron kettles, axes, hoes and knives, blankets and trade cloth, shirts and stockings, stone jugs, firearms and rum. This exchange was not as unequal as it may now seem. Unlike the flat, rich lands of New Jersey and Pennsylvania, which had attracted many more settlers, the forest along the river was hilly and rocky, a beautiful wilderness. When the patent of the English monarchs William and Mary made Frederick Philipse "Lord of the Mannour of Philipsborough" in 1693, no more than twenty families were living on some fifty thousand acres, which included land on the western shore of the Tappan Zee and a large part of what is now the Bronx. The manor was owned and governed by Philipse and his heirs, in succession, Adolph, Frederick II and Frederick III, known as Colonel Philipse. Philip Philipse, the oldest son of the first Frederick Philipse, first purchased the Sing Sing tract, and later deeded it to his father, who survived him. During the Revolution, Colonel Philipse chose to be loyal to the English Crown and forfeited all his property in North America.

11

Philipse Manor House and Sleepy Hollow Mill

Philipsburgh Manor enjoyed nearly a hundred years of comparative peace. By 1740 most of the remaining Indians, their preserves trapped out, had gone elsewhere. Philipsburgh tenant farmers were not moved to rebellion against their landlords, although such conflicts raged around them up and down the river. Their farms were on about two hundred acres each, which they could not own. They did own all "improvements" on the land, including their houses and livestock, and could pass these and their leaseholds on to their heirs. They paid a yearly rent of four to six pounds or one-tenth of their yearly produce and took their grain to be milled at Philipse Upper Mills in the present North Tarrytown. The Philipses in return were obliged to provide the services of a schoolmaster and an occasional clergyman.

Slowly the land was cleared. In 1749 the Swedish naturalist Peter Kalm, in his *Travels in America*, noted the scarcity of settlement on the shores of the Hudson but also wrote: "As we proceeded we found the eastern bank of the river very much cultivated and a number of pretty farms surrounded by orchards and fine plowed fields presented themselves to our view." Much of the local produce was for export and more was transported from far inland to the river landings at Sparta and Sing Sing. The river was dotted with the white sails of market and packet sloops, schooners, trappers' *flyboets*, yachts of the manor lords, English frigates and even some awe-inspiring pirate craft.

By 1763, there were enough residents in the vicinity of Sparta Landing to request "regular preaching" of the Dutchess County Presbytery, and Colonel Philipse donated three acres for the building of a church (noted as "Dutch Presbyterian" on the map of Philipsburgh

Manor made in 1785),[4] at the Sparta Burying Grounds on the corner of Revolutionary Road and the Albany Post Road. This was the third church built in all of Philipsburgh Manor. The first burial in the churchyard was of five-year-old Sarah Ledew, in 1764. Her headstone, beside others of her family with their antique inscriptions, may still be viewed there. The Ledew (also spelled Ladoux) family's 131 acres southeast of Scarborough Road are noted on the 1785 map. In the militia for the Upper District of Philipsburgh Manor, organized under the Provincial Congress in 1775, Abraham Ledew is listed as captain along with five other officers who must have lived within or near to the present village limits: Benjamin Brown, first lieutenant; Jonas Arsor (Orser), second lieutenant; and John Oakley, ensign.[5]

Here Lyes the Body of
SARAH LEDEW Born in the Year
1759 April 26 who Departed
this Life August 15, 1764,
Aged 5 Years 7 mo. and 11 days
daughter of ABRAHAM & ANNA LEDEW

Reuben Whitson "Century Homestead," Chappaqua Road

In the village, particularly near the eastern border, a few houses still stand that were probably built in part before the Revolution. In most of these the oldest portions are disguised and overshadowed by more recent construction. All contain some hand-hewn, mortised beams constructed in the Dutch H-frame fashion, but in the absence of documentary evidence only the spacing of the beams and indications of the size of the original rooms can identify them as Philipsburgh tenant farmhouses.

The Washburn house on Washburn Road is known to date from 1775, if not earlier.[6] The house was damaged by fire and reconstructed, but probably the smallest of the six present bays was pre-revolutionary.

The "Century Homestead," as it is named in the Beers' Atlas of 1867, on Chappaqua Road has been called the Reuben Whitson House. However, since there are no Whitsons on the Mt. Pleasant census rolls before 1830, it was probably another Washburn house. Part of the old Dell farmhouse on Chappaqua Road appears to be pre-revolutionary.

Between 1860 and 1889, the travelling hermit Jules Bourglay sometimes rested from his wanderings in a cave or hut on the Dell Farm. He was found dead there in March 1889. Bourglay was called "the Leather Man" because he was clothed in leather patched together from old shoe tops and the like. A bronze plaque marks his grave in Sparta Cemetery.

The house sometimes known as the Buckhout House and in 1923 named Luthany by the Baroness De Luze, is in part pre-revolutionary, judging by the spacing of the beams and the dimensions of the original four rooms, part of the present cellar and the living room

Buckhout house, Pleasantville Road

Wooden sidewalks in front of "The Elms," Elm Road

above it. The removal of old wallpaper in the dining room, in the 1970s, exposed more hand-hewn beams, a paper containing news of the war of 1812 and the date 1812 inscribed in the old plaster.

The house with a nineteenth-century gable and porch that faces F.B. Hall across Pleasant-ville Road is known to have been the home of the Buckhout family for over a hundred years. The Philipse tenants who farmed the land and probably built the house were members of the Brown family. The house is thought to be of pre-revolutionary construction in part.[7] Walter Law bought the Buckhout land in 1892.

Behind the Titlar (later Comfort) farmhouse on Long Hill Road East, the barn-garage is of typical Dutch H-frame construction and may date from before the Revolution.

Part of the house at 2 Central Drive that was the old Briarcliff Golf Club, a tiny, neat two stories, was at one time tentatively dated at 1790, but because the oldest beams are evidently milled that date has been advanced to around 1840.

The house now gray-shingled and numbered 104 Long Hill Road East, was "all put together with pegs, not a nail in it," Ruth Oakley, who lived there as a child in the 1910s, remembered. The house now contains many nails, as well as two additions, but the oldest beams and the dimensions of the cellar and the present dining room identify it as probably pre-revolutionary. The land the house stands on, which Walter Law bought from the Bishop family in the 1890s, was farmed by Ruth's father, Alvah Oakley, who, old-timer Emil Brown remembered, "had eleven children, lived to be a hundred and smoked Ploughboy Tobacco." Ruth used to walk with her older sister to the top of the hill to fetch a pail of milk from Adkins' dairy farm. When her sister refused to let her carry the full pail down the hill for fear she would spill it, Ruth threatened to run away from home and hid in the cellar while the whole village turned out to search for her. When a neighbor came to console her mother, inquisitive Ruth peeked around the cellar door and was discovered, joyfully embraced and soundly spanked.

The Elms on Elm Road was built in 1810 by Thomas Bailey of Ossining. Some of the Bishop family lived there until Walter Law bought it in the 1890s. It was at one time called the "Ancients" house because alumnae of Mrs. Dow's School stayed there.

*Joseph Washburn house,
Washburn Road*

Few events of great historic interest are known to have happened within the present village limits during the Revolutionary War. A plaque on Hardscrabble Road marks the spot where Major John André is believed to have watered his horse on September 22, 1780. André was riding south toward the British lines with the plans of West Point concealed in his stocking. The plans, which were crucial to the outcome of the war, had been given to André by the commander of West Point, Benedict Arnold, who had also arranged for André to sail back through the lines on the British sloop *Vulture*. While anchored off Teller's Point (now Croton Point), the *Vulture* was fired on by a patriot cannon hastily brought down from Verplanck by Colonel Livingston. The ship retreated down the river, but not before Benedict Arnold had managed to board her and make his escape to join the British army.[8] André, forced to make his way overland, was detained several miles to the southwest of Hardscrabble Road by three local militiamen who turned him over to Washington's forces. He was court-martialed, found guilty of spying, and hanged.

After the battle of White Plains in 1776, General George Washington set up headquarters just north of Peekskill. British headquarters were in New York City. Both armies needed provisions, and some farmers, millers and teamsters were released from active duty to get grain to the Croton River mill and make flour for Washington's army. Other noncombatants, particularly some Quakers, managed to do well, but Westchester as a whole, for some seven years was "Neutral Ground" between the enemy camps, and suffered greatly from raids and pillage by marauders claiming allegiance to both sides. These were called Cowboys and Skinners, because they stole and skinned cattle and sold the hides and meat to the armies. Livestock and provisions of all kinds were stolen and farms were burned and abandoned. When the end of hostilities was declared in 1783, the countryside was in ruins.

The story of a typical atrocity was told by Joseph Bowron Washburn at the 1875 Centennary of Reuben Washburn at his house on Washburn Road in Briarcliff:

Joseph, our grandfather, lived in this house, kept bachelor hall until he was married to Freelove Matthews in 1775. The first of fourteen children was Reuben. This farm belonged to "Philipse Manor" and once a year Joseph went to the manor house near Tarrytown to pay his rent. Joseph, who lived in this place during the war, suffered severely from lawless bands of skinners, who robbed

Washburn family reunion at Washburn house, circa 1875

and beat him nearly to death for his money. He gave them the silver and they beat him still more for his gold. He refused to give that up. He was then hung from an apple tree.

Fortunately, after the rascals departed, Washburn's family returned in time to save his life.[9]

General Washington's army probably camped at Scarborough Corners on its way north along the river to King's Ferry (Verplanck). A rapier and English coins of the period, now in the archives of the Ossining Historical Society, were found at the site of the Scarborough Presbyterian Church.

After the Revolution, Loyalists' holdings, including Philipsburgh Manor, were confiscated and put up for sale in pursuance of an act of the New York State Legislature "for the speedy sale of the confiscated and forfeited Estates within this State."[10] Isaac Stoutenburgh and Philip Van Cortlandt were appointed commissioners of forfeiture for the southern district of the state. Farmers were able to buy the land they had worked as tenants. In the Scarborough region, John Bishop bought 265 acres in 1785, Abraham Orser bought 123 acres in 1786, and Marvil Garrison bought 200 acres in 1792. Tunis Van Houten (Houden, Housen), a Revolutionary War pensioner, bought some 90 acres on Scarborough Ridge. Jonas Orser and the families of Abraham Brown and Job Sherwood bought land they had farmed as Philipsburgh tenants. An entry for 1795 in the minute book of the Town of Mt. Pleasant names the following "Path Masters": "Robert Ossor Path Master from Peter Davids [in Sparta] . . . Job Sheerwood from 33 Mile Stone to the Bridge This Side of the Whitewood Tree. Benjamin Brown from Mud Bridge to Mill [Pocantico] River. Jonas Ossor from the Popple Brook to foot of the Long hill." The path masters were concerned with wandering livestock, and there must have been disagreements to be settled because

Hogs that Sufisently Ringed and yoked are Permitted to Run in the Street . . . [and] . . . no Ram to go at Large from the first Day of august untill the first Day of November and if they should hapen in to Any Person Land he has a Right to Cut [earmark] the Said Ram or Rams and the owner [of the land] to have four Shillings for his Trouble of Cutting.[11]

3

Sparta and Scarborough

THE WAR-RAVAGED farms recovered and entered the nineteenth century in peace and prosperity. Settlers—farmers, tradesmen and boatmen—arrived in increasing numbers, moving out from the city or west from Bedford and Newcastle. Sparta competed successfully in the lively river commerce until around 1820, when dock rentals were lowered at Mount Pleasant Landing, two miles north in Sing Sing, and the Post Road, which had followed the present Revolutionary Road, was straightened at an inconvenient distance from the landing at White Point in Sparta.

Letters written to England by John Burgess portray life in the environs of Sparta in the 1790s. Burgess, a clergyman, had come to Sparta "as the boys had not the small pox, and I thought it too dangerous to stay in the city." He wrote to a friend in 1794:

The land is wonderful fertile—we have very fine horses which seem to be a half breed, good cows and oxen, but not large, hogs exactly like yours, cats and dogs the same, but not many of them, geese and chickens like yours . . . a great many wild ducks, part of the year. No man is denied to carry his gun—rich and poor alike. There are no boundaries to our manors. . . . All belongs to him that kills it, so we don't meddle with a man's private property, what the farmer brings up tame. It is the custom of this country that if a man goeth into another man's house at mealtime, he is always almost to be asked to sit down to eat and drink with the family. If it be a poor man it is just the same. We have a great many farmers what have 100 or 150 acres of land of their own and use it. But I don't know them by their clothes nor by their fat bellies from a poor man. In the summer they wear trousers, but very old ones. Any old stockings and often without shoes. I have seen them at plow without a shoe or stocking. The women go the same, never wear stays, very seldom a cap, common[ly] without shoe or stocking when they are at work, but many of them, when they go out dressed, dress very gay. The women are remarkable for riding. They will set any horse up hill and down full gallop. The men nor the women never go very far afoot. They ride good horses, neat saddles. The farmers have been used to make many shifts: tan their own leather, and make it up when they have done, save all their wool, make all their clothes, both for men, women and children—the same as they did in England in my Grandmother's time. . . . Many good farmers, I mean farmers that use 200 acres of their own land, live in a house not larger nor better than what Sam Packett's house. All their business in a place is dug in a bank, covered with a few boards for a milk house, and you seldom see a house in the country without a bed or two in the room where they live, even in a public kitchen.[1]

The old mustard mill, Sparta

William Kemeys and Josiah Rhodes bought land in Sparta around 1790 and established a gristmill on Sparta Brook. It consisted of three wooden buildings "employed as A mannifactory for the flour of Mustard and for crushing flax-seed," as Rhodes described it in his will. Rhodes and Kemeys both had emigrated from Yorkshire, England. Kemeys, whose name was fixed to the cove where he owned land, came from Scarborough. Perhaps these two early residents were responsible for naming the western part of the present village Scarborough. The line between Sparta and Scarborough was not set until 1813, when the village of Sing Sing was incorporated (the first incorporated village in the county). Many years after the line was drawn, parts of Scarborough were still referred to as Sparta:

Sparta can also boast of being the birthplace of Admiral Worden, who performed the gallant service of sinking the *Merrimac*.
> The *Monitor* went whack into the *Merrimac*,
> And as she went, played "Yankee Doodle Dandy O!"[2]

Admiral John L. Worden was born in 1818 in the stately Greek revival mansion (since demolished) on the southeast corner of Scarborough Road and the Albany Post Road. The house was named Hillside when the J. Warren Rogers family lived there, from 1863 to the 1900s,[3] when Frank Vanderlip bought the property. Admiral Worden commanded the *Monitor* in the first encounter in world history of ironclad warships, in Hampton Roads, Virginia, in 1862.

The Presbyterian congregation moved from the church at Sparta Burying Grounds up the road to Sing Sing in 1800, and until the Reverend William Creighton started to hold services for the first congregations of Saint Mary's Episcopal Church in the 1840s there was no church within present village limits. Residents went for their devotions to the Old Dutch Church at Philipsburgh Upper Mills, to Sing Sing or to the Friends Meeting House in Croton. (Sing Sing Village was renamed Ossining in 1901.)

There was, however, in 1833–1834, a resident prophet—self-proclaimed. Robert Matthews, like his upstate contemporary Joseph Smith, had a vision, not of an angel who led him to the golden tablets of the ancient American prophet Mormon, but of himself as the resurrected New Testament Matthias (Acts:26). He had been preaching on street corners and in and out of prison when he became acquainted with some wealthy men of strong religious inclinations and great credulity. One of these, Benjamin Folger, was his host in the old part of the Webb-Vanderlip Beechwood, in Scarborough. There is some evidence that the house, which Matthias named "Zion Hill," was built for him under his supervision.[4] Folger and a lodger named Elijah Pierson advanced large sums of money to Matthias and deeded the house and land to him, mortgaged at $5,000. Matthias spent their money on clothing and trappings suitable to his divine calling: frock coats "of green lined with white satin or black lined with pink," a vest of "rich silk figures," silk tunics and pantaloons, high topped boots and sandals, a conical leather hat of "black japanned leather, with a visor," the "Sword of Gideon," and the "Chariot of Israel," drawn by a matched team of white horses. His hair and beard flowed long because he believed it wrong to cut them, or his fingernails. His sleeping cap had twelve tassels, each inscribed with the name of an Apostle, and he carried a golden key "to the gates of Heaven."[5] When he ran out of the money that his host and followers had lavished on him, Matthias became violent. Soon after drinking a brew the prophet had prepared for him, Elijah Pierson died. Then the whole

Folger family fell mysteriously ill. Matthias was tried for murder in White Plains and acquitted for lack of evidence, although the exhumed body of Pierson was found to contain traces of arsenic. The prophet was found guilty only of the brutal beating of his grown daughter. He served a short jail term before vanishing from this neighborhood, but the scandal resounded throughout the county and beyond.

Fortunately for the tone of our history in this period, Folger's, and Matthias' nearest neighbors-to-be were evangelists of a very different kind. In 1834, Henry J. Auchmuty, a lieutenant in the United States Navy and nephew of Sir Samuel Auchmuty, a rector of Trinity Church in New York City, bought a hundred acres "more or less"[6] on the banks of the Hudson just south of Folger's land. This estate Auchmuty's widow, Louisa, sold in 1836 to William Creighton, D.D., who, in the words of historian James Elliott Lindsley, "deserves a prominent niche in the iconography of the Diocese of New York."[7] A graduate of Columbia College, Creighton had been rector of Saint Mark's-in-the-Bouerie for twenty years when, because of his wife's ill health, he followed his friend Washington Irving into retirement in the country. In 1837, Creighton established Christ Church in Tarrytown and conducted services there and at Zion Church in Dobbs Ferry. In 1839, with his son-in-law, the Reverend Edward Mead, he established Saint Mary's Episcopal Church. Dr. Mead conducted the first services in a one-room schoolhouse on the corner of Sleepy Hollow Road. Some of the first parishioners lived in Archville, a community of laborers who were building the Croton Aqueduct.

In 1850 the church was built, paid for in part by contributions from wealthy and prominent neighbors such as Commodore Matthew Calbraith Perry, General James Watson Webb, William H. Aspinwall, the shipping magnate, and Ambrose C. Kingsland, mayor

The Croton Aqueduct crossed the Albany Post Road at Archville.

Rev. William Creighton

of New York City in the 1850s. Dr. Mead drew the plans for the church building, relying on his memory of a chapel of thirteenth-century Saint Mary's Church in Scarborough, England, which he and his wife, Jane (Creighton), had visited on a tour of Europe. Built of native granite by local stonemasons, the church has the narrow lancelet windows typical of early English Gothic. Among other special features, the church has a complete set of stained glass windows by John Bolton of Bolton Priory in Pelham, one of the earliest masters of

All Saints Church, at the corner of Old Briarcliff Road and Scarborough Road, 1854

his art in America. It is the only complete set of Bolton windows in existence. The first services were held in the church in 1851.

A second Episcopal church, All Saints, was begun in 1848 by the Reverend John David Ogilby, D.D., professor of ecclesiastical history at the General Theological Seminary in New York, on his summer estate, which he named "Brier Cliff" after his family home in Ireland. While in England, Ogilby had noted the similarity of the corner of his land at Old Briarcliff and Scarborough Roads to the site of the Gothic church at Bremerton, near Salisbury. He resolved to build a chapel at this point on his land to provide services for his neighbors. Architect Richard Upjohn, who had designed Trinity and other churches in New York City, drew up plans for a church like the one at Bremerton.

Dr. Ogilby died before the building was finished, but the work was carried on by his friends Henry and Francis McFarlan. Opening services were held on the 13th of December 1854. Six visiting clergymen took part. The sermon was preached by Dr. Ogilby's brother, the Reverend Frederick Ogilby, and holy communion administered by Dr. Creighton. A church publication of the time described the church as a "small but beautiful stone sanctuary . . . commanding one of the finest views along the whole length of the Hudson."[8] The building was entirely furnished, the interior finished in pine, oiled and varnished. An English friend of Dr. Ogilby's gave the chancel windows in his memory and Sir Robert Ogilby gave money for the other windows. All were of stained glass by Gibson of Philadelphia. The church "was sustained from its beginning until 1874 chiefly by the efforts of the Brinkerhoff family . . . "[9] some of whom lived on Old Briarcliff Road, north of the corner. The Ogilbys, McFarlans and Brinkerhoffs were related, and members of all three families owned houses close to the church. A history of All Saints, exquisitely handwritten by Helena

Rev. John David Ogilby

Bishop's chair and Sedilia, All Saints Church

Duncombe and illustrated by Katherine Figart, which is one of the church's treasures, reveals some details of the relationship of these families. The Brinkerhoffs may also have been related to Henry R. Remsen, who owned the house and part of the property of the present Beechwood from 1850 to 1903.[10]

Besides carrying his considerable duties in three country parishes, the Reverend Creighton continued to take part in the affairs of the Episcopal Church and travelled often to the city for that purpose. This was a period of dissension in the Diocese of New York following the suspension of the fourth bishop, Benjamin Onderdonck, for "improper conduct with women." Creighton was called on again and again to chair contentious diocesan gatherings, and "earned the trust of all." He was nominated and finally elected provisional bishop, but "after prolonged consideration about his age [he was fifty-nine] and family cares, decided he must refuse what must have been the crowning honor of his long life of devotion to the Church."[11]

Creighton named his farm Beechwood and built a house overlooking the river which he shared with his daughter, Catherine Schermerhorn Creighton, and his daughter and son-in-law, Jane and Edward Mead, until the first rectory was built for the Meads in the 1850s. Mrs. Creighton, whose illness was nervous, or mental, lived apart with an attendant in "the Cottage." Like most of the surrounding countryside, those acres had been farmed, perhaps profitably, before Lieutenant Auchmuty bought them.

The inventory of stock and other articles sold to Creighton with the land is typical of small local farms in the 1850s:

Five cows. One Pair of oxen. One Pair of Farm horses. Eight swine. About Thirty head of poultry. One farm wagon. One wood Sled. Set of farm harness. Two Ox chains. Four Ploughs. One harrow. One hay rake. Two shovels. Two iron shovels. Two Spades. Four scythes. Four sneithes. Three hoes. One corn knife. Two Potato hooks. One pair of Steelyards. One garden edging iron. One Pick axe. Two garden rakes. One Trowel. One wheelbarrow. one watering Pot. Three Churns. Three Tin pails. Twenty pans. Two Trays. One Strainer. One Stone boat.[12]

This was a gentleman's farm, not a big enterprise. Other farms in the Hudson Valley had been changing to specialty crops, fruit orchards and dairying, after the opening of the Erie Canal in 1825 started to bring competing produce and livestock down the river from the west and far upstate.

Dr. Creighton did not welcome the "abominable screeching of the locomotive," as Washington Irving called it. His many trips to and from the city on church business must have been by packet sloop—steamboats at midcentury were only beginning to compete—by stagecoach in summer, by sleigh in winter, or by horse and carriage. In any of these conveyances, the journey was long, chancy and arduous. Even with a good pair of horses, from the city to Tarrytown was a four-hour trek on the narrow, unpaved Albany Post Road. But when, in 1848, the Hudson River Railroad Company, authorized by the State Legislature, offered $2,789 for a parcel of Creighton's river front (roughly three acres above and two below high-water mark) plus damages and counsel fees, he refused, although the transaction and the sum had been approved by a jury of his neighbors in the county. In spite of Creighton's refusal, the land was appropriated, the money deposited to his credit in the

American Express Train,
Currier and Ives
lithograph, 1864

Westchester County Bank,[13] and the Hudson River Railroad "screeched" through to Peekskill in September of 1849.[14]

When the Reverend Creighton refused to sell his river-front land to the railroad, he was defying a force whose dynamic enormity he could not have foreseen. Forty years later, Arthur T. Hadley wrote:

The railroads of the world are today worth from twenty-five to thirty thousand million dollars [which] . . . probably represents one-tenth of the total wealth of civilized nations, and one-quarter, if not one-third of their invested capital. . . . The capital engaged in banking is but a trifle beside it.[15]

Wherever there were bankers and large investors, there were officials of railroad companies and railroad money, and Scarborough and Briarcliff Manor soon had their share of both. William Creighton's contemporary, James Boorman, who has been called "the originator of the Hudson River Railroad,"[16] did not live in Scarborough, but his close relatives (probably a brother and a nephew), Robert Boorman and James Albert Boorman, and their families are buried in a separate plot in Sparta Cemetery. The oldest of the Boorman graves is a sarcophagus inscribed: "Mary Boorman, died City of New York, August 1861 and there interred," which is said to have been transported from a cemetery where Boorman graves had been desecrated by grave robbers who stole bodies and held them for ransom. The large Boorman property directly north and east of the cemetery is designated Hollingbourne on maps drawn from surveys made in the 1860s.[17]

C.C. Clarke, who lived on the corner of Old Briarcliff Road opposite All Saints Church, where he was senior warden,[18] was the first vice-president of the New York Central and Hudson River Railroad. The millionaires who came to Scarborough in the 1890s—Elliott

Shepard, James Speyer, Henry Walter Webb and others—were all large investors in rail-roads. Colonel Shepard "did much toward settling the railroad law of the state."[19] It is no wonder that more express trains stopped at Scarborough than at the stations in other villages of comparable size on the Hudson River line.

In "the Matter of the Hudson River Railroad Company and William Creighton," the names of jurors called included some of the oldest in the county: Isaac Purdy of Rye, Andrew See of Mount Pleasant, Joseph Merritt of Newcastle, Michael Varian of West Farms and Bernardus Montross of Yorktown.[20] It seems that the social makeup of the county had not yet changed much since revolutionary days.

With the railroad and increased steamship travel, changes were not long in coming. Gentlemen like Ogilby, Brinkerhoff and Remsen, escaping at least in summer from the increasingly congested city, bought farmland in the region, especially with sweeping river views. As old prints remind us, at that time the views from Scarborough Ridge to the Hudson and east across the Pocantico Valley were one long sweep of field and pasture without woodlands or trees, except around houses and along roads. George Jackson Fisher, M.D., chronicler of the town of Ossining in Scharf's 1886 *History of Westchester County*, describes the

scenery at Sing Sing . . . from the hills and terraces of every portion of the town of Ossining, [as] extremely beautiful. . . . The broad expanse of the Tappan Zee, and of the Haverstraw Bay, divided by the long and narrow peninsula known to the world as "Teller's Point," of Revolutionary fame; the Palisades, far to the south; the triple-headed mountain, known as the "High Taurn," rising eight hundred and fifty feet above the river level, in the northwest; with the distant domes of the rugged Highlands far to the northward, embraces a stretch of over thirty miles, with flourishing villages and hamlets here and there, all in full view; the bosom of the noble river is whitened with the sails of a multitude of craft of every sort.

Dr. James Holmes Holden

Fisher ends this passage with the often-quoted "strain" which he attributes to Alexis de Tocqueville: "I must except the view of the Bay of Naples, out of deference to the opinion of the civilized world, but with that exception, the world has not such scenery."[21] (Tocqueville had travelled to Sing Sing in 1830 to visit the prison, which was a model for its time.) Except that some of the roads were paved, the views remained basically unchanged for a hundred years.

In the middle of the last century, Scarborough Road was "a dirt thoroughfare lined with huge willows."[22] In 1853, Emil C. Becker bought the Thomas Van Husen (Van Houden, Van Houten) homestead, built in 1827, on some ninety acres. In the Alvah P. French *History of Westchester* of 1925,[23] the house was reported "kept in fine condition . . . the dignity of its Colonial architecture unmarred, the only addition having been a veranda . . . entirely in keeping with the general plan." Becker, born in Roden, Germany, in 1911, was "a leading importer of his day."

In 1860 C.C. North purchased from Lydia and Edward Ryder some hundred acres adjacent to the Van Husen-Becker property. The land had been held since the 1830s by members of the Ryder family.

Emily Brush Holden

In 1861 Dr. James Holmes Holden, a New York City dentist, and his wife, Emily Brush Holden, built their homestead high on the ridge east of Scarborough Road on twenty-five to thirty acres purchased from C.C. North. Born in New York City in 1828, Dr. Holden was in his thirties when he settled in Scarborough and must have travelled regularly to his Fifth Avenue office to carry on his practice. He and Emil Becker were among the first, if not the very first, commuters in the neighborhood. The Holdens' sons, J. Henry and George Clarence, married and had, respectively, seven and five children. The two houses with French roofs on the hill below the homestead were built for the two families. George manufactured pressed stone, and J. Henry ran a coal and wood business in the village of Ossining. After the deaths of the elder Holdens, the homestead was rented to a variety of tenants, including the Impressionist painter Abbott Thayer and the Rodney Deans and their four children. (Mrs. Dean later married Harold Pierson of the horticulturist Pierson family and wrote *Roughly Speaking*, the story of her life.)

"Sunset Hill," the Holden homestead on Scarborough Road

Holden House, Scarborough Road

25 / *Sparta and Scarborough*

Ashridge, Scarborough Road

Robert Dinwiddie

When she was a small child, Marion Dinwiddie first came to Scarborough to visit the Beckers for Thanksgiving dinner—"a suckling pig with a string of sausages round its neck and an apple in its mouth." With her father, her sister Florence, her aunt and her grand-mother, she moved to Scarborough from New York City in 1888, just after the great bliz-zard, and lived in the house on the corner of Becker Lane "not in its present form," while her father bought thirty-three acres to the north and built two houses. Her first memories were of the Becker barnyard:

> Grandma Becker would go down every morning after breakfast and look over the barnyard where they had a farmer and Mr. Becker would have given him certain things to do, and Mr. Becker al-ways before he went to New York strolled around his estates and always carried a cup of coffee with him and when he finished the coffee he'd put the cup down on a stone wall or under a tree or somewhere and when Grandma Becker perceived that her china was getting low she would take a basket and walk over her estates and retrieve her cups and saucers.[24]

The big house at Ashridge (the estate now numbered 508 Scarborough Road), originally stood on the Post Road near Saint Mary's Church. The house, which is thought to have been built by George Swords around 1825, was sold in 1862 by J. Butler Wright to C.C. North for $500 with the understanding that it be moved within a certain time. It was tak-en down in sections, carefully marked, loaded on sledges and hauled up the hill over the snow. North called his new home Ashridge, because the only large tree on the ridge was an ash.[25] Butler Wright's own fine house near the original site of Ashridge, part of which is said to have dated from 1779, served as the golf house and, at times, the main clubhouse of the Sleepy Hollow Country Club, until it was torn down in the 1960s.

Holbrook Preparatory School for Boys

In 1866, off the road that bears his name, the Reverend David H. Holbrook founded a school that offered an academic-military education to as many as 137 boys from many parts of the country. After Dr. Holbrook's death in 1899, the school continued as Holbrook Preparatory School for Boys, managed by three Holbrook sons, until it closed in 1915.

By midcentury, at the corner of Scarborough Road and the Post Road, a hamlet had formed, which consisted of a small group of houses and stores facing south and west, and the tavern, grown prosperous, that had incorporated the old Presbyterian church. There was a blacksmith shop and a hay scale which served as a dance floor for the young people on festive occasions. "One small store, owned by a Mr. Higby, supplied the settlement with necessities such as needles, horse blankets, leather boots, grains and meats. Oil cans containing kerosene for lamps and lanterns stood in long rows, each with its potato on the spout to prevent spilling. . . . Back of these buildings was a pond filled with ducks and Calamus reeds in summer and skaters in winter."[26] In 1864 the Scarborough Post Office was established down by the railroad, and Scarborough Road, with the short jog on the Post Road so familiar to commuters, was extended to the railroad station.

Long Hill School

In 1812 school districts had been set up in the county, fourteen of them, and some time later the Long Hill Schoolhouse, District No. 4, was built at the foot of Long Hill Road on the Croton Aqueduct property.[27] "In it there were two simple rooms and two devoted teachers, Miss Charlotte Coburn and Miss Adelaire Wheeler, trying patiently to instruct 70 pupils, not always thirsty for knowledge. If thirsty for water the one pail with its one dipper for all comers sufficed. Its one stove was antique but quite able to roast any pupil on one side while freezing him on the other. There were no illustrated textbooks, no electric lights, and the only school bus was tough shoe leather underfoot. The 'three R's' were

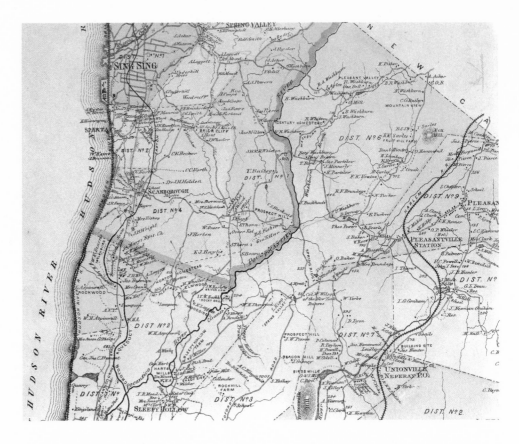

taught, with sewing extra for girls, and, as the reward for merit, gingerbread and cambric tea."[28]

Mr. and Mrs. Joseph Warren Rogers came to Scarborough in 1863, to live in the house where Admiral Worden had been born. They called the house Hillside. They had been teaching in a mission Sunday school in Brooklyn and, finding that the children of their new neighborhood were apparently receiving no religious education of any kind, they started the Scarborough Mission Sunday School with the help of a group of neighbors, including Mr. and Mrs. C. C. North and Dr. James Holden. Classes were held on Sunday afternoons in the upper room of the Long Hill schoolhouse, until it was decreed that religious education could not take place in public schools. At that time the Sunday school moved to All Saints parish house.

4

The Wars

SEVERAL OF THE new gentlemen residents were of the military and served in the Mexican War (1846–1848). Commodore Matthew Calbraith Perry, the great seafaring man who opened Japan to trade with the West and was called the "father of the steam navy" was active in the Mexican War. He was a parishioner of Saint Mary's Beechwood (as Saint Mary's was then called) and gave that church its first bell, which he had captured at the Battle of Tabasco.[1] Lieutenant-Colonel Henry Bainbridge, who in 1857 went down with his ship and crew on the *Louisiana*, lived in the vicinity of Scarborough for a time.

Historical marker on the Albany Post Road

Two Civil War generals, an admiral and two colonels lived in Scarborough. They were: Admiral Worden, born at Hillside at the corner of Scarborough Road (demolished in 1990); General Alexander Stewart Webb, the son-in-law of Henry R. Remsen, who lived in the present Beechwood; Major-General George Webb Morrell, who lived in Creighton's Beechwood; Colonel Swain and Colonel Elliott Fitch Shepard.

General Morrell was commander of the 4th Division, Army of the Potomac. Colonel Swain raised and commanded a regiment of cavalry, the "Scotts 900" (officially the 11th New York), that was President Lincoln's bodyguard. He conducted the regiment to Camp Relief, named for his wife, Relief Davis Swain, at Meridian Hill, Washington. Swain's son, Chellis, served as a lieutenant under his father. Colonel Elliott Fitch Shepard was an aide-de-camp of Governor E. D. Morgan. The 51st Regiment of the New York Volunteer Infantry, the "Shepard Rifles," was named in his honor. When Governor Morgan's term of office expired, President Lincoln offered Colonel Shepard a brigadier's commission, which he declined, "from a sense of fairness to other officers, who had seen more field service than himself."[2] He recruited the 9th Army Corps and, among other good works, helped to secure the passage of laws providing for the allotment of soldiers' pay to their families and enabling soldiers to vote in the field.

Civil War casualties listed for the Town of Ossining include two men who, if they did not live in the vicinity of Scarborough or Whitson's Corners (later Briarcliff Manor), were almost certainly connected with families who did. They were Cassius Bishop of the 7th

New York Heavy Artillery, who died in Andersonville Prison in September 1864, and Private Andrew J. Orser of Company E, 51st Infantry, who died in November 1864 and is buried in Sparta Cemetery.[3]

Two or three men from the village, among them Fred Becker and Bob Grannis of Scarborough Road, served in the Spanish-American War. Marion Dinwiddie remembered seeing the troops off down the road, cheering them on and then greeting them when they returned. It was, as she said, "a very short war."[4]

A window in the Briarcliff Congregational Church depicts Saint George overcoming the dragon. It is inscribed: "In Memory of the Soldiers and Sailors who died in the War with Spain, 1898." The story of Edward Harden's scoop, as a young reporter, of the news of Admiral Dewey's victory at Manila Bay is told in Chapter 13.

5

Walter Law

Whitson's School, Pleasantville Road

INLAND FROM Scarborough Corners, about three miles as the crow flies, were the sleepier beginnings of a community called Whitson's Corners, after the family that owned and farmed some four hundred acres around the junction of Pleasantville and South State roads (the latter then named Unionville Road because it led to Unionville, later named Hawthorne). A one-room schoolhouse, District No. 6, built around 1865, was called Whitson's School after John Whitson, who donated the land near the present Route 9A access road on Pleasantville Road. The Richard Whitson house, now number 857 Pleasantville Road, still stands. Whitson's post office, established in 1881, was for some time in the Joseph Whitson house, called The Crossways (later a teahouse), on the southeast corner where the parish house of the Congregational Church now stands. The first train on the New York City and Northern Railroad (later named the Putnam Division of the New York Central) stopped at "Whitson's Station" in 1880.

In 1867 Whitson's School was replaced by the White School—so called because it was painted white. George A. Todd, Jr. replaced Paris Bowers as the sole teacher of thirty-five students in all grades. Attendance varied with the seasons because the farmers' children stayed home to help with planting and harvesting. Todd worked his own farm at his family home, the old Washburn house on Washburn Road. (The Todds and Washburns were related.) Todd also taught Sunday school and was instrumental in establishing the Congregational Church. Before he retired, almost forty years after he first started to teach, he was the growing school district's first superintendent. Todd School and Todd Lane are named for him.

With the arrival of Walter Law in 1890, great changes suddenly began in the central and eastern parts of the present village. Almost all of the land was farmed, but because farming was less and less rewarding, many young men and women had gone to work in the industries that were growing up in the county, especially along the Hudson River. Walter Law, a vice-president of the W. & J. Sloane Company, had been living in Yonkers with his wife, Georgianna Ransom Law, and their two sons and three daughters when a struggle with tuberculosis forced him, at the age of sixty-one, to retire. He bought Briarcliff Farm, the 236-acre Stillman farm, between Pleasantville and Old Briarcliff roads, for $35,000. Then

31

Walter W. Law as a young man

Walter W. Law and his wife Georgianna Ransom Law

Walter W. Law

*Daughters of Walter and Georgianna Law about 1888
(left to right): Georgie, Martha, Carolyn, and Edith.*

Map of Briarcliff from 1891
"Atlas of Westchester County,"
published by Watson & Company

Interior of dairy barn

Original Briarcliff Farm dairy, Woodside Avenue.

Farm team on Dalmeny Road

"Briarcliff Aristocrat" at Barn C

he added to it, in rapid succession, 160 acres bought from Jesse Bishop, 48 acres from Stephen Buckhout, 106 acres from Aaron Hyatt, 115 acres from John Kip, 90 acres from John Whitson, 112 acres from John Washburn, 368 acres from Emma Minnerly, and a number of smaller tracts. In all he made some forty purchases in less than ten years for sums ranging from $1,200 to $35,000. By 1900, he owned more than five thousand acres, including large tracts in Yorktown, Millwood, Pound Ridge and as far afield as Glenville, Connecticut.

In the Briarcliff Manor-Scarborough Historical Society there is a complete record of these land purchases, and the dates mortgages were paid off, in Law's own neat, spidery hand. Some of the farms were worked on shares with their former owners as indicated by this entry for the Bishop farm: "Third of everything except hay and straw of which *I* get one half."

On this increasing acreage, Law at once set about building his Briarcliff Farms. To those of his new neighbors who were glad to work for him he added others invited down from upstate, until there were some three hundred workers. Briarcliff Farms specialized in pure-bred Jerseys and was one of the first producers of certified milk in America. Besides cattle, there were some five hundred pigs, four thousand chickens, many thoroughbred horses, some pheasants, a few peacocks and a flock of sheep.

There were six main barns: Barn A, near the farm office building (later the operating engineer's office) on Pleasantville Road, housed all the horses, both farm and livery. Surrounding Barn A were the blacksmith shop, wheelwright shop, harness shop and other buildings, including the Briarcliff Steamer Company No. 1, the first firefighting organization in the village. Barns B and C, on Dalmeny Road, housed 78 and 118 head of the milking herd. Barn D, at the junction of Beech Hill Road and Route 117, housed 116 of the milking herd. (This barn later was used as a boarding stable for horses.) Barn E, for another 118 milk cows, was on Pleasantville Road just east of the present Taconic Parkway, and Barn F, on the old Saw Mill River Road, west of the crossing of the Taconic and Route 100, housed 118 more. At each barn there was an icehouse. The ice, used to cool the milk, was harnessed from Echo Lake and Kinderogen Lane (now part of the Girl Scout property). There were also young stock farms throughout the county, one of which was the Cross River Farm of eight hundred-odd acres, later part of the Pound Ridge Reservation.

The three to four thousand quarts of milk produced daily by the milking herd and the cream and butter were processed at the Briarcliff Dairy (the stone building still standing on Woodside Avenue) and sent to New York City every night via the Putnam Division Railroad for delivery the following day. The milk (12 cents a quart), cream and butter were sold at the Windsor Arcade, Fifth Avenue and 46th Street. The milk was also sold by the glass in leading hotels and restaurants. An order for seven pints of milk, seven and one-half pints of cream and two pounds of butter processed at the Briarcliff Dairy on December 21, was put on board the S.S. *Luciana*, reached Liverpool on December 29, was transferred to the S.S. *Carmania* on January 5 and found "fresh and sweet" when the last pint was used in New York Harbor on January 13. The milk won a gold medal at the Paris Exposition in 1900.[1]

Law gave prizes at Christmas time for the best kept barn, the cleanest room in the dalmeny (dormitory) Harmony Hall, which he built for the workers, and for the gentlest handler of his cows. He insisted that cows do better under humane treatment and allowed no shouting or abuse of any kind. A man he saw kick a cow was told to work elsewhere.

Advertisement for Briarcliff Farm products

Law established a School of Practical Agriculture and Horticulture on Pleasantville Road at the present site of Frank B. Hall. "I shall not be satisfied to stop," he said, "until the Briarcliff Farms has placed itself in the forefront of any institution of its kind to be found in the whole country."

Who was this Walter Law, who after "his health compelled him" to retire from business, went on with such energy and care to build a community? "Rugs to riches," a phrase possibly used by snobs of the gilded age to describe William Sloane, Law's employer,[2] is even more appropriate for Law. Walter William Law was born in 1837, the son of a carpet dealer in Kidderminster (carpet country), England. Educated locally and in his father's office, he went to work as a draper at the age of fourteen and at twenty-two travelled to New York City without friends or money to seek the fortune he was well on his way to finding six years later when he became a partner of W. & J. Sloane Company. His first employment in this country was with a carpet company as a travelling salesman at a dollar a day. When he discovered the company was passing domestic carpet as imported, he quit the job. One of the many mottoes by which he lived, "Nothing is good enough if it can be bettered," is well illustrated by the great betterment of American carpetmaking in the course of his buisness career. Many years later, at his seventieth birthday celebration at his Briarcliff Lodge attended by many dignitaries, it was said that Walter Law had played a central role in the shift of control of the carpet industry to this country from his native England.

As a partner, Law developed the wholesale department of W. & J. Sloane Company, and when he secured the account of the Alexander Smith & Sons Carpet Company in Yonkers for marketing moquette carpets, it naturally fell to him to manage the account. The remarkable growth of the Smith Company from that time was largely due to his energy and good judgment, the "dogged perseverance" he called his British birthright.

Horticulture, like dairy farming, was profitable in the vicinity of the growing city, and with the assistance of the Piersons, "of famous name in the rose business," Law took up

rose culture. The greenhouse space soon grew to seventy-five thousand square feet and the annual return from the sale of American Beauty roses went up to $100,000 a year. Twelve greenhouses were owned and operated by Paul M. Pierson and F.R. Pierson. As many as eight thousand roses were cut and shipped to florists daily, packed in long wooden boxes filled with newspapers and ice. Carnations also were grown. While most of the roses were shipped to New York City, some that were sent to Scotland were received "fresh and fragrant" eighteen days after they were cut.

The greenhouses were on the hill between Pine and Sleepy Hollow roads, just above where Fountain Road now runs. There Paul Pierson's foreman, George Romaine, "with God's help and blessing," propagated the pink Briarcliff Rose. Sports taken from a Columbia rose were on the verge of being thrown out when Pierson noticed several were producing flowers that were a decided improvement over the parent plant, at that time considered the leading pink rose. The buds were longer and more pointed, the color was brighter, and every bud was perfect. Pierson had the rose registered as the Briarcliff Rose with the American Rose Society. Romaine and his "loyal and dedicated daily workers" propagated it in quantity, and it became very popular.

In the 1920s, the Romaines lived close to the greenhouses in the second house from the corner of Sleepy Hollow Road. Their granddaughter, Marie Davis (Mrs. Everett) Evelyn, remembers that when she was a child "the highlight of the week" for her family was the Sunday visit with the Romaines. Marie would slip away up the path to the greenhouses, "the magical world of roses, roses, roses," where on Sundays the only sound was the whispering of the steam pipes around the raised rosebeds, the moisture releasing the "fragrance of the living earth and plants." The center path of narrow, wooden boards led to a door outside. Just beyond were steps up to the door to the next greenhouse and then the next and the next. The Romaines had seven children and ten grandchildren, and there was always singing as they gathered around the piano. Grandfather Romaine was a

Briarcliff Table Water, a pure, deep spring product bottled at the spring and delivered in cases, has a large distribution in and about New York. To secure the delivery of Briarcliff table water at your home or office, telephone the New York office of Briarcliff Lodge. 7071 Bryant.

Methodist and always asked to sing hymns, most often his favorite, "Nearer My God to Thee."

For Walter Law, one enterprise naturally led to another, and when he foresaw the potential of Briarcliff's pure water, he formed the Briarcliff Table Water Company on Pleasantville Road, near where Saint Theresa's Church now stands. The water, from reservoirs 250 feet below all surface contamination, was bottled at the well and sold at the New York store of Briarcliff Farms and at other stores in Yonkers, Tarrytown, White Plains, Ossining and Lakewood, New Jersey.

Near the Table Water Company, the Briarcliff Print Shop was kept busy printing dairy information, advertisements, even bottle caps, and in 1900 the "Briarcliff Bulletin," which contained information and articles on agricultural matters. In 1903, "Briarcliff Once a Week," edited and largely composed by Arthur Emerson, first appeared. This booklet was handsomely laid out and illustrated and contained elegant, brief essays on nature, religion and bits of history as well as the social news of Briarcliff Lodge and Pocantico Lodge, listing the occasions and names of guests, who included F. W. Woolworth, J. Pierpont Morgan and Chauncey Depew. Pocantico Lodge had replaced Walter Law's School of Practical Agriculture in the building on Pleasantville Road, which was later Miss Knox's School and still later the site of F. B. Hall.

Walter Law built the Briarcliff Lodge on the highest point of his estate, overlooking the Hudson River and the countryside for many miles. As a brochure that was circulated at the time put it, "Every room commands an inspiring view." A resort hotel, the Lodge, in its first decades, served mostly as a summer residence for New Yorkers. Also convenient for commuters and visitors to the city, it was easily accessible by train either over "the main line of the New York Central" to Scarborough or, from downtown, by way of the Sixth and Ninth Avenue elevated lines to 155th Street, where these connected with trains of the

Putnam Division of the New York Central to Briarcliff Manor Station. (The New York and Putnam Railroad Company merged with the New York Central system in 1913.) The original Whitson's and Briarcliff Manor railroad station was removed to Millwood, where it can still be seen in the 1990s. The new station was built and fully furnished with rugs and tables and chairs in the fashionable Mission style. Lodge automobiles met principal trains at both Scarborough and Briarcliff stations, and touring car and coaching parties ran from Central Park and 59th Street in the city "into the State road of perfect macadam which intersects Briarcliff Manor village." Some Lodge guests also travelled by private motor car and by yacht to Scarborough dock.

Guests at the Lodge enjoyed meals prepared by "the finest chefs" from "choice vegetables and fruits . . . grown in Briarcliff gardens . . . Briarcliff milk, cream and butter and Briarcliff Table Water." They might find there "perfect rest" or enjoy a variety "of delightful recreation . . . to fill their days with pleasure." A golf course "with the start and finish near the Lodge and clubhouse features midway, a music room equipped with a pipe organ and other musical instruments, concerts every afternoon and evening during the season, a swimming pool [indoor], a small theatre, a casino with a billiard and pool room, a library, several parlors, [a ballroom] and lounging rooms for . . . social diversions." Out of doors, there were "well-kept tennis courts and many inviting wood paths." For "the health and happiness of children every provision [was] made in the way of play-grounds, swings . . . and croquette grounds, freedom seldom possible at a large resort hotel, and the best companionship." There was a stable of well-kept saddle horses and many well-shaded dirt roads to ride on, and a baseball field on which a Lodge organization played a fixed-date schedule. For "automobile patrons" there was a special dining hall, with dressing rooms, smoking rooms and "perfect provision for the comfort of their attendants [chauffeurs] and the safe keeping of their machines." There was a garage with a large parking floor, "a repair and supply shop, dining room and chamber service," and "for guests without automobiles

a livery of Fiat touring cars and limousines for use at any time."

Over the years the Lodge had many distinguished guests, including Franklin Roosevelt, when he was governor of New York, Alfred E. Smith when he was governor, Jimmy Walker, mayor of New York City, film stars Warner Baxter, Mary Pickford and Tallulah Bankhead, operatic contralto Ernestine Schumann-Heinck and actress Sarah Bernhardt.

Some longtime Briarcliff residents reminisce about the great days of the Lodge: chauffeurs in blue, gray and purple uniforms to match the automobiles they drove (Margaret Pearson Finne): Sir Thomas Lipton in his Pierce Arrow with the top down; Mrs. Huntington Hartford with her daughter and son-in-law, two granddaughters, three chauffers and a maid; room and board for a servant thirty-five dollars a month (Stanley O'Connor); attendants sweeping the morning dew from the croquet lawns so that the ladies would not get their slippers damp (Joan Goldsborough).

In 1923, Chauncey Depew Steele took out a twenty-year lease on Briarcliff Lodge "with the determination of adding several important attractions and refinements . . . without omitting one single little thing that has made the Lodge so delightful in the past."[3] It was to be "an all-year resort hotel de luxe" with facilities for all winter sports, "one of the notable dance orchestras of the metropolis," and, golf professional (instructor), Gene Sarazen, who held the titles of (U.S.) Open Champion and Professional Champion and had "defeated Walter Hagen in the unofficial match for the World's Championship." To "the sporty nine holes" already at the Lodge was added a new championship course for a total of 18 holes "obtainable only at a few golfing Edens."

As one of the refinements added at the Lodge, Chauncey Steele installed Maurice LaCroix

Louis XV costume ball at Briarcliff Lodge. Far right, Henry Law; front right, Gertrude Watson Law; front far left, Katherine Moran Douglas; left (behind Douglas), Dorothea Watson; third from left rear, Gregory Maue, and to his left, Leila Peacock Maue.

as head chef. LaCroix had entered the hotel business at the age of fourteen as assistant chef at the Hotel Bel Dor in Reims. He emigrated to the United States when he was seventeen and worked at the Astor, Belmont, Knickerbocker and Biltmore hotels in New York City and at the Sleepy Hollow Country Club in Scarborough. At the Lodge LaCroix composed all the menus. Dinner for the "Bonne Annee Carnival," December 31, 1924, was "Grapefruit Pamplemousse, Consomme Viveur, Surprise Ostendaise [the fish], Dindonneau Farci Roti a la Vatel [the turkey], Carrots Glacees Vichy, Pommes Douces Louisianne, Petits Pois Au Beurre, Salade Briarcliff, Florida Iceberg, Friandises, Bonbons, Demi Tasse, White Rock and Apollinaris." The everyday, a la carte menu was somewhat plainer but very complete, including twelve hors d'oeuvres as well as oysters and clams (at 50 cents a serving), seven kinds of soup (45 cents), eight salads, five kinds of ice cream and baked Alaska ($1.25). The most expensive item listed under Roasts and Grill was Roast Long Island Duckling (half) $2.50; (for two) $4.00. Lobster *Newburg* was $1.50. In season, all vegetables were picked in the Lodge gardens. On one occasion Dr. Charles Brieant was summoned to the Lodge in the small hours of the morning. Everyone there, from the humblest scullion to the most celebrated and wealthy guest, was deathly sick. The cause of this sudden plague, it was discovered, was Paris Green, a primitive insecticide, on the broccoli. (This incident was not during the tenure of Chef LaCroix.)

Entertainment at the 1924 New Year carnival dinner consisted of eight acts, including: "MISS BONNIE MURRAY with Mr. John Dolan, Solo and Ball-Room Dances; DELMAR, An Oriental Phantasy from the Land of King Tut-tut; MUSETTE, From the European Concert Stage, A Gypsy Violinist; TRIXIE HICKS, A Flurry of Dimpled Knees, Snap-

Maurice LaCroix, head chef at Briarcliff Lodge

*Original Briarcliff Congrega-
tional Church, 1897*

py Bits of Singing and Dancing.'' Dance music at that New Year's Eve celebration was provided by four orchestras—the Clifford Dance Orchestra in the Mirror Room, Robert Gunther's Briarcliff Lodge Orchestra in the Ball Room, Robert Gunther's Melody Men in the Card Room and Robert Gunther's Rolling Stones in the Stone Room.[4]

In 1930, Chef LaCroix left Briarcliff Lodge for the Concourse Plaza Hotel. He returned to Briarcliff to work at the Sleepy Hollow Country Club from 1939 to 1945.

The lake near the Lodge was converted, in 1912, into a "Roman pool" the largest outdoor pool in the world, in which Gertrude Ederle, the most famous swimmer of her time, and Johnny Weismuller, best known as Tarzan in the first films of that name, tried out for the U.S. Olympics in 1924. In 1926 the U.S. Olympic winter trials took place at the Lodge. A ski jump was constructed from a platform in front of the Lodge down to Dalmeny Road, and the jump and landing covered with snow shipped from Canada by rail, six freight cars full. Some of the snow was discovered to have cinders in it, so three more cars of fresh snow were brought in. Also in the snow, it is happily remembered, were packed some bottles of Canadian whisky, a rare treat in those Prohibition years.

As business prospered, extensions to the Lodge were built, a north wing of sixty-five guest rooms and a west wing with six floors above ground and three below and, from the roof, a view of Manhattan to the south and Stony Point and Bear Mountain to the north.

The Briarcliff Congregational Church was an outgrowth of a Sunday school started in the White schoolhouse by Edgar Johnson, Jr., and others from the Sing Sing Heights Chapel (later the Ossining Heights Methodist Church) on Camp Woods Road. When the schoolteacher, George A. Todd, Jr., became superintendent of the Sunday school in 1896, he approached Walter Law concerning the need for a more permanent and better-equipped church. Law responded with characteristic enthusiasm and generosity; the property at Elm and South State Road was transferred to the church by deed of gift and by Christmas of the same year the southern part of the present building, the Norman tower and the nave, were completed. Law had been an elder and a generous contributor to the First Presbyterian Church in Yonkers, but before deciding on the denomination of the new church he called a meeting of the people identified with the Sunday school and all other interested villagers. Because those assembled were of many different denominations, it was decided that the new congregation should join the Fellowship of Congregational Churches because of the Congregationalists' democratic policy. Some years later Arthur Emerson wrote: "Within the population of the place nearly or quite all forms of Protestant belief were represented, but a canvass showed that there were no Congregationalists . . . and all other creeds were disarmed and rallied to the standard of active support."[5] That former affiliations of members continued to be diverse is shown by the clerk's list at the time of the fiftieth anniversary of the church in 1946. Twenty-three denominations were represented, including "four Lutheran groups . . . Protestant Episcopal, Parish Church of Scotland, Free Church of Scotland, Friends (Quakers), German Evangelical, German Dutch Reformed, Unitarian, Finnish Evangelical, Swiss Reformed, Calvary Evangelical, Disciples of Christ and a Jew."[6]

To his initial gift to the community of the church property Walter Law added the manse, two pipe organs, and the northern part of the church, consisting of the transepts and the original Sunday school rooms, dedicated in 1905. He also gave four Tiffany windows, the first, the "Joseph Window" in the front of the church, dedicated in 1898 to the memory of his longtime friends Mr. and Mrs. William Sloane of New York City. He said of the church, "My heart is here." When the Premier of Canada asked him for a tour of Briarcliff Farms at eleven o'clock on a Sunday morning, Law replied that he hoped the Premier would visit some other time because he had "an engagement every Sunday morning at 11."

Enrollment in the Sunday school, about sixty in 1898, quickly increased. The Women's Society, a philanthropic group, and a Young People's Christian Endeavor group were established early. The church became an important social center for young people in the village and beyond, and residents of various faiths and neighborhoods still remember and speak with pleasure of social activities there. Eileen (O'Connor) Weber and Joan (Borough) Goldsborough, who were Catholic, would attend mass and then go over to the Congregational Church. When she was in high school, Eileen "ended up on the Executive Board." She remembers the "turkey suppers . . . with Henry Law, James Minshall and Alfred Pearson carving and Mrs. Wolf, Mrs. Pearson and Mrs. Courreges serving mashed potatoes." And at Christmas there was always a present for her under the tree.

Houses for Briarcliff Farms workers on Dalmeny Road, built in 1901

As Walter Law's several enterprises prospered, the hamlet of Whitson's grew, and with it the need for municipal services. After Law's attempt in 1899 to incorporate Scarborough failed for lack of the three hundred persons per square mile required by state law, he turned his attention to the property east of his house on Scarborough Road and arranged for houses to be built and sold to the farm workers on generous terms. He held the mortgages himself. On May 15, 1901, he wrote his attorney, William A. Arthur, that he had a parcel of land of "some one and 11/100ths of a square mile with some 331 persons residing" and would soon have the petition of twenty-five adult freeholders necessary to start incorporation.

The square mile included land in both the towns of Ossining and Mount Pleasant (as allowed by state law) and within two school districts (as required by state law). The two town supervisors met with the freeholders on September 2, 1902, in the offices of the Briarcliff Farms. An election was held on September 12, the vote was favorable, and the village was officially incorporated on November 21, 1902.[7] Walter Law's friend Andrew Carnegie had called him (accurately) "The Laird of Briarcliff Manor," a title that appealed to all concerned, and so this latter day manor found its name.

The *New York Times* reported the event the following morning:

BRIARCLIFF MANOR ON STATE MAP ONLY 25 VOTES CAST BUT THEY ARE UNANIMOUS FOR THE NEW HONORS.

Enjoying the distinction of being one of the few American millionaires to own villages of their own, Walter W. Law, the prominent carpet manufacturer and popular club man, now waits with interest the election for the village officers to be held in Briarcliff Manor on the Hudson next week.

Until yesterday Mr. Law did not own a village. His possessions in Briarcliff Manor consisted simply of a large tract of improved and unimproved but unincorporated land. Yesterday the place assumed the dignity of a village. As Mr. Law owns all but two small parcels of land in the manor and employs almost all of the 100 persons who live in the village limits he had a vital interest in the result of the election to decide whether Briarcliff Manor should assume corporate airs.

The vote in favor of such a move was unanimous. The tract now forming the new village is one mile square, and part of it was [*sic*] in the town of Ossining and the remainder in Mount Pleasant. Only 25 votes were cast, 23 from Ossining and 2 from Mount Pleasant.

Mr. Law, the owner of the village, who can at will wipe out practically its entire population by discharging it, is a member of the Alpine Club, the Players', the Century Association, American Fine Arts Society, Ardsley Casino and the Metropolitan Museum of Art. He takes keen interest in municipal improvement and, it is said, will spend much money to make Briarcliff Manor a model village.

The residents of Scarborough, intent, then as later, on maintaining a separate identity, held out for a year or two before petitioning for annexation to the village of Briarcliff Manor in order to receive municipal services. In 1906, annexation was granted.

On his seventieth birthday, in 1907, Walter Law, in an address to the men of Briarcliff, "all his larger family," told the story of his life, from his "sweetest" childhood memories of praying with his mother to his struggles with tuberculosis and starting the first farm. If it had not been for the "urgent and repeated, and earnest requests" of Mr. MacColl, rector of the Briarcliff Congregational Church, he said, he would not have spoken of himself, although he would gladly have talked about Briarcliff, for, as he said, "I love it with all my heart." He closed the address with the following words:

You see, I did not find an ideal condition in the country. Yet, it has been given to me to work it out and to make an ideal country life up here, which I have been endeavouring to do. But what of the future? It may be that I shall not be able to speak to you again in this delightful way, for the shades of Life's evening are drawing around me, or I should say that the glimmer of the Beulah Land is already dawning. But I have strong conviction that with the golden rule always in the ascendant Briarcliff Manor will go on to increase both in numbers and moral power, each member of it as one happy family, filled with charity and thoughtful consideration for his neighbor, and above all, having the blessing of the Lord. "It maketh rich and addeth no sorrow thereto." A veritable Garden of Eden, where God Himself will love to dwell.

PART III

THE MILLIONAIRES' ESTATES

*V. Everit Macy with his staff at
Chilmark Farm*

6

The Elliott Shepards

I N THE EARLY 1890s Colonel and Mrs. Elliott Fitch Shepard came to Scarborough, to live in Woodlea, the 140-room Renaissance Revival mansion designed for them by Stanford White. The Shepards had been married in 1868 and had six children, five of whom lived to maturity. Mrs. Shepard was Margaret Louisa Vanderbilt, one of the eight children of William Henry Vanderbilt, the oldest son and principal heir of Commodore Cornelius Vanderbilt, who had been the richest man in the nation. After William Henry Vanderbilt's death in 1885, all eight Vanderbilt heirs built palaces where they could live, as Louis Auchincloss put it, "in the style to which Vanderbilts rapidly began to accustom the newspaper readers of their day. . . . By 1893 [they] had probably between them more beaux arts palazzi, more wide-ranging rural demesnes, more yachts, pleasure domes, greenhouses, and servants than any other group of siblings since those of Napoleon Bonaparte."[1]

Elliott F. Shepard

Colonel Shepard was admitted to the bar in 1858, and for twenty-five years "organized and was counsel for banks, savings banks, insurance companies, churches, and commercial and other enterprises . . . [and did] much toward settling the railroad law of the State. . . . In 1876 he was a founder of the New York State Bar Association, of which he became president in 1884."[2] In the same year he gave up his law practice to devote himself to travel and writing. His best known pamphlet "Labor and Capital Are One" was translated into various languages and sold more than a quarter of a million copies. In it he called the modern corporation "one of the greatest blessings of the nineteenth century, and a distinguishing mark of its civilization." In 1888 Shepard bought the *Mail and Express* from Cyrus Field and managed that newspaper, shaping "its policy on every question and writing many of the editorials," until his death in 1893. He aimed "to introduce the Christian spirit into journalism."[3]

Louis Auchincloss describes Colonel Shepard as "a strict Presbyterian who had not wanted to allow the municipal bus lines in which he invested to operate on Sundays. He was a hard, autocratic man, possessed of much worldly ambition; he wanted the great house that he had erected in Scarborough, New York, to be the seat of a dynasty. It is now the Sleepy Hollow Country Club.

"Shepard, who dissipated all of his wife's money that was not tied up in trust, was not popular in the family. He told one of his daughters that her personal deformity was a punishment from God."[4] Margaret Shepard, on the other hand, was much loved by all the family.

A cousin and close friend of the Shepards' daughter Edith, Adele Sloane, visited Edith at Woodlea three weeks before her marriage to James A. Burden. (Adele was also the granddaughter of William Sloane, Walter Law's sometime employer and friend.) She made the following entry in her diary:

Scarborough, Sunday, May 12 [1895]

I spent most of last week here and came up again early yesterday morning. This will be my last Sunday with Edith until I am married. I only have three more to spend as a girl, only three weeks and four days left of my girl life. I have felt very serious and very quiet these last few days. I am realizing so much more the reality of leaving this first part of my life and starting on the second,

the fuller, larger, more earnest life of the future. God help me to make it all that it now is in my dreams.

How wonderfully beautiful the country looks! The fresh green trees, the long stretches of green lawn, the orchards of white apple blossoms, the smell of lilacs, the blue violets, the wonder of it all! . . . Tomorrow will be my last day in town, tomorrow night the last night in my room. . . . It is very hard to be sensible and calm with all these thoughts crowding on me. Mr. [Chauncey] Depew gave me a dinner Friday night, also the last dinner I go to as a girl.

Chauncey Mitchell Depew for fifty-nine years an attorney in the service of Commodore Vanderbilt's New York & Harlem Railroad and its allied lines, and for twelve years United States senator from New York, was a frequent guest at Briarcliff Lodge.

Adele Sloane's diary continues:

My wedding presents are beginning to come in faster and faster. . . . Papa gave me a gorgeous diamond sun, the largest one I have ever seen. Mother gave me a diamond and sapphire necklace,

The family of William Henry Vanderbilt painted by Seymour Guy in 1873. Left to right are William Henry, Frederick, Marie (Mrs. William Henry), George, Florence, William K., Lila, Margaret Shepard, Elliott Shepard, a servant, Emily Sloane, another servant in rear, Alice (Mrs. Cornelius II), William D. Sloane (buttoning Emily's glove) and Cornelius II.

Adele Sloan with her first cousin Edith Shepard in 1894. Edith is in mourning for her father.

one that she has worn a little herself and therefore all the dearer to me, and from Uncle Corneil [Cornelius] a most gorgeous stomacher of diamonds and one enormous pearl . . . enough to turn my head and quite spoil me. . . .

LATER. Edith and I have just come back from a walk together and such a nice long talk. I am sure that the talk we had that day in Marguerite's still quiet room [Marguerite Shepard died of pneumonia January 31, 1895, at the age of fifteen] with her peaceful white face smiling near us, brought us closer together than we had been in years. I only hope that we will not grow apart again, never lose the sympathy which makes the perfect understanding of friendship. A woman in her married life needs her friends just as much, perhaps more than when she is a girl. The sun has just set behind the hills, and there is such a beautiful glow of light on the river. There is such tremendous happiness inside of me that the world seems almost supernaturally beautiful.

As the community of workers and artisans who had come to Scarborough to build Woodlea grew more numerous, they indicated a desire for church services. Colonel and Mrs. Shepard bought the country store and "the Corner" as the site for a new church. The little store was enlarged and remodeled with new diamond-paned windows, new floors, "huge" kerosene lamps, side lamps with reflectors and new porches. Starting late in 1892, church services were held in the former store, with the Reverend Frank Fenton Blessing, a graduate of Princeton Theological Seminary, in charge.[5]

The congregation applied to the Westchester Presbytery in Mount Kisco, and the Scarborough Presbyterian Church was organized. On the recommendation of Stanford White, the architect of Woodlea, the Shepards engaged the firm of Haydel & Shepard to draw up the plans. Augustus Dennis Shepard of that firm was Colonel Shepard's brother, a vice-president of the American Bank Note Company,[6] and, later, the colonel's executor. Carpenters, masons, stonecutters and many other skilled craftsmen began the giant task of preparing the ground and building. Quicksand at the back of the property made it necessary to excavate thirty feet below the surface for a solid concrete foundation. A special side-

*Architectural sculpture above
doorway of Scarborough Presbyterian Church*

Wedding of Edith Shepard and Ernesto Fabbri, October 20, 1896. The wedding party is on the steps of Woodlea.

track was added to the two-track railroad to deliver great slabs of granite, Indiana limestone and wood.

Among the new residents the building of the church brought to Scarborough was John Smith, who came from Scotland to take charge of all the stonework. His family grew up in the neighborhood and, in due course, his two sons, William Murchieson and George McNeil Smith, married two Holden sisters, Helen and Harriet. When their sister, Euphemia Smith, was married to Scottish John Duncan, a master gardener, a band of pipers in kilts and tartans marched up Kemeys Avenue playing appropriate Scottish airs in celebration of the event.

Elliott Fitch Shepard, Jr., the son of Colonel and Mrs. Shepard, laid the cornerstone of the new church on October 13, 1893, with a suitably engraved, silver trowel. Colonel Shepard died in the spring of the same year, but Mrs. Shepard continued with their plans and the completed church was dedicated in May of 1895. The local paper described the event as follows: "In the large company that thronged about the building . . . one saw the loving neighbors and helpers of Mr. Shepard come at his bidding to bless his work for them and to mingle their tears of sorrow at his untimely death with their grateful acknowledgment of his generous deeds and purposes which are already assured and imperishable.[7]

Scarborough Church is described by Frank Sanchis in *American Architecture: Westchester County, New York*, as follows:

Panels of carefully laid small-scale fieldstone (on the exterior walls) are contained by borders of smooth-finished granite and Indiana limestone. Italian Renaissance details are appended to a straightforward, traditional plan featuring a square tower . . . at the front center of a simple, gable-roofed nave. Of particular interest . . . are the cupola and the arched entryway set into the tower, with a finely carved relief sculpture in the Tympanum. . . . The interior . . . contains an exceptional, coffered-wood ceiling over the entire nave. The wood is finished in a natural, dark tone and contrasts with the delicate plaster treatment of the balance of the interior. The nave terminates in a semi-circular chancel lighted by a skylight and containing an unusual, built-in wood seat along the entire perimeter.[8]

The Scarborough Church organ, made around 1894 "by J. J. and C. S. Odell & Company at a cost of $7,357 was the first all electric action organ in the world. There were 1498 pipes in it, the longest . . . sixteen feet and made of Michigan pine . . . the smallest . . . one-half inch in length."[9] In addition to the orchestra, organized shortly after the church was built, the choir, for the first ten years, was a paid quartette. There was a choir of men and boy sopranos, then one of boys and girls, who sang at the evening services.

The first wedding in the church was Edith Shepard's, on October 20, 1896. The bridegroom was the son of Ernesto Fabbri, partner of Drexel, Morgan & Company, who had met Edith in Europe. The event was reported in *The New York Times* as "one of the most brilliant weddings celebrated in Westchester County." The church was decorated with banks of chrysanthemums and asparagus fern, the stained-glass windows and the aisles were wreathed and garlanded. A special train brought two hundred guests from the city. The bride wore a Worth gown, and favors for the bridesmaids and ushers were diamond and emerald pins. "An immense number of presents were received by the young couple. Ex-detective Sgt. Charles Heidelberg with ten picked men from New York will guard them until they can be removed to the city. Festivities on the estate were concluded by a dinner to the 150 employees."[10] During the ceremony the church was crowded with members of New York Society, "while outside stood the members of this little community, having come on bicycles and afoot."[11]

The Church House, given by Mrs. Shepard and designed by Augustus D. Shepard, was completed in 1908. During his pastorate at the church, Mr. Blessing lived with the Misses Dennis, cousins of Mr. Shepard, whose home was on the site of the Arcadian Shopping Center. With the arrival of the second minister, Benjamin T. Marshall, a manse was established in the house Dr. Holden had built for his son George Clarence Holden on the hill

The church house of the Scarborough Presbyterian Church completed in 1908

"Camelot Circle" of Scarborough Presbyterian Church about 1922

between the Holden homestead and Scarborough Road (later the Easton house). The present manse, next to the Sparta Burying Grounds on Revolutionary Road, was given by Mrs. Shepard and completed in 1913. It was designed by William C. Holden, son of George C. Holden, who was the builder, and who owned and operated the Ossining Pressed Stone Company on the river front in Ossining village.

Scarborough Presbyterian Church became as busy a social center as any church in the village. Elizabeth Smith, the church organist, daughter of William and Helen Holden Smith, remembers her family walking down Scarborough Road to the church two and three times on Sundays. The Women's Missionary Society, the Ladies' Aid and the Christian Endeavor were organized during the pastorate of Mr. Blessing. The boys' group called themselves the Knights of King Arthur and the girls were the Camelot Circle. Well before Christmas, the Sunday school teacher would ask the children what they wanted, and on Christmas Eve they would find whatever gifts they had asked for, a sled or a new suit, under the tree in the Church House. (Betty Smith always asked for a book.) Mrs. Shepard, their principal benefactor, would be at the Christmas party, sitting quietly on the sidelines. Other annual events were an all-day Fourth of July celebration, with races and games, fireworks and late-evening refreshments, and an excursion to Coney Island and Rockaway on a rented steamboat that sailed from Scarborough Dock, with music for entertainment and dancing provided by the church orchestra. A long afternoon at the beach and amusement park would be followed by a moonlight voyage back up the Hudson.

Among the ministers of Scarborough Church were Edmund Melville Wylie (1938–1947), who wrote several chancel dramas, two of which were presented in the church by parishioners, and Robert Patton Montgomery (1947–1956), who while in Scarborough started the School for Skeptics, which became known nationwide. Montgomery left to undertake special work at Princeton University, where he was appointed director of the Westminster Foundation.

During the pastorate of Roger A. Huber (1956–1963), a fund drive was undertaken to remodel the Church House. New classrooms, kitchen, minister's study, and office were built and the Fellowship Hall remodeled. This was the first building program to be accomplished by church members without assistance from the Shepard family. Mr. Huber left Scarborough to accept a call from the Riverdale, New York, Presbyterian Church.

"Knights of King Arthur" of the Scarborough Presbyterian Church watching the high jump on the Holbrook School playing field on July 4, 1910. From left: Frank Brigham, Arthur Slater, Chet C. (?), and William Holden.

Scarborough Presbyterian Church group on steamboat outing with church orchestra

7

The V. Everit Macys and Chilmark

I N 1896, V. (for Valentine) Everit Macy
bought several large tracts of land just north
and west of Walter Law's Briarcliff Farms.
Macy, then in his mid-twenties, was the son of an official of the Standard Oil Company,
a descendant of prosperous Nantucket whalers, and nephew of a founder of R. H. Macy
& Company. He and his bride, Edith Carpenter, set up housekeeping in their newly built
Tudor-style stone and stucco mansion set on the highest hill of their estate, overlooking
the Hudson. They named it Chilmark, after the Macy family's ancestral home in England.
The Macy's property, added to over the following quarter of a century, amounted to some
300 acres bounded, roughly, by Old Briarcliff and Pleasantville roads on the east, Croton
Avenue to the north and Holbrook and Scarborough roads on the south and west, with
some lots on its western border within the Village of Ossining. The old gate house, now
missing its porte-cochere, still stands at the corner of Holbrook and Scarborough roads.
The mansion was surrounded by gently sloping lawns planted with shade trees and shrub-
bery, meadows and woodlands. Great stone barns housed Guernsey cows, givers of prize-
winning milk, and Hampshire Down sheep. There was a greenhouse for the gardens, a
carriage house with apartments over it for the help, a chicken house, a stable of spirited
ponies, a polo field (the Holbrook School football field), squash courts, a swimming pool,
two tennis courts and a small but challenging (par 27) nine-hole golf course.

*Macy gatehouse with porte
cochere at the corner of Holbrook
and Scarborough Road*

At Chilmark the Macys raised a family, two sons, Valentine E., Jr., and J. (for Josiah)
Noel, and a daughter, Editha. Everit Macy was a member, and for a time treasurer, of Saint
Mary's Beechwood. Mrs. Macy, like her husband's Nantucket forebears, was a Quaker,
but, Marion Dinwiddie reminisced, "She sent her little daughter Editha down to church
for the second service on Easter and they were singing, 'He is risen! He is risen!' and the
little girl got very excited and turned to her neighbor and said, 'Oh, He is risen! Does Mother
know?'"

Marion Dinwiddie also remembered that, "The first automobile around here was one
that was driven by Everit Macy . . . and we would sit up on this hill and watch Mr. Macy
dash down the road and then we'd wait half an hour and we would see Mr. Macy walking
back, and after a suitable interval his coachman would go down with a team of horses to

haul the thing back, and Mrs. Macy said, 'I am not fond enough of walking to go out riding with Everit!' "

The Macy family devoted much time and effort, as well as money, to social welfare and civic programs of many kinds. V. Everit Macy in 1913 was elected county superintendent of the poor (the title later changed to commissioner of public welfare). Perhaps because of his early enthusiasm for automobiles, he was a founder of the Westchester Parkway system, and in the four years before he died in 1930, president of the Westchester Park Commission. Mrs. Macy was a founder of the Westchester Children's Association and a force in the Girl Scout movement. As a memorial to his wife, in 1925, Macy gave 265 acres just over the village line on Chappaqua Road for the establishment of the Edith Macy Training School, operated by the Girl Scouts of the United States. The school later became the national headquarters of the Girl Scouts.

Valentine E. Macy, Jr., and his brother J. Noel, helped to found the Macy Westchester Newspapers, later the Westchester Rockland Newspapers, with the avowed intention of perpetuating the social and civic programs their parents had helped to establish. While an undergraduate at Harvard, J. Noel worked on the *Lampoon*, and he was later a reporter for the Yonkers *Statesman*. The Macy chain, as the group of newspapers was commonly called, grew to include nine dailies and five weeklies. It was sold in 1964 to the Gannett Company.

The Village of Briarcliff Manor is perhaps most indebted to the Macy family for the intelligent planning of the conversion of their estate to a community of homes. In 1930, by means of the Deed Realty Company, 250 acres of Macy land were marked off as "Chilmark Park" with zones established, roads laid out and provision made for all public utilities. The family recreation center, with its swimming pool, squash and tennis courts, was made officially available to all residents of the "Park."

In its first decade, while under the control of the Macys, Chilmark was "restricted": Some members of minority groups were barred from buying property there. Hedges were allowed, but no fences could be built, and a family might wake up one morning to find a crew of men planting a large tree in their front yard to hide their house from the Macy's view.

Chilmark Park was a small, close community, as may still be seen in a film, *Hot and Bothered*, made in 1932 by Robert Gowen, who was a pioneer in radio broadcasting and an award-winning filmmaker. Gowen's films were twice selected as among the ten best films of the year by the Amateur Cinema League. A print of his film, *Ossining in Wartime*, is in the Library of Congress. Robert Gowen's father, Charles Sewall Gowen, came to Ossining to assist in supervising the rebuilding of the aqueduct and the Croton Dam. The Gowens lived in their house on the corner of Overton and Underhill roads some years before Macy bought the surrounding acres.

Another distinguished resident at the time the film was made was Herbert Gerlach, Ossining town supervisor and later county executive. Gerlach figures in the film as the peace of his summer Sunday is repeatedly disturbed by telephone calls from distraught neighbors complaining about some supposed mischief of the neighborhood children. Gerlach's exasperation mounts with the temperature of the July day. Residents and children in various states of agitation and undress run in and out of their fine houses, along dirt roads and leafy lanes, through gardens and meadows, handsome young Noel Macy, mounted on a thoroughbred, displays his horsemanship, and the plot is at last resolved when the children are discovered to be as angelic as they look, reading Bible stories aloud down by the club. Chilmark, we gather, was a sunny enclave of innocent affluence in that dark Depression year.

Chilmark is still a model suburban community, zoned for single family homes, except for the shopping center on Pleasantville Road and the apartments behind the Ossining Water Commission. In the 1980s these apartments and those for senior citizens on North State Road were the only rental units in Briarcliff Village. The Chilmark Club, originally for residents only, became a membership club after World War II and in 1980 was taken over by the Briarcliff Department of Parks and Recreation. The land that stretches from the environs of the Macy mansion, now much reduced and modified, to the backyards of Holbrook, Macy and Scarborough roads in the 1980s was the largest tract in the village that was still undeveloped. Apparently that land was still being held as an investment.

8

Briarcliff Manor, 1902–1930

THE INCORPORATION of the Village of Briarcliff Manor in 1902 was an essential preliminary to change, the last great change in the landscape from a few, very large estates to the much more numerous smaller lots of a suburban residential community. Walter Law, who in the space of little more than a decade had transformed many unprosperous farms into one large profitable estate, appears to have foreseen the next change and made ready for it. In 1907–1908 the Briarcliff Farms was removed upstate to Pine Plains, New York. The Briarcliff Realty Company, the combined real estate holdings of the Law family, had been started in 1901 in the office of the Briarcliff Farms on Pleasantville Road.

One of Walter Law's criteria for the excellence he insisted on in all his commercial ventures—locally the Briarcliff Farms, Briarcliff Lodge, the Briarcliff Greenhouses and the Briarcliff Table Water Company—was that they should be profitable. The prize Jersey cows of the Briarcliff Farms must be gently handled in barns kept scrupulously clean so that they would give better milk and more of it, for more profit. Briarcliff Lodge, built to satisfy "in every particular the most exacting taste," attracted an elite clientele. In this expectation of profit from activities associated with his residence, Law was unique among the millionaires of this region. V. Everit Macy, James Speyer and Frank Vanderlip were outstanding contributors to causes more or less distant from their estates in Briarcliff and Scarborough; Macy, Vanderlip and the Shepards were generous and conscientious members of the community; but the means of their beneficence was generated elsewhere.

The Village of Briarcliff Manor, center of a countryside that was very little developed before the 1890s, because of its founder's foresight and business acumen, soon took the form of a residential suburb. Essentials of the village developed quickly. A government was set up and departments to provide municipal services. At the first election, held in November 1902, two trustees, Walter W. Law, Jr., and J. Sidney Bayliss, and a president, William DeNyse Nichols, were elected. The number of trustees was soon increased to four, and the title was changed from "president" to "mayor." Among those who held this office in early years were V. Everit Macy, William McGowan, Henry H. Law, Dr. Dwight Holbrook,

William C. Holden and Isaac Hotaling. Walter W. Law, Jr., succeeded Nichols as president in 1905 and was succeeded in 1918 by his brother, Henry H. Law, who served until his death in 1936.

Henry Law's term as mayor, the longest in Briarcliff by at least ten years, was distinguished by his whole-hearted concern for the people of his father's village. Young and old felt free to go to him with their troubles, and their trust was always rewarded. He "gave all the prizes for the Village Field Day on Labor Day, and was known to take the young in his Model T Ford home for ice cream in the summer and cocoa in the winter. Many a hospital bill was paid, rent was paid, assistance was given in getting employment, and help given to many to get a college education."[1]

Walter Law, Jr., a graduate of Yale University Sheffield Scientific School and Albany Law School, represented the Third Assembly District of Westchester County in the New York Assembly from 1914 to 1918, when he was elected state senator and served in the higher house of the state legislature until 1920. The younger Walter Law lived in Mamaroneck with his wife and five children, but continued to serve as vice-president of the Briarcliff Realty Company.

In the minutes of one of the first meetings of the Board of Trustees of Briarcliff Village, there is a reference to the establishment of an open primary, and since that time open nonpartisan primaries have been held. This system, formalized by state law in 1946 as the People's Caucus party, yearly solicits all interested persons to run for village office. Any resident of the incorporated village who is a U.S. citizen, at least eighteen years of age and attends a meeting of the caucus is a member of the caucus and may seek nomination. The village, like Scarsdale, Rye and Pleasantville, set up and has maintained the tradition of unpaid elected officials, which has provided a long line of dedicated, hardworking public servants.

There has been a salaried village manager since 1967. Max Vogel, who had served nearly fifteen years as an exceptionally conscientious and exacting engineer and building inspec-

Henry H. Law, president and mayor of Briarcliff from 1918 to 1936

Dedication of the first municipal building on July 4, 1914. Walter Law, Jr. presented the key to the fire chief.

"Ready for the parade" at the corner of Central Drive and former section of Dalmeny Road. Building at left is the first firehouse.

Fireman's parade, 1914. Drivers are Howard Bishop and James Fleming.

tor, was appointed the first village manager. Lynn McCrum was appointed village manager in 1974. Anthony Turiano, who worked with Max Vogel from 1957 to 1967, succeeded him as village engineer and building inspector.

The first village budget, for 1903, was $3,050, the tax rate $5 per $1,000 of assessed
valuation, and the total assessed valuation of the village $61,000. In the first fifty years of
village government the budget increased to $156,265, the tax rate to $14.93 per $1,000
and the assessed valuation to $10,466,570. The village budget adopted in April, 1990 was
$6.6 million.

The Briarcliff Steamer Company #1 was organized in 1901 under the leadership of
Frederick Messinger with a horse-drawn steam-operated pumper and a hose wagon contributed by the Briarcliff Realty Company. This new apparatus took the place of a hand-
drawn chemical outfit. The Steamer Company became the official fire department of the
village on January 1, 1903. Messinger was elected first chief, an office he held three times.
The new department, which was housed in the old blacksmith shop near Barn A on Dalmeny
Road, counted forty-two members, all volunteers. In 1907 the Steamer Company was reorganized and incorporated as the Briarcliff Fire Company, and held its first election of officers, who were: President James Fleming; Vice-President Henry H. Law; Treasurer T.
Everett Bishop; Secretary L. B. Jones. In April 1908, a hook-and-ladder truck and a com-
bination hose and chemical truck, both horse drawn, were purchased from the American
La France Company.

Of many difficult local fires the Briarcliff Fire Company fought, the most memorable
were the Knox School fire in 1912 and the Dalmeny Road dairy barn fire in 1913, right
next door to the fire company. As it does today, the department also worked closely with
neighboring departments in Ossining, Pocantico Hills, Archville and Pleasantville. The firemen then were not much different from firemen in the 1980s. In the intervals of their difficult, even dangerous, firefighting, they got together to play pool, hold monthly parties and
march in parades. In 1910 they took part in a parade across the river in Kingston, travelling there by boat from Sparta dock with two pieces of apparatus and the Briarcliff Band.

In 1913, village residents voted to approve a bond resolution to build a village firehouse and buy motorized apparatus. The first municipal building, at 1133 Pleasantville Road, accommodated the Police Department, the Department of Public Works, and the Fire Department. The building was dedicated on July 4, 1914, with a great celebration. The bell, in the tower that still tops the building, for many years summoned volunteer firemen, and tolled the end of two world wars. In the 1960s, the bell was removed to a pedestal in front of the new firehouse, at 1111 Pleasantville Road.

The Briarcliff Manor Police Department began in 1906 with the appointment of patrolman L. H. Bayley and several volunteers, operating from an old barn back of the Briarcliff Realty Company office. The first official chief, Edward Cashman, was appointed by the Board of Trustees in 1907, with, shortly thereafter, two paid assistants. They patrolled the village on foot until a bicycle was purchased, followed by a motorcycle in 1908. In 1909 a notable decrease in burglaries was reported. Forty-three arrests were made during that year, twenty of disorderly persons and two of "incorrigible children."

In 1910, the founders of the Sleepy Hollow Country Club and the village officials established a joint-venture telephone for the use of patrolmen in the Scarborough region. Watchmen's punch clocks were installed at various locations to assure the Board of Trustees that rounds were being made. The first automobile, a Ford runabout, was purchased in 1923.

In 1927, Charles A. Johnson, Jr., of the Briarcliff police force, in pursuit of rum-runners at Scarborough dock, was pushed off the running board of a police car. Johnson brought the rum-runners in but died later of injuries. He was the brother of Arthur W. Johnson, chief of police from 1939 to 1963, and the uncle of Arthur W. Johnson, Jr., chief of police from 1984 to 1990.

At the first business meeting of the village in December 1902, John Hotaling was appointed street commissioner. This was the start of what was to become the Department of Public Works. Hotaling did most of the road work himself, hiring men, horses and wagons to help him as needed. At that time nearly all the roads in the village were owned by the Law enterprises. Later, as they were paved, they were turned over to the village one by one. Since 1902, many of the roads, including Pleasantville, South State, Scarborough, Long Hill and Sleepy Hollow roads, have been substantially realigned. Dalmeny Road then ran through to Central Drive, Elm Road was named Tarrytown Road, and there were parts of Washburn Road that have since disappeared altogether. Ridgecrest Road was laid out in 1932.

When, in 1914, the Village Board asked Street Commissioner Arthur Brown if an automobile would help him in his work, he replied that he preferred a horse but would use an automobile if they bought one. They did not.

The Briarcliff Table Water Company distributed water in the village through an ever-growing system, and when Briarcliff Farms moved upstate, in 1908, the village bought the water company for $75,000. Patrick Manahan, foreman of the Table Water Company, became superintendent of the village water department. Under the direction of the Village Board, Manahan created one of the finest, small-town water systems in the country. A steam pump took water from the Pocantico Brook Pond, deep wells were driven near the high school (now Pace University Village Center), and there was a reservoir on the hill between

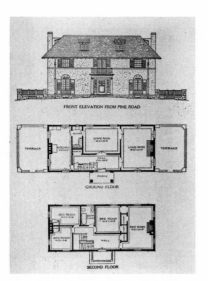

Front elevation and plan of
55 Pine Road

Pine and Dalmeny roads. When Manahan died, in 1940, his son Irving Manahan became head of the department, and served in that position until 1967. The new village also took over the first sewer system from Briarcliff Farms. The road commissioner and assistants took over snow clearing in the 1920s. During a heavy snow in 1918, employees of the Briarcliff Garage attached a board to the front of a truck and plowed all the roads in the village—for $6.00. The Public Works Department was not formally established until 1941.[2]

The removal of Briarcliff Farms left much former farmland vacant. The Briarcliff Realty Company, relocated on the site of the dairy building, which had burned in 1901, set to work promoting residential development. In "Briarcliff Once-a-Week" residential lots were advertised, along with the services of "the builder of the new Lodge at Briarcliff," Briarcliff Milk and Farm Products, Briarcliff Table Water, Frederick C. Messenger (*sic*) Plumbing, Heating and Tinning, William McGowan, Nurseryman (of Briarcliff Farms), and "inexpensive but durable carpets" from W. & J. Sloane (Walter Law's former employer). Almost everything a prospective resident might require was to be had right there in Briarcliff.

The December 29, 1907, issue of "Briarcliff Once-a-Week" published plans and a sketch of the front elevation of one of three "Briarcliff Cottages Now Building" of "a pure type of Italian renaissance . . . beautifully located on the new Pine Road. . . . Foundation porches are of stone, house of fireproof tile and cement, roof of Spanish tile . . . showing to the outside world that country home construction in Briarcliff is finding expression in the very latest words of the building vocabulary." Two houses built from the plans shown are now numbers 55 and 71 Pine Road. One, Number 55, was the home of the parents of Henry Law's second wife, Gertrude Watson. The other, Number 71, was for a time the home of the opera singer Kitty Moran Douglas and her husband, James Forsythe Douglas. The plans for "Barham Cottage," on the west corner of Elm and Pleasantville roads, were published in another issue of "Briarcliff Once-a-Week."

The wedding party of Edith Law and Fritz Brockelman on the grounds of the Walter W. Law estate.

Front elevation of "Barham Cottage," at the west corner of Elm and Pleasantville Roads

Six Gables, Scarborough Road

Hungerford residence, Central Drive

Mt. Vernon House, Scarborough Road

Brae View, Central Drive

Hillcrest, Scarborough Road

*Number 2 Central Drive, clubhouse of
the Mount Pleasant Golf Links*

Briarcliff prospered and residential building flourished. In 1902, Walter Law built houses on Scarborough Road for his three children: Six Gables for Walter W. Law, Jr.; Mt. Vernon for Edith Law Brockelman; Hillcrest, on the corner of Sleepy Hollow Road, for Henry H. Law. This house was for many years the home of Mayor George Kennard. The house on the opposite corner of Sleepy Hollow Road dates from around 1830 and belonged to the Ward family, who in 1891 owned thirty-seven of the surrounding acres. Two farmhouses on Sleepy Hollow Road around the corner from Henry Law's house were remodeled by Mortimer Flagg around 1910. Flagg, a Philadelphian who was related to the Wanamaker family, was active in the affairs of All Saints Church.

From 1902 on, one large house after another was built in the vicinity of the Briarcliff Lodge, mostly by former guests at the Lodge: High View, built by U. T. Hungerford of Chase Copper & Brass; Brae View, built by George McNeir; Treetops, on Scarborough Road, home of the Hilton family; and the homes of the Case and Albright families, who were associated with the F. W. Woolworth Five and Ten Cents Stores. Number 2 Central Drive was the clubhouse of the Mount Pleasant Golf Links across the road, which was used by Lodge guests before the complete course of the Lodge was laid out.

Several houses, sometimes referred to as "the village houses," on the south side of Pleasantville Road east of Route 9A, were built in 1903 by the local contractors Ayers and Simpson. One of these houses was purchased in 1915 by Barrett Clark, distinguished critic and author of many articles and books on the drama, and his wife, pianist Cecile Smith. The Clarks came to Briarcliff because Ms. Smith taught piano at Mrs. Dow's school. She also taught at the Juilliard School in New York City. They bought the house, which then stood on a double lot with a very large backyard, for $3,000. Their son Barrett tells how they changed it:

Like many of the houses along that road, the main porch was on the front of the house and my parents didn't like it there, so they had it moved around to the side. . . . When you walked into the house there was a living room and behind it was another room about the same size, a wall with a single door in it between them. The story is that they had a few beers one night with an old friend of my father's, H. R. Baukhage, writer and for many years the well-known radio news broadcaster from Washington, D.C. They decided to take the wall down, which they did, just by running at it with their shoulders. And, oh, the plaster dust! It was all over the house! So they had a nice living room. It was a pretty room, very long and quite narrow but a nice room with space for this piano and lots of books, of course.

The population of the village, 331 at the time of incorporation, had in 1910 increased to 950, with the annexation of Scarborough and new residents. In 1920, after the annexation of the eastern portion of the village, the population was 1,027. In 1930 it had increased to 1,794.

There was no official zoning in the village until 1928, but covenants in the deeds of the Briarcliff Realty Company served the same purposes. The June 29, 1901, deed for the home of Alfred H. Pearson at 1326 Pleasantville Road is typical. This deed, signed by Walter Law and Georgianna, his wife, includes the following covenants:

First   That the said premises conveyed hereby shall be used solely for the purpose of a private residence.
Second   That no business of any kind whatsoever shall ever be conducted on said premises.
Third   That no liquor, beer, ale or wine shall ever be sold or given away on said premises.

Stores on Pleasantville Road, circa 1910

Briarcliff Laundry cars and trucks, all Model T Fords, in the early 1900s

Briarcliff Laundry workers, 1920s

Fourth   That no stable, piggery, cow-pen or nuisance of any kind shall ever be constructed or
         maintained on said premises.
It is expressly understood and agreed that the said several covenants herein above specified shall
attach to and run with the land.

The owner of this house, Alfred Pearson, who had come to work at Briarcliff Farms
as a boy of seventeen, was village clerk from 1921 to 1952.

In 1904 the first streetlights, twenty-nine electric lights for the whole village, were installed. The original Briarcliff Manor Power and Light building, later used by Consolidated
Edison, still stood on Park Road in the 1990s. In 1906 three stores with apartments overhead were built on the corner of Pleasantville and North State roads: a drugstore (now Briarcliff Manor Pharmacy on the same site), a luncheonette and a general store.

The Briarcliff Steam Laundry on Woodside Avenue, founded in 1909 by Fred P. Stafford,
at its peak employed more than one hundred people to cover twelve routes in Westchester,
Connecticut and New York City. The finest hotels used its deluxe service. Drivers of the
laundry's delivery vans wore chauffeur's uniforms. Stafford also operated a coal, lumber
and supply business from the same location. For the laundry workers, he built, around the
corner on North State Road, two-family houses, which still stand. His own residence was
at 1210 Pleasantville Road.

There was no liquor store in the village until 1946, when Henry Law's son, Theodore
Gilman Law, the last of the Law family to be active in the village, gave special permission
to David Taddeo to open his Briarcliff Wines & Liquors in part of the big garage on Pleasantville Road. In the 1990s, Taddeo's business was still going strong, although there was a
competing liquor store, Manor Wines and Spirits, a short distance down the road. It is
remembered that there was, at one time, a speakeasy toward the end of South State Road.[3]

9

The Schools

THE STUDENT population grew with the village, from 108 in 1905 to 273 in 1923. The school that was built in 1898 on the site of the White School, although it had been enlarged in 1903, did not meet the requirements set by the state commissioner of education. In 1908, the village bought land adjacent to Law Park on Pleasantville Road to build a new school, which was opened for students up to the eighth grade. Those who wanted to go on to high school went to Ossining until 1918, when the first advanced curriculum was offered at Briarcliff. Four high school graduates were awarded diplomas in Briarcliff in 1923.[1] By 1928 the number of high school students had increased so much that a second building was added behind the first on Pleasantville Road, in the same Spanish renaissance architectural style. (Both buildings became the Pace University Village Center.)

The enlarged school accepted students from Millwood, Hawthorne, Valhalla, Croton and as far away as Granite Springs. The Hawthorne boys filled out the athletic teams; the Croton students, some of whom came from the progressive Hessian Hills School, brought to Briarcliff some qualities of their liberal, intellectual parents. Graduates of the late 1920s and 1930s affirm that they had a "very special education at Briarcliff." They studied French in the 5th and 6th grades, and theater and music. They were taught to behave with dignity, and were forbidden to chew gum or to run in the corridors. The girls' field-hockey team, after matches on the home field, poured "tea for the visiting teams, with little sandwiches, watercress and so on, which they made themselves."[2]

Otto E. Huddle, who was principal from 1921 to 1945, is given much of the credit for the excellence of the school in those years. "He really made the school!"[3] Huddle was of slender build, not tall, and prone to movements and gestures so vivacious as to suggest effeminacy. And he wore a tam. However, as one student recalls, when two hefty basketball players got into a fight and could not be separated, Huddle went out on the court and very quickly stopped them. "He decked one of the guys. . . . The story went around the school like wildfire."[4]

Dedication of the public school built in 1898

Original 1909 school, Pleasantville Road

Briarcliff Public School gym class, 1921

Briarcliff High School football team, 1936

Mary Elizabeth Dow, who had been headmistress at Miss Porter's School in Farmington, Connecticut, started a school for girls at the Briarcliff Lodge in 1903. Two years later Walter Law gave Mrs. Dow thirty-five acres on Elm Road and built the chateauesque brick building that was later Dow Hall, center of Briarcliff College. When Mrs. Dow retired in 1919 at the age of seventy-six, her assistant, Edith Cooper Hartmann, who had already initiated a college preparatory department in the school, became headmistress. Mrs. Hartmann later introduced the two-year postgraduate course. The junior college charter was issued to the school in 1933. However, there were persistent rumors about the private life of Miss Doris Flick, president of the college. Rules of student deportment in the 1930s were stringent: "Noise in corridors . . . talking after lights . . . absence from tea on Sunday, absence from prayer or hymns . . . leaving the grounds without a hat, tam or beret," and so on, were "regarded as serious delinquencies."[5] Rumors, however unfounded, about the president of such a school were disastrous and, with the Depression, brought enrollment to an all-time low before 1942, when Mrs. Tead became president.

The School of Practical Agriculture, established by Walter Law in 1900, moved upstate in 1903, and for two years the building was a small year-round hotel called Pocantico Lodge, another of Walter Law's enterprises. Alice Knox, who had worked at Mrs. Dow's school, opened her own school in the Pocantico Lodge building in 1905. When the building burned down in 1912, Louise Houghton, headmistress at the time, moved the school to Tarrytown and later to Cooperstown, New York. All that remains of the original building is a stone retaining wall that stands in front of the stone house built for Dr. Rufus P. Johnston in 1925 and designed by Oscar Vatet, architect, of Pleasantville and New York City.[6] Later the home

Mrs. Dow's School, Elm Road

Dysart House,
Pleasantville Road

of Dr. Arthur O'Connor, the house was sold in 1959 to Cognitronics, a company that made learning devices. About five years later, that company moved to Connecticut and sold the property to Frank B. Hall, Incorporated.

In 1897, Walter Law built a large guest house on Pleasantville Road on the hill across from the railroad station. He named this lodging Dysart House, probably after Dysart House in Kirkcaldy, Scotland, where roses from the Briarcliff Greenhouses were sent at one time.[7] After 1902, when Law's guests could be accommodated at Briarcliff Lodge, the Misses Tewksbury conducted a school for young boys and girls in the house. Their school was taken over in 1913 by Mrs. Frances Scharff Marshall's Day and Boarding School for little girls. There are still school bells in the former Dysart House, which was the classroom building, while boarders lived in the house next door. The cost of each student's board and tuition was $900. Piano lessons cost another $20.

In 1913, Mr. and Mrs. Frank A. Vanderlip started the Scarborough School for their own six children and the children of friends and neighbors. (See Chapter 12 in this history.)

In October 1936, Dr. Matthew H. Reaser brought Edgewood Park, the school he had established in Greenwich, Connecticut, to Briarcliff Lodge. The Lodge, badly hit by the Depression, leased its facilities to Reaser for the winter months, but could continue to operate for only two more summers. In 1938, the school bought out the Lodge.

Dr. Reaser was assisted by his three daughters, Mrs. Shannon Wallace, Mrs. Norman Sowell and Mrs. Gilbert Temple, together with a staff of forty teachers and administrators they brought with them from Greenwich.

Dr. Reaser, a pioneer in women's higher education, believed there was a need for educational opportunities beyond the high school level for young women who lacked the means or the scholastic ambition for a four-year college course. The school combined a preparatory school for four-year colleges with a two-year program designed to prepare high school graduates for semiprofessional occupations without neglecting general culture. Training was offered in the fine arts, commercial art, costume design, interior decoration, merchandising, speech, home economics, medical assistance, kindergarten and secretarial work. In addition to their academic work students were encouraged to take part in local civic affairs. They acted as nurses' aides and assistants in the dietary departments of Grasslands Hospital, did practical teaching in Briarcliff schools, and helped the Red Cross and various other benevolent causes. The school also served the community by acting as host to performers and lecturers to whom most residents would not otherwise have been exposed. One of these was the modern dancer Martha Graham.

Edgewood Park was Christian but nonsectarian. Bible courses and chapel exercises led by the school chaplain and visiting ministers were an integral part of the curriculum. The enrollment was around 300, including students from forty-eight states and twenty-five countries.

Briarcliff kindergarten, circa 1926, beside the Congregational Church. Helena Duncombe is standing at the left.

10

The Community

IN 1910 THE village bought the 1898 school building to establish a community center. "The Club," as it was called, incorporated in 1921, aimed to promote the "mental and moral improvement of men and women" and "to help make Briarcliff a better place to live." The Club is remembered with great affection by people who lived in Briarcliff at the time. In it were the library and a gymnasium-auditorium. Truly the social center of the village, it was the site of many dinners, dances and variety shows. In 1928, shortly after the building had been marked for demolition to make way for the Briarcliff-Peekskill Parkway (Route 9A), it burned down. The building on Woodside Avenue that later housed the Thalle Construction Company became the new recreation center.

Even before the village library had its first beginnings at the Lodge, some residents maintained extraordinary private libraries. Walter Law's own library, as described by his business associate George McNeir, was "an immense room about 25 by 75 feet in size, filled with bookcases, books, easy chairs and sofas. Here, lost to the world, with head embedded in the book of some favorite author, at peace with all men . . . may most frequently be found the owner of Briarcliff, Walter W. Law."[1] The library pavilion and ballroom designed for Frank Vanderlip at Beechwood by Welles Bosworth were lined with books. Both Frank and Narcissa Vanderlip counted many writers among their friends and guests. One of these, Albert Q. Maisel, amazed at the quantity of books in Vanderlip's library, asked, "Have you read all of these?"

"Some twice," Vanderlip replied.

The club publication "Community Notes" for June 19, 1914, announced: "The Library is now open for the loaning of books. So far six cards have been taken out." Less than a month later, some cardholders were being urged to return overdue books, including *The Honorable Peter Sterling, The Count of Monte Cristo* and *Uncle Remus*. There followed several years of haphazard management until the club was incorporated in 1921 and the library, under the club's sponsorship, was registered with the New York State library system. The 1,900 volumes catalogued at this time had grown to 3,000 in 1926 and to 6,000 in 1939. The registration of the library and increasing interest in it are credited largely to the efforts

*Annual men's dinner at the
Briarcliff Community Club,
October 1910*

of Mrs. Alfred Bookwalter, then a newcomer to Briarcliff and a lover of books and libraries.

Mrs. Bookwalter and her family lived at the end of Horsechestnut Road in the stone house that Alfred Bookwalter built, among others in the vicinity, including several between the old school and the municipal building. At that time the house was surrounded with gardens reaching down to the Pocantico River behind it.

In 1924 the village trustees voted $500 for the library, and additional funds were raised by subscription and fund-raising concerts and lectures. Among the notables who starred in these events were Ruth Draper, the popular diseuse, and Barrett Clark.[2] Ruth Draper often visited her sister, Mrs. E. C. Carter, who lived on Horsechestnut Road.

After the Community Club burned down, there was an insurance adjustment of $5,000. Following much discussion of village priorities, this money was given to the library and was used over the years as a source fund for library equipment. The library was housed in the tower room of the Briarcliff Realty Company (later the Operating Engineers Building) for two years and then moved to the new high school in 1930. In 1958, it finally found its home in the former railroad station in Law Park.

In the 1920s several families who were associated with the Y.M.C.A. came to live in Briarcliff. The Herseys, the Sweetmans, the Deans, the Herschlebs, the Rayburns, the

Early photo of Boy Scout Troop 1 of Briarcliff Manor. Mrs. George Wolf, Sr. remembers that her husband was a Boy Scout in 1919, but the actual date of the Troop's charter seems to be history's secret. Several sources have named Bill Buffum as the first Scoutmaster and John Hersey, the first Eagle Scout. Troop 18 has been active for at least 70 years. Today, under the leadership of William Ventura, it continues that tradition.

Girl Scout Troop 28, Memorial Day Parade, 1945. According to Susan Colby McKenna's album for Troop 28's records (circa 1947), the first Girl Scout troop in Briarcliff Manor was formed in 1917 by Mrs. Alfred Jones and Miss Louise Miller. In 1929, the Brownie troop was started, and the National Council issued the first charter. Mrs. Edith Brockelman, Walter Law's daughter, was the first Commissioner under the new charter. In 1955, the Briarcliff Manor Council gave up its charter and joined the Northern Westchester Girl Scout Council, Inc. The troop's current Community Director is Mrs. West Friedman.

Briarcliff Realty Company Build-
ing, later the Operating Engineers
Building, Pleasantville Road

Briarcliff Manor Public Library,
formerly the railroad station

Portrait of Grace (Mrs. Roscoe)
Hersey, by her son Roscoe, Jr.

Rhodeses and the Sheltons are credited (with Mrs. Bookwalter), with the renewed interest in the library and considerable influence on the intellectual and social life of the community. "Briarcliff was special because of the Laws but also because of the Y.M.C.A. people," Mrs. Norman Babcock used to say. They joined the Congregational church and worked for it. Mrs. Roscoe Hersey became full-time librarian in 1928 and "for the next quarter of a century skillfully maintained the growing collection of books and other publications."[3] Mr. Hersey and Mr. Sweetman had served the Y.M.C.A. in China. Mr.Rayburn and Mr. Dean worked for the Y in New York City. Don Odell Shelton was an official of the International Y.M.C.A. Associations of New York, the first president of the National Bible Institute, a teacher and conductor of Bible conferences in many American cities. He was also the author of many books on religious subjects. Shelton's house, on the north corner of Elm Road where it turns west, was acquired by Briarcliff College after Shelton's death in 1941.

The Briarcliff Lodge brought many Irish Catholic immigrants, as employees, as well as some Catholic guests, to the village. In the early 1900s a priest, supplied by the Dominican Fathers in Pleasantville, travelled by bicycle on Sundays to hold masses in the shed of the golf house at number 2 Central Drive. In the 1920s, the parish was joined by several influential families, including the Randal Boroughs, the Edward Whites and the Norman Babcocks. The demands of the Pleasantville parish also increased, until the fathers could no longer spare a priest. In 1926 Cardinal Farley, Archbishop of New York, authorized a new parish at Briarcliff Manor, to be named Saint Theresa of the Infant Jesus. Our Lady of the Wayside Church in Millwood, built in 1926 on land donated by Walter Law, was transferred from the Chappaqua parish to become the mission church of Saint Theresa's parish. Father James F. Kelly, assistant pastor of Saint Raymond's in the Bronx, was appointed first pastor of Saint Theresa's, and held his first mass in the parish in the garage of the Briarcliff Lodge on July 4, 1926. At the same time the Sunday school was opened by a group of Maryknoll sisters.

Saint Theresa's Church, Pleasantville Road

Father Kelly, impressed by the Lodge and the four fine stone churches already in the village, was ambitious for Saint Theresa's. He obtained loans from the Archdiocese and other sources and chose the site of the former Stillman farmhouse, which had been Walter Law's office, on the corner of Central Drive and Pleasantville Road. Part of the house was torn down to make room for the church, and the main section, used as a temporary chapel, later became the rectory.

Building of the church began in 1927, and Father Kelly, who was often seen lending a hand, held midnight mass on Christmas Eve of that year in the church, although there were no windows or heat in it as yet. The formal dedication by Cardinal Hayes took place in September of 1928. The congregation grew until the Briarcliff Lodge closed, some eight years later, in the depressed 1930s. It took thirty years of fund raising to pay back the loans Father Kelly had taken to build the church.

Father Kelly is remembered as a big, ruddy-faced man, "right over from Ireland." Standing at the church door greeting parishioners before the services, he would reach into the folds of his cassock and produce a hard candy for each of the small children. He never had his services interrupted by a crying child. The children were all busy with their sweet mouthfuls, known as "Father Kelly's Hush Candy."

Father James F. Kelly

Father Kelly continued his efforts to beautify the church, and before his death in 1946 two shrines were installed on the lawn with statues of Saint Theresa and Our Lady, which he had designed and donated. They were surrounded by flowering trees and shrubs donated and maintained by the Fitzgerald family.

Frank A. Vanderlip bought Woodlea, the Shepard mansion, in 1910. In 1911 he sold the mansion and surrounding acres to his fellow organizers of the Sleepy Hollow Country Club. They purchased adjacent land owned by William Rockefeller, making a total of 338 acres. The first twenty-seven directors of the club included some of the richest men in the United States—John Jacob Astor, Cornelius Vanderbilt, Oliver Harriman, William Rockefeller, James Stillman and Harrison Williams—as well as Frank Vanderlip, V. Everit Macy and Edward Harden.[4] Vanderlip "got Charley McDonald, a famous golfer, to lay out the course."[5] A letter sent to prospective members described the club: "The house has a very large dining room capable of seating over 200 persons . . . there are salons suitable for lounging and reading and 18 large double bedrooms with bathrooms. In addition there are 21

*Golf course at Sleepy Hollow
Country Club, circa 1939*

*Italian Garden at Sleepy Hollow
Country Club*

smaller rooms suitable for bachelors." There were stables, a garage, and grounds for polo, tennis and other sports. The lower nine-hole golf course was added in 1929. "The holes have names! Headless Horseman, Ichabod's Elbow and Haunted Bridge."[6]

Henry Law established the Briar Hills Country Club on the site of the old Briarcliff Golf Club in 1921. A clubhouse was built and an eighteen-hole golf links of 6,366 yards was designed by golf architect Devereux Emmet. The 150-acre property was bounded roughly by Dalmeny, Poplar and Pine roads, with a strip south of Pine extending behind Tuttle Road to Long Hill Road East. The grounds included the Christie, later Melady, property and the large white house named Elderslie, which for a time served as the clubhouse. Two generations of the Law family, Henry and, after him, Theodore Gilman Law, directed the club until some years after World War II, when it was sold and became Briar Hall Country Club. "Besides . . . golf, tennis, riding, skiing, toboganning, skating and coasting, the Club . . . [offered] every facility for indoor entertainment."[7]

Under the proprietorship of Chauncey Depew Steele, Briarcliff Lodge in the late 1920s doubled as the Metropolitan Masons' Country Club. Three years after Walter Law died in 1924, his residence, "the Manor House," on Scarborough Road just east of All Saints Church, became the clubhouse of the Metropolitan Masons. It was advertised as "second to none for beauty and appointments. It contains twenty-five rooms, eighteen fireplaces, a library of 5,000 volumes, bowling alleys, billiard room, dining rooms, etc., and is furnished completely with rare taste and elaborateness."[8] Members of the club were offered all the athletic and social opportunities (including trout fishing and ski-jumping), that were enjoyed by guests of the Briarcliff Lodge.

Starting in 1907, a club car came down from the Croton railway yards every weekday morning and returned every evening. In it members could relax in Pullman-style armchairs, waited on, in the early years, by a white-coated porter. There was always a bridge game going. The club was called the North River Association and was truly a private club. Members had to be proposed and voted on. Residents of the community, however affluent, who were not popular were not admitted. A former club president remembered that Harry Helmsley, the real estate magnate, who in the 1950s lived with his wife, Eve, at the top of Ridgecrest Road, was for some time denied admission to the club, explaining that Helmsley was not popular because he contributed little to local charities and other community affairs.[9]

One of the duties of the club president was to give a party in the car early in the Christmas season. The club car was discontinued in 1984.

Briarcliff Automobile International Road Race 1908

In the spring of 1908 the village sponsored the Briarcliff Automobile International Road Race. The competing cars were waved past the starting point in front of the Briarcliff Lodge at one-minute intervals. Spectators from far and near crowded the roadsides and even hung from tree branches over the course. Local authorities were well prepared for trouble of any kind. County Sheriff Charles M. Lane detailed many deputies to assist local sheriffs "for the duty of preserving the peace only, AND IN NO CASE DO YOUR DUTIES RELATE TO KEEPING THE COURSE CLEAR." These temporary deputies were further instructed "to make arrests only for misdemeanors that are committed in your presence. . . . You are in no case to use your club except in self-defense, or to prevent a prisoner from escaping, after having been arrested, or to prevent his rescue by other people."

"Briarcliff-Once-a-Week" published the following account by a native son:

BRIARCLIFF AUTOMOBILE INTERNATIONAL ROAD RACE by R. Everett Whitson . . . At 4:45 a.m. on April 24, 1908, the American International Road Race for stock cars competing for the Briarcliff Trophy, valued at over $10,000 given by Mr. Walter W. Law, Sr., was started.

More than 300,000 people witnessed the race and Briarcliff had over 100,000 visitors that day. Special trains on both the Putnam and New York Central Hudson Division ran all night before the race. Large grandstands were erected at the finish line near the center of the Village.

The course covered was from Briarcliff to Kitchawan through Mt. Kisco, Armonk to Kensico and on to Briarcliff, a distance of about 35 miles over dirt roads.

The autos competing in the race were Lozier, Fiat-Panhard, Thomas, Simplex, Isotta-Franchina, Stearns, Renault, Mercedes, and others. Among the drivers were the well-known Strang brothers (Louis and Arthur), Ralph De Palma, Barney Oldfield and many others.

Each racer had his own crew of mechanics in various barns at the Briarcliff Farms weeks before

Barney Oldfield driving Stearns car in Briarcliff Road Race, 1908

the race.

Speeds of over 60 miles per hour were obtained on straightaways.

Arthur Strang, driving No. 4 in the Isotta-Franchina car, won the race. Total elapsed time for 256 miles was 5 hours and 15 minutes.

The writer, at the age of eight, had the privilege of covering this course with Ralph De Palma on test runs before the race.[10]

On November 12, 1934, the Automobile Racing Club of America held another race on a 100-mile course which included Tuttle, Long Hill East, Sleepy Hollow, Scarborough, Pine, Birch and Elm roads. Thousands of spectators lined the route to watch the Bugattis, Whippets, Willyses, MGs, Austins, a Lancia Lamboda and a Riley negotiate the hairpin turns.

1934 road race finish

One of the sixteen entrants in the race was a woman, Mrs. Carle Conway of Scarborough. Langdon Quimby, driving a Willys 77, won the race with a time of two hours, seven minutes and thirty seconds.

On June 23, 1935, the Racing Club held another Briarcliff Trophy Race. Langdon Quimby won for the second time with a time of two hours, three minutes and six seconds.[11]

"Pinkerton man putting a gambler's plant out of business" during the 1908 road race

11

Beechwood

IN THE LAST decades of the nineteenth century, the house and fifty to one hundred acres surrounding the present Beechwood were bought and sold, bequeathed and inherited by members, and connections by marriage, of the distinguished Webb family. In the 1890s, Henry Walter Webb bought Creighton's Beechwood and the adjoining Remsen property. The railroad that the Reverend William Creighton had resisted in the 1840s as an abominable intrusion on his peaceful farm was Webb's principal business and source of income as vice-president of the New York Central and Hudson River Railroad. The Remsen house, which Webb chose to live in, was further up the hill from the river, and the railroad tracks, than Creighton's house.

The Webbs' Beechwood connection had started when Alexander Stewart Webb (Henry Walter Webb's half-brother) married Anna Remsen, the daughter of Creighton's neighbor, Henry Rutgers Remsen. From 1850 until the 1880s, the Remsen family spent summers almost certainly in the very house, on some eleven acres, where Benjamin Folger had entertained the infamous Matthias. (See Chapter 3)[1]

In 1866, Catherine Creighton married General George Webb Morell (Henry Walter Webb's cousin). In his will, Dr. Creighton (after various other bequests, including $500 to "Mrs. Margaret Short the attendant of my afflicted wife"), gave

All the other portion of my farm Beechwood . . . to my youngest daughter Catherine Schermerhorn Creighton & together with the land all improvements thereon viz. Dwelling houses Barns & Carriage houses; the farm stock, farming utensils, poultry, pigs, cows, horses & carriages—all the furniture of the house & all the Library books. Also half the plate & half the pictures & one of the two silver pitchers presented to me by the Widow of Peter G. Stuyvesant. The remaining half of all the plate & pictures & the other of the two Pitchers I give & bequeath to my daughter Jane C. Mead.[2]

As executor of his will, Remsen named his son-in-law, General Alexander Stewart Webb.[3] Remsen's neighbor, George Webb Morell, who survived his wife Catherine Creighton Morell and was her principal heir, named as executors of his will his cousin, Henry Walter Webb, and John Webb Chester, Morell's nephew.[4]

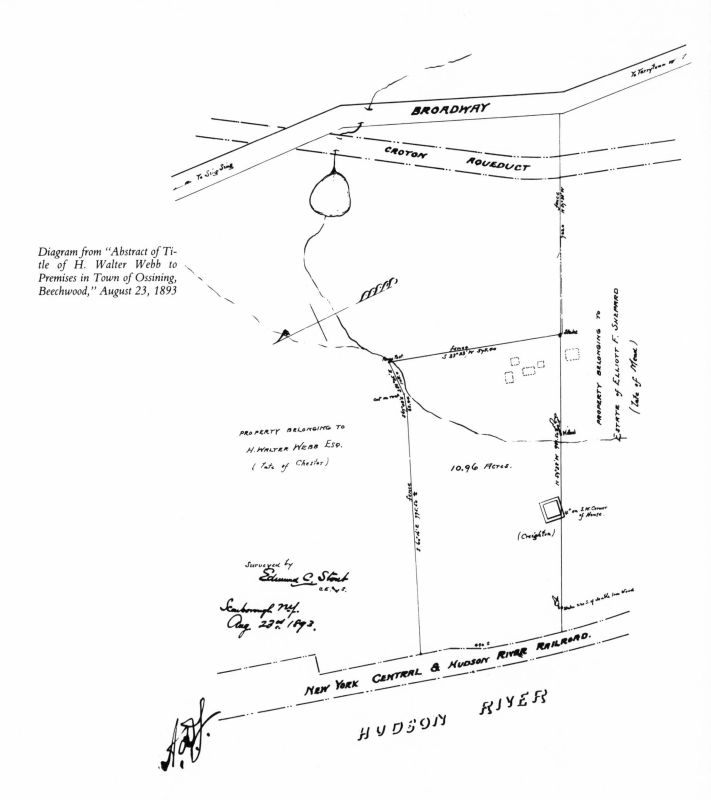

Diagram from "Abstract of Title of H. Walter Webb to Premises in Town of Ossining, Beechwood," August 23, 1893

The Webb family had its share of high-ranking military men. General Samuel Blatchley Webb was an aide to George Washington in the Revolutionary War. His son, James Watson Webb, was made a general when he entered the diplomatic service at the outbreak of the Civil War in 1861. After youthful adventures in the military among hostile Indians in Michigan and Illinois, James Webb had been a newspaper editor and proprietor, "one of the most influential editors in that age of personal journalism." In 1848 he built Pokahoe, "a stone mansion" on "some sixty acres of finely wooded land,"[5] where Philipse Manor is today. He sold Pokahoe to General John Frémont when he was named minister to Brazil, in which post "he. . . . through his intimacy with Napoleon III, aided in procuring the withdrawal of the French from Mexico."[6] Webb was twice married and fathered eight sons and two daughters.[7] A son of the first marriage, Alexander Stewart Webb, was awarded the Congressional Medal of Honor for "distinguished personal gallantry in the battle of Gettysburg."[8] In 1861–1862 Alexander Webb and his cousin, George Webb Morell, both served in the Army of the Potomac, Webb as assistant to the chief of artillery, Morell (twenty years older than Webb) as brigadier general of the United States Volunteers. After the war, Alexander Webb was elected president of the College of the City of New York and served in that office until 1902. Before he settled with his family in Riverdale, New York, two of his children, Henry Remsen and Elizabeth Remsen Webb, were born in Scarborough.[9] In 1866, General Morell settled at Creighton's Beechwood and until his death in 1883, devoted himself to farming and neighborhood affairs, such as the supervision of Saint Mary's Beechwood when that church was without a rector from 1877 to 1882.[10]

James Watson Webb

The younger sons of General James Watson Webb, who came of age in more peaceful times, took up nonmilitary professions and careers, mostly in finance, particularly of railroads. William Seward Webb was educated at Colonel Churchill's Military Academy in Sing Sing before going on to Columbia College, and studying medicine there and abroad. Then, abandoning his medical practice, he established the Wall Street firm of W. S. Webb & Company. He married Lila Vanderbilt, Mrs. Elliott Shepard's sister, and, at his father-in-law's request, took over the management of the Wagner Palace Car Company, reorganized it, and became its president and "a director in several railroad companies."[11]

Henry Walter Webb went to Columbia College and practiced law in New York City until 1882, when he joined his brother's banking firm. In 1890 he became a vice-president of the New York Central and Hudson River Railroad Company.[12] In 1893 he purchased the Remsen house on some twelve acres for $20,000.[13] He enlarged the house, adding a "south wing whose Colonial Revival central portico and details were sympathetic extensions of the original Federal core."[14] He bought General George Webb Morell's property, including Creighton's house, from Morell's heirs, and, after Colonel Shepard's death in 1903, some ten more acres from the Shepard estate.[15] Shepard, expanding his Woodlea Kingdom, had purchased Jane Creighton Mead's share of her father's property from her heirs and proposed to name the whole Shepard desmesne Woodica. Webb took the name Beechwood for his own reassembled estate. He became a warden of Saint Mary's Church in 1895. Marion Dinwiddie remembered a church fair in the Webb barn, when she won a prize for pinning the tail on the donkey.[16]

Alexander Webb

Henry Walter Webb died in 1904, in his forties. In 1905, Frank A. Vanderlip bought from Webb's widow, Leila Howard Griswold Webb (then remarried to Ogden Codman), the house Webb had named Beechwood on some twenty-three acres,[17] " and also the furniture and other property listed in the annexed inventory and situated in the dwelling-house . . . for a total price of Eighty Thousand Dollars. . . ."[18]

The inventory lists the contents of every room in the house: on the third floor one double and seven single servants' bedrooms, one bath, a sewing room, storerooms and two "Men's Rooms" (for visiting valets and chauffeurs?), all the bedrooms furnished with white or black iron bedsteads with mattresses, springs, and pillows, carpets and small rugs, bureaus, tables, side chairs, rockers, Swiss sash curtains and shades, washstands with five- to seven-piece toilet sets, and scrap baskets. On the second floor are listed: "End Guest Room . . . Bath . . . Bed Room next End Room . . . Yellow Guest Room, Bath, Writing Room, Pink Bedroom, Blue Bed Room, Bath Room adjoining, Mr. Codman's Room, bath adjoining, Small Guest Room, Bath Room opposite, Maid's Room, Mr. Walter's Room, Dressing Room adjoining, Store Room, Mr. Griswold's Room, Square Hall outside Mr. Griswold's Room, stairs to First Floor, Hall outside small Guest Room, Hall, Main Staircase." The guest and family bedrooms were furnished with Brussels carpet and rugs, framed mirrors, chiffoniers, commodes, mahogany chairs and desks, chintz or velvet portieres, candlesticks, vases and inkstands, all itemized down to the last chintz lambrequin and "china hair receiver forgetmenots." Furnishings for fireplaces are listed for the Pink and Blue Bedrooms. A handwritten note at the end of the inventory—"Mrs. Codman's Bedroom. Blue silk damask portiere. Blue silk damask hangings to bed"—seems to indicate that the blue bedroom was Mrs. (Leila Howard Griswold Webb) Codman's. Rooms on the first floor, for which full and elaborate furnishings are listed, were: "Main Staircase . . . Main Hall . . . Entrance Hall . . . Middle Hall and Staircase . . . Library . . . Piazza . . . Library Telephone Room . . . Drawing Room . . . Dining Room . . . Breakfast Room . . . Butler's Room [with bed] . . . Pantry . . . Room next Pantry . . . Hallway outside Drawing Room . . . Back Hallway with staircase and Hall outside Breakfast Room . . . Back Telephone Room . . . School Room . . . Servants' Sitting Room . . . Servants' Dining Room . . . Kitchen . . . Pantry . . . House Laundry . . . Laundry."[19]

The Webb-Codmans took with them little more than their personal attire and one or two beds, leaving the pictures on the walls and many decorative knickknacks. This indifference to the Webb family furnishings may be explained by Ogden Codman's profession. An architect, he was, beyond that, a pioneer in the "reform in house-decoration" in America.[20] With his friend the novelist Edith Wharton, he wrote *The Decoration of Houses* (Scribner's, 1902). A reaction to "the vulgarity of current decoration," the excesses of some of the Vanderbilts and others, this work advocated interior decoration as a function of architecture and cited many European, especially French, authorities. It was addressed to "those whose means permit" because, "when the rich man demands good architecture his neighbors will get it too."[21] Wharton did the work of writing the book, but she deferred to Codman's dicta, as is illustrated by an anecdote in R. W. B. Lewis's biography. A young woman who had been coolly received by Wharton "as she was struggling with her snowshoes in the vestibule . . . heard the novelist say in a very different voice, warm and humorous: 'What do you think, Ogden—could one in a little house like this allow a Chippendale clock on the hall table, or should it be only a card tray?'"[22]

When Edith Wharton was planning her house in Lenox, Massachusetts, in 1901, "Codman, who had been prospering visibly . . . demanded what Edith regarded as exorbitant advance payments even for his rough sketches."[23] They remained friends, but she engaged another architect.

12

Frank and Narcissa Vanderlip

IN 1910 Frank A. Vanderlip bought Woodlea, which he referred to as "the Elliott F.
Shepherd (*sic*) estate." He wrote, "It was a
great place, on which about $2,000,000 had been spent and I picked it up as a bargain, paying,
I think, about $165,000 . . . but . . . Mrs. Vanderlip was unwilling to live there; it was too
grandiose." She preferred to remain at Beechwood.[1]

Frank Vanderlip, like Walter Law, was a self-made millionaire whose energetic benevo-
lence had great impact on the village. His career, quite as extraordinary as Law's, was in
journalism and banking rather than manufacturing and, at that career's height, he and his
wife Narcissa Cox and their growing family settled at Beechwood in Scarborough.

Vanderlip's autobiography, *From Farmboy to Financier*, tells his admirable story. His happy
boyhood on an Illinois farm ended before he was twelve years old when his father died,
the farm failed and he went to work in a relative's wagonworks in Aurora, the sole support of his grandmother, mother, sister and two maiden aunts. He continued to read and
study, while working, and saved enough money ($226) to attend the University of Illinois
at Champaign for two years. Then, in response to a help-wanted ad, he became "city editor" of the *Aurora Evening Post*, where he learned typesetting and reporting. In 1886, when
he was just twenty-two, he took a job as secretary to Moses Scudder, a broker and investors' agent, a sort of pioneer in investment banking: "Scudder had gone into an uncharted
sea of commerce"[2] and Vanderlip got his first financial training examining mortgages and
bond issues, mostly for insurance companies. Through his friend and preceptor Joseph
French Johnson, he was hired as a reporter for the *Chicago Tribune*. Those were adventurous
days in journalism, and Vanderlip often covered stories in the company of such great hu-
morists as George Ade of the *News* and Finley Peter Dunne of the *Herald*. He succeeded
his friend Johnson as financial editor of the *Tribune*, then, in 1894, became editor of the *Econ-
omist*. His work there attracted the attention of Lyman Gage, who, on his appointment as
secretary of the treasury in the McKinley cabinet, invited Vanderlip to be first his secretary
and then assistant secretary of the treasury. As a junior cabinet officer, Vanderlip had various extraordinary experiences, including editing Theodore Roosevelt's speeches at the request of that man of the hour. After Vanderlip's successful handling of the $200 million

Frank and Narcissa Vanderlip

bond issue during the Spanish-American War, James Stillman, president of the National City Bank in New York, offered him a vice-presidency of that bank. He accepted the vice-presidency in 1900, rose to the presidency in 1909 and remained in that position for twenty eventful years. So "in six moves [he] got out of overalls and became president of the nation's biggest bank."[3]

Vanderlip's experience and gifts as a journalist made him "the publicist banker," unique among financiers of the time. He wrote articles and made speeches which gave the bank a reputation enabling it "to cast a big shadow." He worked with J. P. Morgan, E. H. Harriman, Woodrow Wilson, Jacob Schiff, Henry Clay Frick and other great men of the era. His accomplishments—helping to draft the Federal Reserve Law, creating a system of War Savings Certificates as a Washington, D.C. dollar-a-year man in World War I—are history. He was equally active and influential in his home community of Scarborough.

Narcissa Cox Vanderlip was a social feminist and philanthropist, as distinguished for her own achievements as for those she shared with her husband. When she met Vanderlip in 1903, she was an honor student at the University of Chicago and editor of the university paper.[4] While living in New York City after her marriage, the young Mrs. Vanderlip celebrated the first birthdays of her eldest daughter, Narcissa, with parties for tenement children. In World War I, she served as treasurer of the National Women's Liberty Loan Committee. She was an "American godmother," corresponding with fighting men who had lost contact with their families. To control venereal disease and prostitution near military camps, she supported the Girls' Protective League and the Social Hygiene Association. She conducted a New York state government skill-index census of Westchester County residents, supervising four thousand women and providing a personnel resource listing, thereby saving thousands of dollars in labor costs and demonstrating the ability of women to organize and complete a great task. As vice-chairman of the Women's Land Army in the state, she recruited women to work on farms. She demonstrated food conservation by installing a dehydrator at Beechwood, where a unit of the Women's Land Army, "the Farmerettes," resided. Also at Beechwood, she entertained hundreds of furloughed soldiers and sailors after the Armistice, providing for their transportation from New York City.

Mrs. Vanderlip was best known at that time and earlier as a suffragist. She campaigned throughout the state for the ratification of women's suffrage, logging some eight thousand miles in her chauffeur-driven touring car and many more miles on night trains. Her son Frank remembered sitting in that open car full of children singing, "Rah, Rah! Give our mother the vote." When the Federal Suffrage Amendment was ratified in August 1919, Mrs. Vanderlip, in *The New York Times*, likened that day to Armistice Day: "The great war and the battle for women's vote were very much alike. The League of Women Voters will continue to function as a national body, devoting itself to urging legislative reforms and educating the new women voters regardless of party lines." At the first convention of the League in Albany, she was elected chairman. In a magazine interview, she was asked, "Will most women vote as their husbands vote?" She replied, "Thinking women will probably make research into candidates and measures and report to husbands so that husbands will vote like their wives."

In those first years of the League of Women Voters, Mrs. Vanderlip worked for legislation of child labor, the minimum wage, the eight-hour day, maternity and infant care clinics, health insurance, birth control, citizen literacy tests and the eligibility of women for jury duty. A digest of legislation, "City-State-Nation," was originated by her long-time associate Esther Lape. She recruited Eleanor Roosevelt, "unskilled but willing," to assist Esther Lape. Vanderlip supported his wife in all her undertakings with large financial contributions and in every other way he could. Among the many good works they undertook together was the establishment of scholarships for students in Near-East colleges.

In later years, Mrs. Vanderlip was most concerned with the New York Infirmary for Women and Children, a hospital staffed by women doctors, which was established in 1857 by Dr. Elizabeth Blackwell. In the 1920s the Infirmary encountered financial problems, a new board of trustees took office and in 1929 Narcissa Vanderlip was elected president. Under her leadership the Infirmary survived the Depression and expanded. The cornerstone of a new building was laid in November, 1953. As women doctors became accepted elsewhere, the Infirmary was obliged to employ men doctors and "Women and Children" was dropped from the name. Later, by merger it became the New York Infirmary/Beekman Downtown Hospital. Until shortly before her death in 1966 at the age of eighty-seven, Mrs. Vanderlip commuted to the city regularly to attend to the business of the Infirmary.

With all her work for the public good, Narcissa Vanderlip was also an active hostess. Vanderlip seldom returned from the city without guests for the evening or the weekend. Officers of the bank, heads of corporations, distinguished foreign visitors and a variety of other notables from Woodrow Wilson and Henry Ford to Sarah Bernhardt were invited to Beechwood. Vanderlip wrote, "I brought someone nearly every night, and at least part of my reason was my pride in Beechwood."[5]

Vanderlip increased his property to more than 125 acres, buying the remainder of Creighton's Beechwood as well as land north of Station Road and east of the Albany Post Road. Some of this land he bought from William Rockefeller, John D. Rockefeller's brother, a director of the City Bank and a large landholder in the neighborhood of Scarborough.

Isadora Duncan dancers at Tea House in Italian Garden at Beechwood

Virginia Vanderlip with rabbit

He engaged Beaux Arts architect William Welles Bosworth to design the addition to Beechwood of the library-pavilion north end and to redesign the living room and solarium south end. Bosworth also designed the main building of the Scarborough School and the Beechwood Playhouse, the garage, and Little Beech (the guest house, since demolished), and in 1920 planned the Italian Garden and landscaped the swimming pool lawn.

The firm of Frederick Law Olmsted, designer of Central Park in New York City, laid out Linden Circle, and in the 1920s, Donald Armstrong remembered, "many lovely houses" were built around it—"Bemis, Durrell, Currier, Kies. Durrell's had . . . a genuine Maine hunting lodge occupying its third floor. Gossip at the time was that the most expensive poker game ever played occurred there."[6]

When the First National City Bank, at 55 Wall Street, was remodeled in 1907, two huge Ionic columns were discarded. Vanderlip, then a vice-president of the bank, had the columns shipped to Scarborough, and Bosworth incorporated them in the main entrance complex of Beechwood. He solved the problem of their disproportionate height by digging one-third of them into the ground. A wrought-iron elevator shaft with a vaulted roof was also discarded by the bank, and Vanderlip had the top of this made into a cage for his children's pet rabbits. The rabbits dug their way out, but with the addition of a concrete foundation the elegant cage contained them very well.[7]

William Welles Bosworth, who had worked for the firm of Frederick Law Olmsted, designed the gardens of John D. Rockefeller's estate in Pocantico Hills, and the main buildings of the Massachusetts Institute of Technology in Cambridge, Massachusetts. After World War I, he oversaw the restoration in France of the palaces of Versailles and Fontainebleau and the cathedrals of Reims and Chartres.[8]

About the Scarborough School, Vanderlip wrote, "I was 46 when I had this experience of becoming a millionaire. . . . I never bought a yacht, I never bought a stable of horses. . . . Education was what I had yearned for always and they [his six children] should have it right at their front door. . . . Eventually there was a school with 300 pupils and all told I contributed to it about half a million dollars. That, I confess, was luxury."[9]

When their children were very young, in 1912, Mr. and Mrs. Vanderlip pioneered the Montessori method at the Harden's residence in Tarrytown. In 1913 the school moved to the River Gate House at the north end of River Road, and in 1916 moved into the new big building on the Albany Post Road. In the meantime the Vanderlips, judging that the Montesorri method was inappropriate, sponsored a more formal approach, with more discipline, although there was "still more than average freedom in the classrooms." The school was designed for classes of ten, to accommodate 120 children, but as it grew they had to add "another building [burned down in 1959] for the younger children and then a lunchroom and then a shop and a studio."[10]

Vanderlip himself had "some grand fun" in the school teaching simplified political economy by playing Swiss Family Robinson on an imaginary island with students, to "experience in play the development of capitalism."

The lunchroom was run by Mrs. Vanderlip, who served good simple food, but gave some of it fancy names. Rice pudding with raisins was called Bête Noire à la Bolshevik. There were always farm animals nearby for the children to see and play with and a gorgeous circus carousel to ride on. Dedicated teachers, Frances Sheridan, Ethel Daniels and Fulton Main taught (respectively) second grade, third grade and science for many years, Miss Daniels for more than fifty years.

Scarborough School, Beechwood, on the Albany Post Road

For almost sixty years, members of the Vanderlip family, particularly Virginia Vanderlip Schoales, continued to play an important part in the administration of the school. A development plan adopted in 1959 included construction of a new primary school, new science facilities, expansion of the library and the creation of an organization for alumni, of whom there were more than a thousand living in 1977. Unable to obtain sufficient funding, the school closed in 1978, and in 1980 the buildings and property were taken over by The Clear View School for mentally disabled children.

The J. Warren Rogers house (called Hillside on the Watson map of 1901), birthplace of Admiral Worden, which Vanderlip had purchased, served for a time as a dormitory for a few Scarborough boarding students. Before that it housed some junior employees of the National City Bank. One of these, Dudley N. Schoales, married Virginia Vanderlip, and they raised a family in a remodeled barn (since demolished) between River Road and Creighton Lane. Dudley Schoales, who became a Morgan Stanley partner, was the last owner of Beechwood before the estate was sold to MTS Associates, developers, in 1980.

Among those who were attracted over the years by the fine reputation and progressive policy of the Scarborough School was Louise Randall Dean (later Pierson). She and her first husband, Rodney Dean, then an officer in the National City Bank, moved to Ossining in order to send their children to the school. In her autobiography, *Roughly Speaking*[11] Mrs. Pierson devotes some chapters to a highly colored description of the Scarborough community during Frank Vanderlip's time:

It was the Promised Land. The burning question was: to whom had it been promised? The Intelligentsia or the money-grubbers? Mr. Vanderlip . . . went hopefully forward on the theory that there was no great gulf between the bright and the rich. . . . Community activities were practically ceaseless. There was something for everyone: a gymnasium class, an amateur theater group, folk singing, a swimming pool, an Economic Forum. . . . Mr. Vanderlip, a tall stooped man with a leonine head of white hair, led off the first meeting of the forum with a subject he'd been thinking about for a long time: the wisdom of levying heavy inheritance taxes. He was a convincing speaker. He said it was unwise for a man to leave great sums to his children who had not had the foresight to earn it and would not know how to conserve it. He thought it was better for children to start from scratch and earn their own living.

This speech proved a bombshell. . . . The money-grubbers received it in dour silence. Could it be that Mr. Vanderlip was a traitor to his class, a socialist? The intelligentsia were too smart to applaud openly. Though Dr. John Kingsbury, Secretary of the Milbank Memorial Fund, and Mr. Harry Hopkins, Assistant Director of the Association for Improving the Condition of the Poor, were smiling broadly.

But it gave the forum a lift. Everybody showed up for ex-Commissioner Frederic C. Howe's talk on immigration. . . . Mr. Howe's theme was "the Melting Pot." He said the millions of foreigners being assimilated would be the making of America. It would enrich her culture and supply new blood. This was the year after Sacco and Vanzetti were arrested and Mitchell Palmer, the Fighting Quaker, had rounded up six thousand Reds. . . . "It's about time we put a stop to these foreigners pouring in," somebody shouted. "America for the Americans!"

"You're locking the stable door after the horse is gone," said the ex-Commissioner. "The America you're talking about no longer exists."

"You're a radical," someone yelled. . . .

"We had a frank discussion," said Mr. Vanderlip, mopping his brow after the meeting had disbanded. "But both sides seemed rather intolerant."

In the original Scarborough School building, because Vanderlip particularly wanted his own theater, Welles Bosworth included the Beechwood theater, a replica of the Little Theater in New York City, which was designed by Winthrop Ames. Although small, seating around 250 people, the theater was perfect in every detail. The lighting equipment, the scene lofts and fly gallery, the dressing rooms, the stage floor designed especially for dancing, the excellent acoustics and ideal theater proportions made it possible to mount almost any kind of production with professional ease.

The Beechwood Playhouse was opened and dedicated on January 2, 1917, with a concert by Ignace Paderewski, world famous pianist and statesman. During his performance the "Black Tom" explosion took place at a munitions works in New Jersey, more than thirty miles from Scarborough. Frank Vanderlip, Jr., recalled the event in a 1952 newspaper account:

I was about ten, and it was a great concession for me to be allowed to go . . . Paderewski sat in a special chair with tassels on it, somewhat like a Steig drawing. The house was jammed . . . in the middle of the program a terrific detonation shook the building. Paderewski played on as if nothing had happened. The automatic fire doors at the top of the Theater sprang open, and two men had to be sent aloft to sit on them until the end of the performance to prevent a cold draft from sweeping onstage.

The theater served the school for assemblies, plays, concerts and lectures. As the home of the Beechwood Players it also served a large adult community and continues to do so (see Chapter 17). From the first years, Broadway professionals when not otherwise engaged found it convenient to work there. Among these were Sylvia Sidney, Laurette Taylor, Lynn Fontanne, James Dean, Judson Laire, and Parker Fenelly ("Pepperidge Farm remembuhs"). Lecturers and performers in the theater included Sarah Bernhardt, Robert Frost, John Masefield, Vachel Lindsay, Eleanor Roosevelt, H. G. Wells, Stephen Vincent Benet and the King of Siam.

One local resident active in the Players from the beginning was John Gowen, an engineer who was by avocation a poet and actor. He was the brother of the filmmaker Robert Gowen (See chapter 7). The Players put on several plays a year, summer and winter. Some of these plays were written by Eunice Armstrong, who was the second practicing lay Freudian analyst in this country. One of her plays, *Technique*, went on from the Beechwood Playhouse to Broadway, and is listed in Burns Mantle's *Best Plays of 1930–1931*.[12] Mrs. Armstrong, with her husband, the physician Donald Armstrong, built one of the first houses on the river side of River Road in the 1920s and moved there from Sparta. The Players put on several plays by G. B. Shaw and Tennessee Williams, especially during the 1950s, when they were joined by the Brandywine Players, so called because they first performed *The Glass Menagerie* at Brandywine (the Spiegelberg, then Barksdale estate) on Sleepy Hollow Road. They were John and Mary Douglas Dirks, Barrett Clark, Jr., Betty Myers and Lou Gallo.

Louise Pierson wrote of the Beechwood Players:

There again the intelligentsia were at odds with the bourgeois-capitalist world.
The Players gave six plays a year, with three-night runs. They had started with three one-act

plays but had graduated to full-length dramas. During the confusion resulting from the changeover from short plays to long ones, the intelligentsia. . . . got the upper hand. Mr. Tom Cleland, an artist who designed covers for "slick" magazines, had put on a Chinese play. He adapted it, painted all the scenery, designed the costumes, and played the principal part. Artistically it was a gorgeous thing. The trouble was nobody came to see it but Mr. Barrett Clark, dramatic editor of *Drama* Magazine. . . . Mr. Cleland stubbornly maintained it was Art. Mr. Louis Westerman, whose firm illustrated the Sears Roebuck catalogue, said if nobody came to see it, it wasn't art.

At this point, the Players achieved real distinction by giving a first performance of Lulu Vollmer's *Sun-Up*. Miss Vollmer was then an unknown ticket taker in a southern movie house, who had sent her manuscript to the committee in the crazy hope that they might produce it. This play pleased the simple-minded bankers and brokers and got under the wire as "folk-drama" with the intelligentsia. More, it was bought by a Broadway producer and had a long run. . . . We put on a dank thing called *Black Waters*, in which Rose Hobart played the lead. The hero, who had to carry her in dripping after a suicide attempt, sprained his back. . . . We had counted on a dash of incest in the play to put it over, but it was to the word "bastard" that it owed its success. When the word "bastard" rang through the auditorium, Mrs. Walter B. Mahony, Nicholas Murray Butler's sister, got up and stalked out.[13] We were horror-struck. Should the play be abandoned?

"No," said Mr. Westerman firmly, "The play is made. If we are smart we'll hire a couple of other Confederate soldiers to stamp out every night when the word 'bastard' is said."

It wasn't necessary. The aisles were jammed.[14]

In the first decades of this century, the proximity of Vanderlip's Scarborough to the hamlet of Sparta became uncomfortable. First settled in the late seventeenth century, Sparta had been a busy river port and a stable small-industrial and middle-class community. But after the Croton Dam was completed in 1905, many immigrants moved there to work in the quarry, the limeworks and a nearby shoe factory. Some worked as gardeners, some in the Pierson nursery and greenhouses (Arcadian Gardens) on the Post Road. Many also worked as employees of Sing Sing prison, with which drug and liquor smuggling were associated. The hamlet was crowded and as local enterprises failed, incomes fell and the crime rate rose.[15] Vanderlip described Sparta as "something of a center of wrong-doing[16] . . . a very tumbled-down town, a place without electricity, without gas, without baths and possessing not a single hot-water heating plant. It had been left behind, skipped over by modern conveniences and comforts."

The Vanderlips' uneasiness about nearby Sparta and the prison can be inferred from this anecdote told by Frank Vanderlip, Jr.: One night in the autumn of 1918, the whole Vanderlip family was asleep on the sleeping porch at Beechwood. (They were great believers in the health-giving powers of fresh air.) They were awakened by the prison sirens sounding, once, then again, then continuously. Then the bells of the churches rang and continued to ring. The din was awful. They assumed there had been a prison break, a big one. The children had never seen their mother so frightened. "There were tears in her eyes." After a fearful night, Vanderlip called his office and asked if there was anything in the papers about a prison break. "Haven't you heard?" was the reply. "The war is over. It's the Armistice."

That night, Frank Vanderlip believes, his parents' resolve was formed to do something about Sparta, their "doorstep problem." After Vanderlip's resignation from the presidency of the National City Bank in 1919, decreasing demands on his time and energies allowed him, with Mrs. Vanderlip, to set about rectifying that problem. Aware of the hamlet's antiquity and latent charm, they undertook "remodeling a few old houses in order to preserve something of their architectural beauty and make them livable. . . . The houses will be occupied by teachers at Scarborough School and other desirable people."[17] Vanderlip had owned some property in Sparta for at least ten years and now quietly bought more, twenty-nine parcels in all.[18] Some of these houses were demolished, others moved—back from the streets or to face the river view. Several were thoroughly remodeled (with sleeping porches) to the plans of Arthur Loomis Harmon, a well-known architect.

Vanderlip's rehabilitation of Sparta has been called the first urban renewal. The project attracted a great deal of public attention at the time. One newspaper described it in these distorted terms: "VANDERLIP BUYS VILLAGE—WILL MAKE MODEL COMMUNITY.... He has bought the entire village and plans to remodel its present houses, build new ones and ask the undesirables to leave."[19] In actuality the work was accomplished with taste and tact, in some cases even with stealth, and it is not recorded that any of the residents were offended or much disturbed.

Some teachers at Scarborough and other schools did live there, and some artists. Some still do. Harry Hopkins of the Roosevelt administration lived in one of the remodeled houses for a time, as did Donald and Eunice Armstrong and their family. Louise Randall Pierson lived there with her first husband, Rodney Dean, and their children before renting the Holden homestead above Scarborough Road.

Some Sparta residents who would not sell to the Vanderlips were the family of Pete LaLuna, who owned the Pine Tree Restaurant at 6 Rockledge Avenue. Some fifty years later, in 1971, the Vanderlips' grandson, Dudley Schoales, bought LaLuna's restaurant, remodeled it, painted the house purple, and opened Dudley's of Sparta. He and his wife, Cecile, operated the restaurant until they sold it and, in 1978, moved to Connecticut. LaLuna had already sold the house before Dudley bought it, but he still held a small mortgage on it. Ceely remembers that he would come in once a month, always around eleven o'clock in the morning, to collect his mortgage payment. Dudley would sign the check with his full name, Dudley *Vanderlip* Schoales, and LaLuna would have a good laugh over that until Dudley hurried him and his aromatic cigar out of the restaurant before the lunch crowd came.

Shirley Hibbard concludes her "Investigation of the Vanderlip Preservation Project at Sparta":

As Vanderlip was a friend of Henry Ford and the Rockefellers it is impossible to imagine that the Sparta project did not play some definite role in the evolution of village restorations which followed. Sparta may justly be seen as a step in the development of the preservation movement in America.

When the National City Bank acquired a controlling interest in the Continental Can Company, the bank directors put Carle Cotter Conway at the head of the company. The Carle Conways lived in a large house on the east corner of Linden Circle. Their son Norton, who was six-feet six-inches tall and on the Yale football team, married Charlotte Vanderlip in June 1927, a few weeks after the wedding of her sister Narcissa to Julian Street, Jr. The Streets were married in the New Church, a small Georgian edifice on 35th Street in New York City, "in one of the largest and most brilliant weddings of the spring."[20] At the Colony Club reception, there were more than fifteen hundred guests, including the Franklin and Archibald Roosevelts, assorted Vanderbilts and Goulds, Bernard Baruch, Edna Ferber and James Montgomery Flagg.[21] The Conways were married in Scarborough, their "nuptuals bordering on the pageantry of Medieval days, in a setting of transporting beauty on the lawns at Beechwood.[22] The bridesmaids' gowns were of chiffon in various shades

of blue, and they carried bouquets of blue delphiniums. A brick house in the South African Dutch style was built for the young Conways just below the Italian garden at Beechwood. This handsome house was designed with some unusual features: a loft in the garage where the young couple could hang their sails after cruising on Long Island Sound and an outdoor hearth for barbecues in the big south chimney. Charlotte and Norton Conway had two children, but their marriage broke up, their house was sold and, after World War II, the small building (Beechtwig) in the corner of the Beechwood wall on the Post Road was remodeled for Charlotte and the children.

A friend of the Vanderlips who attended many parties at Beechwood in the 1920s describes that decade as "the fabulous years! . . . One Christmas in the Library the Vanderlip family gifts looked like a "Dynasty" scene—Ermine and mink coats, jewels, crystal—and a new car for Virginia in the driveway."[23]

Frank Vanderlip, Jr.'s memories of Christmases at Beechwood are somewhat different: "There was *one* ermine coat—no minks. N. C. V. got a new pearl necklace from F. A. V., and a pregnant goat from her children. She preferred the goat. It had three kids, one black, one white and one gray, which played on the lawn where the goat was tethered the next summer. Pa loved to see them scamper around their mother."

In the depressed 1930s, after the death of Frank Vanderlip, most of the assets of the Vanderlip family estate were in real estate rather than cash. Accordingly, Scarborough Properties, the family realty corporation, under the direction of Harry Benedict, set about developing the river-front land west of Beechwood. River Road was extended, Creighton and Woodlea lanes laid out and a sewer system, water pipes and fire hydrants installed. Scarborough Properties offered to dedicate the road and lanes, with improvements, to the village of Briarcliff Manor with the understanding that they would be reimbursed $88,933.38, less depreciation of 2%, for the cost of the improvements in a transaction like those made routinely between the village and the Briarcliff Realty Company. At the request of the board of trustees, village officials Valentine and Manahan investigated the improvements made by Scarborough Properties and reported that $50,438.33 "represented their fair and reasonable cost." When Scarborough Properties promptly confirmed this figure, the village took possession of the roads without paying Scarborough Properties and started collecting charges for their use from owners of adjacent property. Scarborough Properties took the case to court, judgment for them was affirmed, but the village appealed and, with what today reads like a legal quibble, won. The judgments were reversed and the complaint dismissed, with costs in all courts. Attorney Herbert Gerlach of Ossining (See Chapter 7, Chilmark) represented the village.[24]

This case and others like it help to explain the division, and occasional antagonism, between the two overlapping but distinct parts of the small village of Briarcliff Manor. As is noted in the 1977 history of the village, "residents of Scarborough have steadfastly held on to their identity," and when, some years after the annexation of Scarborough in 1906, a sign reading "Briarcliff West" was put up by the railroad at the Scarborough station, it was thrown into the Hudson River and replaced with the Scarborough sign. In a similar episode, a proposal to discontinue the Scarborough post office or make it a branch of the Briarcliff office was met with a storm of protest, a mass meeting and a lengthy study of the volume of mail handled by the Scarborough post office. Rather than change their address from Scarborough-on-Hudson, N. Y. 10510 to Blank Road (or Lane or Circle), Briarcliff Manor, N. Y. 10510, Scarborough residents, even some former residents who had moved away, preferred to go to the post office every day to pick up their mail.

13

Friends, Relations and Neighbors

OF THE MANY friends who surrounded the Vanderlips at Beechwood, several were business associates, some were relatives, some were both. Among them were the Philip Henrys, the James Speyers, the Edward Walker Hardens, the Carle Conways, Eugene and Lulu Ailes, the Isaac Newton Spiegelbergs, Dr. Percy Norman Barnesby and "Uncle William" Rockefeller.

In 1906, the National City Bank united with the banking firm of Speyer & Company to finance and oversee the building of a railroad in Bolivia. As head of the construction company, Vanderlip selected Philip W. Henry, "an engineer of wide experience,"[1] and the husband of Narcissa Vanderlip's sister, Clover. Some years later the Henrys built, on the north lot of Linden Circle, a handsome stone house designed by the architect Bertram Grosvenor Goodhue. Philip Henry's choice of architect may have reflected his years in South America, for Goodhue is noted for his revival of the Spanish style, particularly in southern California. Henry must have seen examples of Goodhue's work while visiting the Vanderlips on their Palos Verdes property, near Los Angeles.

Milton E. Ailes, who succeeded Frank Vanderlip as assistant secretary of the treasury, was "his eyes and ears"[2] in Washington, a devoted friend and trusted associate. Eugene Ailes, Milton's brother, bought the Kemeys house at the head of Kemeys Cove in Scarborough. There were six Ailes children who went to the Scarborough School. Miss Lulu Ailes, sister of Eugene and Milton, taught fourth grade and ancient history at the Scarborough School for many years.

In the 1940s, the Kemeys–Ailes house was the home of Nina Baekeland Roll, her husband, Phillips Wyman, who had been a publisher with the McCall Corporation since 1923, and their children from former marriages. Mrs. Wyman was the daughter of Leo Hendrik Baekeland, who in the 1900s invented a substance known as Bakelite, which made him a fortune. (Her nephew Brooks Baekeland, a grandchild of the inventor, was the father of Anthony Baekeland, who, in London in 1972, killed his beautiful, glamorous mother, Barbara.)[3] The younger children went to the Scarborough School. In World War II Phillips Wyman served as a lieutenant in the Air Force. In the 1960s, the house was converted to

102

a nursing home, and there Mrs. Vanderlip spent the last months of her long, illustrious life. In the 1970s, the house was demolished and the Kemeys Cove Condominiums built on the site.

The James Speyers

James Speyer's country estate Waldheim (Forest Home) occupied a large tract of land between Scarborough Road and the Albany Post Road. The estate's brick wall still borders Holbrook and Scarborough roads as far south as the entrance to Philips Laboratories. Speyer was born in New York City in 1861 and educated in Germany, at Frankfurt-am-Main, where at age twenty-two he entered the family banking house. He later transferred to Paris and London to enlarge his experience before returning to New York to become a partner in his Uncle Philip's Speyer & Company (founded in 1837). James Speyer was senior partner of that firm until 1939, when it went out of business. From his "high-ceilinged, Old World office in a Pine Street building modeled after the Palazzo Pandolfini in Florence . . . [he] operated a patrician one-man banking house."[4] He is described in Birmingham's *Our Crowd* as "a small, dapper, starch-collared, and rather prickly man. . . . [his] personal bearing so Old World . . . so Continental, as to have seemed downright exotic."[5]

It is remembered that alone among local millionaires he conducted the Waldheim household in the aristocratic European manner, with, for example, a footman stationed behind the chair of each guest at the dinner table. He was an officer and director of many companies, a member from 1891 to 1941 (and twice vice-president) of the New York Chamber of Commerce, and so active in many charitable and educational enterprises that he became

House on Linden Circle designed by Bertram Grosvenor Goodhue

better known for these than for his banking career. He was "the guiding spirit" behind the Museum of the City of New York. From 1900 to 1932 he was a trustee of Teachers College of Columbia University, to which, in 1902, in his wife's name, he presented the Speyer School. He was a founder of the Provident Loan Society, of the Salvation Army, and of the American Society for the Control of Cancer. "He was a director of Mount Sinai Hospital, a steady donor to Jewish charities and an outstanding critic of clubs and schools that practiced racial or religious discrimination. Yet he was a member of the Racquet Club, where other Jews were not even welcomed as guests of members."[6] In 1897 he married Ellin Prince, a gentile of old American stock, and gave her name to one of the first (and still the foremost) animal hospitals in New York City.

The June 1908 issue of "Briarcliff-Once-a-Week" confirms Mrs. Speyer's concern for animal welfare in a report on the second annual New York work-horse parade on Memorial Day:

The official list of the Auxiliary [of the A.S.P.C.A.] carries many of the most prominent names in New York City as its elective officers, executive committee, Patrons and subscribers, among which it is noted that Briarcliff has representation in the persons of Mrs. James Speyer, treasurer, and Mrs. Robert G. Mead and Mr. James Speyer contributors.

Briarcliff had other reasons to be proud of the parade:

Honors fell to Briarcliff's New York store. Superintendent Tuttle, of the Farms Department, who is himself a lover of the horse, approved of two entries for the parade, and Manager Crockett, of the New York Store, helped forward the entries in every way possible. In division A of class 30, "Milk and Cream," entry No. 539 by Briarcliff Farms included a team of seven-year-olds, "Louise" and "Minnie," driven by John Corcoran, which was awarded a white ribbon of honor, and in division B, same class, entry number 541 by Briarcliff Farms secured first prize in a list of sixteen entries, for "Nigger," a faithful veteran of fourteen years, driven by Cornelius Sullivan.

Waldheim, the James Speyer estate on Scarborough Road

Parade for the Hudson Fulton
Celebration in front of Briarcliff
Lodge, 1909

A public-spirited, generous American, James Speyer was also a truly international banker. An anecdote in *Our Crowd* about Speyer "lunching with the old Kaiser Wilhelm," illustrates his cordial relations with that monarch: "Mr. Speyer mentioned his sorrow at having no sons to carry on. 'But surely there are some Speyers left in Frankfurt,' said the Kaiser. 'None,' said Speyer sadly. 'This will never do,' said the Kaiser. 'There must always be a Speyer in Frankfurt!' And he conferred the title 'von Speyer' on Speyer's brother-in-law."

At James Speyer's invitation, Kaiser Wilhelm's son, Crown Prince Wilhelm, came to Briarcliff for the Hudson-Fulton Anniversary celebration in September 1909. It was the centennial of the first voyage of Fulton's first steamship *Clermont* on the Hudson River and the tricentennial of Henry Hudson's discovery of the river. There was a naval parade of 1,542 ships, including replicas of the *Clermont* and the *Half Moon*, the Navy's entire Atlantic fleet, and ships from many other nations.[7]

The German battleship that conveyed the Crown Prince to these shores, anchored off Scarborough dock, inspired the awe of Frank Vanderlip, Jr., who was a small boy at the time.

The Crown Prince led a Prussian regiment in a spectacular parade in honor of the anniversary in New York City. In Briarcliff, as in towns all up and down the Hudson River, a parade was held, starting from the Lodge. Eileen O'Connor Weber remembers looking at the photograph of the parade and asking her widowed mother, Mrs. Lillian O'Connor, why her father, Daniel O'Connor (front row, left), was so dressed up. "Because the Crown Prince of Germany was visiting Briarcliff," she was told. Eileen also remembers that memories of this event, and Speyer's part in it, were less enthusiastic a very few years later, during World War I.

The Spiegelbergs

In 1909, Isaac Newton Spiegelberg built a forty-nine room Tudor style mansion on some twenty acres off Sleepy Hollow Road and named it Miramont Court (Spiegel-mirror, Berg-mountain). The house still stands as part of the Brandywine Nursing Home. Outbuildings, including a seventy-five-foot water tower, and plantings form a courtyard around the facade of the house. From the porte-cochere an entryway leads directly into the "great hall," which is wood-panelled, with a large fireplace and set into the ceiling in terra cotta the initials of the Spiegelbergs, I.N.S. and S.F. (Stella Friedlander) S. To the right is the Music Room, in which there were a stage with a piano on it; an organ; a big window with seats cushioned in red velvet; a small balcony in the back; and, seated on an overhang around the ceiling, child-size cast or carved and painted cherubs with their feet crossed, looking down. Many concerts and theatricals took place and special occasions were celebrated in the Music Room, including the marriage of the Spiegelbergs' daughter Marie to Alan Harcourt Black.

Isaac Newton Spiegelberg was born in the United States to a family of wholesale clothing merchants who had prospered during the Civil War, but, like Speyer, he was educated in Germany. Trained as an engineer, he worked for a time on the St. Gothard Railway in Switzerland before returning to this country, where he worked, mostly in Oklahoma, on the Atlantic & Pacific Railroad. In 1884 he gave up engineering for the brokerage business with the firm of J. & W. Seligman. His "keen business judgment . . . combined with his high sense of honor in all business as well as personal relationships soon won him recognition as one of the leading brokers of Wall Street. In 1886, he purchased a seat on the New York Stock Exchange and . . . began to trade independently."[8] He was a member of Temple Emanu-El in New York City, where he also maintained a residence.

Miramont Court was the summer residence of Spiegelberg, his wife Stella, and their children, Marie and Stanley. Spiegelberg took great pleasure in the gardens there. Pierre Courreges was superintendent of the estate, and his daughter Kay, who grew up there, remembers the large flower and vegetable gardens and the arbors of "special" grapes, from which her father made wine. Courreges was assisted at all times by at least three other gardeners. Many plants were imported for the gardens, mostly from Japan, because local nurseries were comparatively undeveloped at the time. The house had a grand view—from the

Indoor staff of Miramont Court, the Spiegelberg mansion. This building is presently part of the Brandywine Nursing Home

Stella F. Spiegelberg with her granddaughter

Harden-Vanderlip family group. Adults left to right (rear): Narcissa Cox Vanderlip, Frank A. Vanderlip, Edward Harden, Ruth Harden; (center front): Aunt Sarah Marilla Cox.

Edward Walker Harden

lawn and tennis courts in the foreground, across the gardens, a vineyard, a pond and a strip of woodland, to the Hudson River and the hills of Rockland County on the horizon. On fine afternoons Stella Spiegelberg took tea in a treehouse in the garden. She had to climb steep steps up into the treehouse, but there was a dumbwaiter to convey the tea and accompanying delicacies to her there.[9]

Isaac Spiegelberg died in 1927 and a year later his heirs sold the estate to Mrs. Ethel Barksdale, a sister of Pierre du Pont, from Delaware. The Barksdales bought more land, built a studio (some of the family were artists), a greenhouse and kennels, remodeled the interior of the house, threw out the cherubs and named the estate Brandywine. Mrs. Barksdale, with her daughter and son-in-law, John Dublois Wack, lived there until 1931.

The Edward Walker Hardens

Edward Walker Harden was a friend of Frank Vanderlip's from his newspaper days and succeeded Vanderlip as financial editor of the *Chicago Tribune*. When he was assistant secretary of the treasury, Vanderlip arranged for Harden to go on the maiden voyage of the cutter *Hugh M'Culloch* to the China coast in 1898. In Vanderlip's words, "That was all I had to do with Harden's feat."[10] The feat referred to was the scoop of all the newspapers of the world with the news of Admiral Dewey's destruction of the Spanish fleet at the Battle of Manila Bay. The Spanish cable to Hong Kong had been cut, and the *Hugh M'Culloch* was picked to be the dispatch boat. Two other reporters and Admiral Dewey's flag lieutenant, with his official dispatches, were aboard. At Hong Kong dock, Harden was first off the boat and managed to get a forty-word bulletin containing the essence of the great news through to the *Chicago Tribune* more than five hours ahead of the official dispatches. An editor at the *Tribune* telephoned the White House at four-thirty in the morning and got President McKinley out of bed to tell him of the victory.

A variation on this story attributes Harden's newspaper scoop to his friendship with Filipino insurrection leader Emilio Aguinaldo, who issued Harden a special pass through insurgent lines to get on the first boat out of Manila Bay after the victory.[11]

When the Edward Hardens moved to Westchester County, perhaps to be near Ruth Harden's brother, Frank Vanderlip, and his family, Harden was no longer a newspaper reporter but a Wall Street broker, a member of the New York Stock Exchange and a director of many big corporations. In Tarrytown the Hardens built the mansion at 200 North Broadway that later became the administration building of the Tarrytowns' public schools. While living in Tarrytown, Harden gave the village the land for Dean Park, on the corner of Broadway and Main Street, after the Dean house was demolished in 1912. A decade later the park was sold to business interests.[12]

In the 1920s Harden sold the Tarrytown house and bought the property in Briarcliff between Long Hill Road West and Sleepy Hollow Road, adjacent to Spiegelberg's Miramont Court. The previous owner, Joseph Ulman, a stockbroker, had built a group of Saranac-style cabins connected by covered ramps. These the Hardens tore down, all but one, and built a stone mansion, in the Italian renaissance style, and named the estate the Wilderness. In the 1980s the estate became the Rosecliff development. Like the Vanderlips, the Hardens traveled extensively in Europe and the Middle East and collected many antique furnishings. An upholsterer and a cabinetmaker were for some years steadily employed in the basement of the mansion at the Wilderness. The Hardens "spared no expense in creating a lovely, homey place, with parts from the Italian past."[13] The driveway and courtyard of the house were paved with Belgian cobblestones. Shortly after the house was built, Rosemary Harden was married in the formal garden. Kay Courreges remembers, "We were little kids. We all climbed up the tower at Brandywine to watch. It was a lovely wedding." The water tower at Brandywine at that time had a conical roof and a circular walkway commanding a sweeping view.

In the 1930s the Hardens bought Brandywine from the heirs of Mrs. Barksdale, and a road was built connecting it to the Wilderness. Courreges became the superintendent of the combined estates. Harden also bought land on the east side of Sleepy Hollow Road across from Brandywine. Some of this acreage he presented to the Vanderlips' eldest daughter, Narcissa, and Julian Street, Jr. ("son of the celebrated author")[14] when they were married in April 1927. The young Streets preferred a more secluded property that Vanderlip owned on Long Hill Road West, and they sold the land on Sleepy Hollow Road to Curtis and Anna Roosevelt Dahl. The house that architect Wallace Harrison designed for the Streets, now 710 Long Hill Road West, was one of the first in contemporary style that was built in the county.

There was a stone wall around the property on Sleepy Hollow Road because, as Frank Vanderlip, Jr., remembered, "Uncle Eddy [Harden] never bought a piece of land without building a stone wall around it." The Dahls removed a section of the stone wall in order to build an entryway. "Uncle Eddy was a very funny man," and he flew into a comic mock rage and let everyone know how he felt about this damage to his wall. The Dahls, when their house was half built, sailed for Europe to buy furniture for it, "as everyone did." When they were halfway across the Atlantic Ocean, a radiogram brought them the news that the house had burned down. The morning after the fire, Harden burst into the club car exclaiming, "I did not start that fire!"[15]

The Dahls rebuilt their house and in 1929 moved into it. For a time their two children, President and Mrs. Roosevelt's grandchildren Buzzie and Sistie Dahl, went to the Scarborough School. When the Dahls were divorced, a bank took over their house and rented

Ruth Vanderlip Harden

*Portrait of Virginia Vanderlip at
entrance to Beechwood
library-ballroom*

it out. Susan Cullman remembered with pleasure visiting the Dahls there, and in 1936 she and her husband Joseph Cullman (of Philip Morris, Inc.) bought the house. "The only furniture was in the big living room—one small square rug in the middle of the floor with a rocking chair at each corner." The Cullmans named the place Sleepy Hill, and over the years added only a porch, which was later enclosed.

Dr. Barnesby

Dr. Percy Norman Barnesby was the medical director of the City Bank and Frank Vanderlip's personal physician. Vanderlip built a brick house for Dr. and Mrs. Barnesby at the south corner of River Road and the Post Road. Later, under the name of Marie Fayant Hall, the house was given to the Scarborough School and served as a girls' dormitory in the 1940s and as headmaster's residence for some thirty years after that. In his autobiography, Vanderlip tells the story of a line-fence quarrel between William Rockefeller and Dr. Barnesby, who "had become the squire of six acres, wedged like Belgium between Beechwood and Rockwood Hall."[16] The boundary between the Barnesby and Rockefeller properties was a broken-down fence and a ragged growth of scrubby bushes, all rooted in Rockefeller land.

One day as the Barnesbys stood in their garden [they] . . . discovered that a heavy-set stranger who rested his elbows on that troublesome fence was no less a personage than the master of Rockwood Hall·. . . accompanied by Hawks, the estate superintendent. Barnesby strolled over and said, "How do you do, Mr. Rockefeller? I am Dr. Barnesby." There was no word, only a piercing look from the granite-featured gentleman. Dr. Barnesby cleared his throat and spoke his piece anyway: "Would you mind if I took down these scrub bushes and planted a nice row of trees in place of them?"

At that, Mr. Rockefeller, who was really tall, reared himself high above Dr. Barnesby. Not until he had buttoned his coat did he speak, and even then he simply growled: "See Hawks" and strode away, closely dogged by Hawks.

When Barnesby's rage had cooled, he hired half a dozen Italian laborers and directed them as they cleared away the scrubs. Then it was Vanderlip's turn to rage—at his friend Barnesby, for fear Rockefeller's dignity had been so "seriously affronted" that he might "salve it through some action against me or the bank" (the City Bank, of which Rockefeller was a director).

Rockwood Hall, the William Rockefeller estate in North Tarrytown

William Rockefeller

William Rockefeller, the brother of John D. Rockefeller, had bought Rockwood, the estate of William H. Aspinwall, shipping and railroad magnate, from General Lloyd Aspinwall. Rockefeller tore down the Aspinwall mansion and built a grander one, which he named Rockwood Hall. While it was being rebuilt he lived at Edgehill, "the Brick Villa," which was designed by Stanford White, on Sleepy Hollow Road just south of the town line.

Rockwood Hall in Rockefeller's time is described by Tarrytown historians as "unparalleled in Westchester for magnificence."[17]

The three oldest Vanderlip children were allowed to take turns accompanying their father to the train at Scarborough Station on weekday mornings. Briarcliff Lodge and the Sleepy Hollow Country Club both sent large chauffeured touring cars to the station in those days, and it must have been a grand sight to a small boy. When young Frank was about six years old, he had seen his father off to the city and was on his way home when "Uncle William" Rockefeller came by in his electric car and offered him a ride. Frank accepted and was driven to Rockwood Hall, where he was treated to an illustrated lecture on how to run a large estate economically. Rockefeller had one of the first gasoline-powered mowing machines and had paved the estate roads with blocks of a special composition containing tar for resilience which, set close together, kept out weeds. Meanwhile, in the Vanderlip household there was growing panic at Frank's disappearance. When Rockefeller's butler

was made aware of this, he suggested that his employer telephone Mrs. Vanderlip. He did so, with a look on his face that Frank read to mean: What more can I do to annoy her? He took the boy into the big morning room and ordered the butler to bring champagne, which both were sipping when Mrs. Vanderlip arrived to rescue her son and heir.[18]

Marion Dinwiddie, speaking of Saint Mary's Church, reported more favorably on William Rockefeller. He was

not an official member but a very much loved member of the congregation. . . . He and Mrs. Rockefeller used to come up every Sunday except one Sunday in the year when they went to the Baptist Church. . . . While he always gave very generously to everything we were raising money for, he would give what he thought was his proper amount, owing to the fact that he probably had more money than anybody else, then he would say, "If you don't get all you want, ask me again," and he would make up the difference. Mrs. Rockefeller was a wonderful member of the Guild. She would shop like mad and she could tell you where you could get all the bargains in New York, I'll tell you that![19]

Frank Vanderlip, Jr.

14

Other Distinguished Residents

ASHRIDGE, THE porticoed Greek Revival house on the ridge above Scarborough Road, was smaller when, in 1862, C. C. North had it moved from the Butler Wright estate on the Albany Post Road (see Chapter 3). The interior of the house was divided into many small rooms. Before it was remodeled, Ashridge had one distinguished resident, Benjamin Church, chief engineer of the Croton Aqueduct Commission, who made his country home there around the turn of the century.

Church had been working, in charge of the impossible task of supplying water to the growing city through the leaky old Croton Aqueduct, as far back as the 1850s. The tunnel had to be inspected frequently for cracks and leaks, and on one occasion water was let in during an inspection. "A group of men grabbed a ladder forming a human chain to keep from being swept away. One of them tried to get out before his turn and had to be pulled back. By the time the last man was out, the water had reached Church's neck, but the crew had been saved."[1]

Giles and Flora Whiting

Giles Whiting and his wife, Flora Ettlinger Whiting, bought Ashridge from C. C. North in 1910. In 1913 and 1926, increasing their property to some hundred acres, they bought more land from Annie C. Smith, widow of Augustine Smith, whose forebears in 1785 had owned 629 acres on and around the ridge. Whiting was an architect and manufacturer of "Persian" rugs. Mrs. Whiting was described as "a slender, diminutive woman with sharp hazel eyes and a head for figures."[2] She was the daughter of printing magnate Louis E. Ettlinger, who was a director of the Crowell Publishing Company, publishers of *Collier's Weekly, Woman's Home Companion*, and several other magazines. Ettlinger in 1902 had "purchased Boscobel, the Henry Ward Beecher estate in Peekskill, where he made his summer home and continued the famous preacher's work of transplanting and cultivating trees from foreign countries."[3]

In the 1930s the Whitings had the house remodeled by Aymar Embury II and greatly enlarged by the addition of wings. The Whitings' 1910 purchase included, as well as the stables and the other outbuildings of a working farm, a house in the Federal style built in

Ashridge, Scarborough Road, after remodeling

the early 1800s. This may have been the Smith farmhouse or the "Old Ryder Homestead" mentioned in the 1860 deed of C. C. North.[4] Jesse Ryder had owned land in the vicinity at least as far back as 1824.[5] This handsome little house, which the Whitings remodeled and used for guests, is most often referred to as "the Cottage," or "Hoover Cottage," after Mrs. Whiting's friend President Herbert Hoover, who stayed there on his several visits to Ashridge.

Giles Whiting died in 1937. Mrs. Whiting lived on at Ashridge and in her Park Avenue apartment in New York City into her nineties, sixty years in all . She was a woman of many interests, a dedicated moviegoer, Canasta player, stock market watcher, world traveller, philanthropist—particularly generous to the Girl Scouts—and hostess of "formal dinner parties at which as many as 10 or 12 of the nation's outstanding museum curators and collectors, including Henry du Pont, would be gathered."[6] Mrs. Whiting's greatest interest was the collection of American antiques, in which she was a pioneer. Her friend Joseph Butler of the Sleepy Hollow Restorations (later Historic Hudson Valley) said of her, "She would always spot the best thing in a shop instantly." She furnished the Cottage with the simpler country antiques and displayed more formal pieces in the paneled rooms of the mansion and the New York apartment. According to Joseph Veach Noble, a director of the Museum of the City of New York, "All three of [her] homes were crammed with things— especially the attics and basement in the country."[7]

Flora Whiting

In 1972, a year after Mrs. Whiting's death, the Parke-Bernet gallery conducted an auction at Ashridge. The antiques she had amassed in her lifetime of collecting brought more than half a million dollars, considerably more than the gallery's top estimate. This "confirmed suspicions that a boom [was] building for just the sort of Federal furniture Mrs. Whiting collected."[8] The Metropolitan Museum bought fifty major pieces of furniture and about

Holly Hill on Scarborough Road was formerly named Weskora.

a hundred and forty-six decorations. The State Department of the United States paid more than $5,000 for an eighteenth-century camelback sofa, and the Museum of the City of New York bought twenty-five pieces of furniture, including ten Duncan Phyfes, twenty-five period appointments, and paintings by George Innes and Childe Hassam. All the furniture is on display at the museum in the Whiting Room, created in Mrs. Whiting's memory, as specified in her will.

In the late 1930s, the Whiting's only daughter, Ann, eloped with a young man who was making a very modest living selling neckties in a department store. Mrs. Whiting was seriously displeased and threatened to disinherit her daughter. But the marriage lasted, mother and daughter were eventually reconciled, and the grandchildren enjoyed visiting at Ashridge. Lisa Thomas, Mrs. Whiting's granddaughter, told *New York Times* reporter Rita Reif that the year she and her brother, W. Giles Murray, lived in the mansion while their mother was ill was "the greatest time of my life . . . we watched the boats go by on the Hudson and yes, on a clear day you could see as far as the Delaware Water Gap, fifty miles away." She said she thought more about "how homey" the mansion was than how rare the antiques were. "It was such a friendly lived-in house and that's the way I want to remember it."

The Hubert Rogers Estate

In the 1920s Hubert Rogers, a New York City lawyer, purchased properties on Scarborough Road that had belonged to the Grannis and Crawford families, among others. This new estate stretched from the Dinwiddie land, well below the corner where Scarborough Road turns east, to the backs of properties on Sleepy Hollow Road and to the Becker and Whiting properties to the south. Rogers named the estate Weskora, after the legendary Indian chief. One house built in 1913 on the Rogers property remains as Mrs. Vincent Astor's gardener's cottage. Rogers had another house torn down and replaced in 1928 by a residence designed by William Adams Delano of Delano & Aldrich, architects of several outstanding mansions, including the John D. Rockefellers' Kykuit in Pocantico Hills. William McGowan, nurseryman at the Briarcliff Farms, supervised plantings, particularly of young holly trees, on the estate. Rogers died in the early 1960s, survived by his wife for a year or two. When Mrs. Rogers died, in her nineties, Nelson Rockefeller called Mrs. Vincent Astor to tell her the Rogerses' son did not want to live in Scarborough and Weskora was for sale. Mrs. Astor's country estate at the time was in Rhinebeck, inconveniently distant from the city. "You couldn't invite people out there just for lunch." She went to see Weskora, within days contracted to buy it, and renamed it Holly Hill after McGowan's now well-grown holly trees. Mrs. Astor altered the name but not the handsome house, except for one large window and an indoor swimming pool in a low wing on the courtyard, not visible from the outside. She feels that Delano, the architect, would not have been offended by these changes.

The William J. Burns Family

When William J. Burns bought Shadowbrook, on Scarborough Road, in 1917, he was already an international celebrity. He was the supersleuth. More than a detective or the head of a detective agency that was growing at a tremendous rate, he had become the national watchdog, carrying out assignments that exposed corruption in state and local governments. In 1911, when Burns had solved the case of the bombing of the *Los Angeles Times*, *The New York Times* called him, "the greatest detective . . . perhaps the only really great detective, the only detective of genius this country has produced."[9] Burns was of medium height but compact, with red hair and a red mustache, and seemed to be always in motion. He was gregarious, shrewd and witty, an accomplished mimic and a flamboyant performer.

In 1888, when he was thirty, Burns left his father's tailoring business in Columbus, Ohio, and set up as a full-time private investigator. In 1891, he became an operative of the United States Secret Service, which was at that time a division of the Treasury Department and

William J. Burns

mostly concerned with counterfeiters. Burns' exploits in apprehending just about every corrupt master engraver in the western world have been the inspiration of countless mystery writers.

In 1903 President Theodore Roosevelt, suspecting that the nation was being cheated out of vast tracts of public land in Oregon, transferred Burns to a new position in the Department of the Interior. Roosevelt's belief that he had hired the one investigator who would bring him the truth was justifed when Burns proved that the United States General Land Office was "corrupt at every level . . . corrupt to the very core."[10] The new position created for Burns was the forerunner of the Federal Bureau of Investigation. Years later, at the end of his career, Burns was director of the F.B.I. J. Edgar Hoover was his aide.

Burns went on to solve the San Francisco graft case, in a three-year struggle, and the case of the bombing of the *Los Angeles Times*, exposing the domination of the California government by corrupt railroad officials.

In 1910 Burns left government service and established the Burns National Detective Agency in Chicago, with his son Raymond as manager of the headquarters and a network of some two dozen regional offices. Burns's own office was in a Pullman car because he was constantly travelling.

Unlike its archrival, the much older Pinkerton Agency, the Burns Agency was never involved in strike-breaking operations. Burns favored neither capital nor labor. Accused by Clarence Darrow, the leading labor lawyer, of masterminding a capitalist conspiracy in the case of the McNamara brothers, Burns told a reporter:

I'm no respecter of persons when they're criminals. . . . If I'd found evidence in this case to implicate the president of the largest corporation in the United States, and the board of directors, I'd have been right after them all. . . . When I'm employed to find out who committed a crime, I go out to find him. I don't care a row of red apples who he is or where he is. These people who are calling me an "enemy of labor" for running down these dynamiters [the McNamaras] are as muddleheaded as the jawsmiths in San Francisco who called me an "enemy of capital" for going after big fellows in the graft investigation out there. When I have my case against a criminal, I put clamps on him just as quick whether he has diamond rings on his fingers or callouses as big as hoofs.[11]

In 1913–1914 the Burns Agency became international, with offices in Montreal, London, Brussels and Paris. Burns moved his family to Westchester County, to Bronxville and then to Scarborough. Shadowbrook, just south of James Speyer's Waldheim and across from the Dinwiddies on Scarborough Road, was "a lovely, rambling brown-shingled house with a glassed-in sun porch and many bedrooms."[12] There were gardeners to care for the many gardens on thirteen acres, servants and bells to summon them. But Mrs. Burns preferred to do most of the cooking herself. Burns entertained famous friends there, including governor of New York Alfred E. Smith, the showman John Ringling and Owen Johnson, author of the stories of "Detective McKenna," for whom Burns was the real-life model. Owen Johnson also wrote the popular Hickey books, about boys at the Lawrenceville preparatory school, and *Stover at Yale*, "which attacked the solemn mumbo-jumbo of senior societies and the intellectual incuriosity of the average undergraduates [at Yale] in no uncertain terms."[13]

The big house at Shadowbrook could not be seen from the driveway entrance above it on Scarborough Road, where a lush growth of rambler roses often attracted the attention of Sunday afternoon motoring parties. Motorists who stopped to admire and perhaps

Three generations of Burns International presidents: William J., Raymond, and William J., Jr.

pick some of the roses were suddenly horrified by a sonorous, apparently disembodied voice saying, "That's private property! Don't you dare touch those roses!" The voice, amplified by a megaphone, issued from the shadows of the Dinwiddies' veranda. Mr. Dinwiddie had found a Sunday afternoon pastime nearly as absorbing as Everit Macy's automotive exploits of earlier years.

The Burns family was extraordinarily close and devoted. George, Raymond and Sherman Burns, from boyhood on, ably assisted their father in his work. After a particularly strenuous assignment investigating homestead claims in the mountains for the land frauds case, George contracted tuberculosis and died. Raymond and Sherman, with their own sons and some grandsons, carried on with the agency after their father's death. In 1960, after the Briarcliff Village Board adopted a "floating zone ordinance" (see Chapter 16) to permit office and laboratory use of land parcels of ten or more acres, the Burns agency established headquarters at 320 Old Briarcliff Road, where they remained until the building and land were sold in 1985 to Great Lakes Carbon Corporation. The elder Burnses lived in Scarborough less than ten years, moving to Florida in 1925 because of Mrs. Burns's chronic bronchitis, but their son, Sherman, and their oldest daughter, Florence, married to the artist Randal Borough, built houses in nearby Ossining in the 1920s.

Sherman Burns had three sons, W. Sherman, Jr. (nicknamed Bunny), Ashley J. and Bruce. Bunny and Bruce played football and baseball on Briarcliff High School teams, the "Bears," or B.B.C. Bunny was named on the Westchester County Class C all star football team. Bruce and Bunny played with the B.B.C. baseball team for several summers. "Few forget the fine play of Bunny in the infield, smooth play and a fine arm, while his brother was always one of the best hitters."[14] On July 23, 1943, Second Lieutenant W. Sherman Burns, Jr., was killed in service when his plane crashed during a routine training flight over the Mojave Desert in California. His bride of only four weeks, the former Elsie Dineson, of Ossining, was with him in California at the time of the accident.

Sherman Burns, Sr., was president of Sleepy Hollow Country Club in the late 1940s and the 1950s, guiding the club through the crucial years when it became a family club rather than a "gentleman's club," as it had first been established. Randal Borough became art director of a leading advertising firm in New York City.

Walter L. Johnson

Walter Lathrop Johnson began his long career on Wall Street as an office boy. He became a partner of Shearson, Hammill & Company, president in 1918 of the New York Cotton Exchange, president from 1915 to 1953 of the Commodity Clearing Corporation, then vice-president of the New York Stock Exchange from 1924 to 1928 and again in 1937 and 1938. An Ossining resident for many years, in 1916 Johnson married Isabelle McWilliams, daughter of the pastor of the Ossining First Presbyterian Church. The cross on the south steeple of that church was installed to honor his lifelong service to the parish.

In the early 1920s the Johnsons moved to Oakledge on Central Drive in Briarcliff and lived there until the house burned on January 1, 1961, when they moved to 175 Holbrook Lane.

Johnson started and led the drive to build Phelps Memorial Hospital in North Tarrytown, and when it opened, on January 7, 1956, he became chairman of the board. In 1960, when he was eighty-six years old, he was instrumental in raising $2 million for the new wing of the hospital.

Roger Wallach

In 1924, Roger Nestor Wallach, distinguished chemist and business executive, bought the Tudor-style house just below the Don Sheltons' on Elm Road and lived there with his wife and two daughters until his death in 1941. The house had been built in 1919 by a Mrs. League, a relative of the Bonnell Tappans, who also built the house just below it. Wallach was born in Mulhouse, Alsace-Lorraine, in 1882, educated there and in Switzerland, and worked in his father's dye company. He was an officer in the German army, but when war broke out in 1914 he was unwilling to fight against France and England and came to the United States with his fiancee, Marguerite Schweighofer. He obtained financial backing to set up a dye manufacturing plant in Wappingers Falls, New York, and Marguerite taught French and German at Mount Saint Mary's. They were married in 1916. When the United States entered the war, Wallach's company made all the khaki dye for the United States Army. In 1919 he sold the company and joined the Grasselli Chemical Corporation as executive vice president. One of his responsibilities was supervision of Bayer Aspirin, then located in Albany, New York. In 1929 he founded the Sylvania Industrial Corporation of New York City and Fredericksburg, Virginia, of which the principal product was sylphrap, similar to the cellophane made by the du Pont Company and its chief competitor. He was also one of the founders of Stauffer Chemical in Elmsford, New York.

Roger Wallach

Wallach was a brilliant and cultivated man, an accomplished cellist, a great reader and a poet. His art collection included works by Sir Joshua Reynolds and various old Dutch masters and modern French painters. As an anonymous benefactor, he sent many boys through college and supported three French war orphans to manhood. He was made a chevalier of the Legion of Honor by the French government.[15]

The Wallachs' daughter, Carrie Garrison, who grew up on Elm Road, remembers that after the Community Club burned down in 1928 the young people in the neighborhood played on her family's tennis court, under the supervision of the Reverend Stanley North of the Briarcliff Congregational Church.

Haymont, the W. W. Fuller residence, now the Maison Lafitte restaurant

W. W. Fuller

Haymont, high on the hill north of Chappaqua Road, was built around 1910 by William Whitehead Fuller. The central section, with its pediment and huge pillars, was balanced by long three-story wings at both ends, the present parking lot was a formal garden and the mansion stood on some two hundred acres that in 1901 had belonged to the Ryder family. Fuller, a native of North Carolina, was general counsel, and for a time, president, of the American Tobacco Company and other corporations. When he was fifty-four years old, in 1912, he retired from business "to devote himself to farming and country life" until his death in 1934.

In the 1940s the Fuller estate was occupied by Bernard Van Leer and his Holland Classical Circus. An historical sketch in the April 28, 1970, *Citizen Register* tells the story of a fire near the stables that was extinguished by Briarcliff firemen, "as the flames were licking the barn in which were quartered a prize retinue of 16 world famous Ippanzer [*sic*] horses imported from Holland and four elephants, the grateful owner . . . working with the Briarcliff Fire Council decided to stage a circus, the profits to be used for an ambulance." On the very day of the circus the tragedy of the death of President Roosevelt "clouded the entire country," but "it was decided that the 'show must go on' and go on it did, with all the thrills of the finest traditions: elephants, clowns, hot dogs, pop corn and the famous Ippanzer horses. The circus realized the handsome profit of $2,174.11 and with this as a starter the ambulance was ordered." (See also Chapter 15.)

After the war Van Leer and his circus moved away, and J. Henry Ingham, who had been mayor of Briarcliff Manor from 1936 to 1941, bought and worked the Fuller farm. Ingham owned the gasoline and oil concessions of a string of service stations on the Taconic Parkway.

J. H. Ingham and his son J. H. Ingham, Jr.

In the 1950s, Robert and Pauline Morin operated a riding stable called the Walk, Trot and Canter Club, on the Fuller property. Morin sold the property around 1960 and went into real estate.

In 1963, Giovanni Susech, a native of Trieste, Italy, opened a restaurant in the Fuller mansion, by that time missing the two lateral wings. Even without the wings, the restaurant rooms, the lobby and the terrace (for summer luncheons) were spacious and handsome. The a la carte Continental cuisine menu was as extensive as that of any hotel dining room in the city. In the 1980s the main dining room was done over with wood paneling and hung with 19th-century American oil paintings provided by art dealer Rudolf Wunderlich, a long-time Ossining resident and executive of the Kennedy Galleries (in New York City), which was founded by his grandfather in the 1870s. Giovanni named his restaurant the Maison Lafitte, perhaps as a souvenir of his many years of service on the high seas, starting at the age of fourteen, as bartender and cook on oceangoing ships and liners. He had also worked in the bars and kitchens of several New York City hotels. At the celebration of its twenty-sixth anniversary in 1989, Giovanni Susech's Maison Lafitte was doing well.

Luthany

In 1923, The Baroness De Luze bought from William Reynolds one of the oldest houses still standing in the village, on twenty acres just west of Pleasantville Road. (In 1968, some eight of these acres were purchased by the village to improve the access to the new Briarcliff High School from Pleasantville Road.) The Baron De Luze was a brewer of malt beverages. The baroness, born Ruth Farnum, named the house Luthany in his honor and lived there with her family for many years. She was a member and generous patron of the Briarcliff Congregational Church. "She loved the house and had the money and good taste to make it a beautiful home." Her gardener, Philip Downton, landscaped the surrounding acres with ornamental shrubs and a bed of lavender at the center of the driveway turnaround.

An apartment in the garage housed a couple who did the laundry and tended the garden. The baroness added a porch and a kitchen to the old house, and ornamental wrought iron at the front steps.[16] The garage, extensively remodeled, became a separate residence.

The Buckhout House

Before the baroness named the estate Luthany it was commonly referred to as the Buckhout house. Extensive research by Mount Pleasant historians John Crandall and Carsten Johnson II found no Buckhouts among the several owners of the house from 1851 to 1921. However, the house further along the road toward Briarcliff village facing F. B. Hall is known to have been occupied by John Buckhout and his descendants for over a hundred years.[17] This house was acquired in 1892 by Walter Law in one of two purchases, of forty-eight acres and seven acres, from members of the Buckhout family,[18] and in the house the young ladies of Mrs. Dow's school conducted a school for handicapped children. During World War II, Judge Charles P. Robinson of the Briarcliff Police Court lived there. The Victorian facade on Pleasantville Road is a relatively recent addition to a much older house.

Woodledge

Woodledge, Pleasantville Road

The Baroness De Luze's nearest neighboring estate to the east of Luthany was Woodledge, a large Tudor-style house on the wooded hillside above Pleasantville Road. The stone gateposts and a metal name plaque still stand by the road. The house, on some thirty acres, was the summer home of Percy S. and Edith A. Straus, of the department store and banking Straus family. They sold it in 1919 to Leo Greendlinger, founder and head of the Alexander Hamilton Institute of New York City, one of the first business schools to be conducted through the mail. The Greendlingers shared the house with in-laws, among them Bernard Lichtenberg and his family, as a summer home, until year-round country living was advised for young Ruth Lichtenberg after an illness in the early 1920s. Ruth, now Mrs. Norman Simon, remembers daily walks along Pleasantville Road to the Briarcliff post office, with her younger sister in a baby carriage and their nursemaid. Between Hardscrabble and Larch roads, they passed no more than three houses and the stone retaining wall and steps at the site of Miss Knox's School. The stone house on that site, now part of F. B. Hall, was not yet built. Ruth Simon remembers with pleasure the gardens and vineyards at Woodledge and the massive home-preserving of the produce. Members of the Greco family, neighbors to the northeast, also made wine, which, in those Prohibition years, they sold. Their transactions and accompanying merriment so disturbed the Greendlinger family that they bought eleven additional acres to put more space between themselves and the "jolly bootleggers."

In 1928 Leo Greendlinger sold Woodledge to Briar Hills Estates, Incorporated of Ossining, John Stephenson, president. The plans of Stephenson and his partner, Robert Lent, to build a number of houses on the property were abandoned during the Depression and left no trace but the name of Stephenson Place. The house at Woodledge was destroyed by fire. The name of Ledgewood Lane off Hardscrabble Road may be a backward souvenir of the vanished Woodledge estate.

The Leland Rosemonds

In the 1950s, Hillside (Admiral Worden's birthplace) became the residence of Mr. and Mrs. Leland E. Rosemond. The stately pillared house on the corner of Route 9 and Scar-

borough Road, had been the Warren Rogers residence and, when Frank Vanderlip owned it, a dormitory, first for young Morgan Stanley bond salesmen and later for Scarborough School boarding students. The land between the house and the corner of Scarborough Road was an open field circled by a track for the Rosemonds' riding horses. Rosemond, a distinguished audiologist, developed his "Otarion Listener," the world's first eyeglass hearing aid, which in the mid-1950s was manufactured in the former Bernarr McFadden School (later the Tetko site), a short way down Route 9 toward Ossining Village. Rosemond served on the President's Commission on Employment of the Handicapped and was active in rehabilitation of the handicapped in Westchester County.

Grey Ledges

Todd Lane climbs from Pleasantville Road to one of the highest points in the village. Just below and to the north of the crest, a large house was built in the 1910s as a rest home for working women by a group of young lady philanthropists, including the daughter of J. P. Morgan. On the crest, in the 1920s, Asa Geeding built Grey Ledges, one of the finest houses in the village. Associated with the Briarcliff Realty Company and active in the Congregational Church, Geeding "had a finger in just about every pie that was cooking in the village," one old-timer remembered.

Geeding sold Grey Ledges to Mr. and Mrs. Barclay Acheson. Acheson was the brother of Lila Bell Acheson, who with her husband, DeWitt Wallace, founded and directed the *Reader's Digest*. Acheson had been Wallace's roommate at Macalester College in St. Paul. He worked for the *Digest* for many years, as roving reporter and later as director of foreign editions.

More recently, Richard Rosenthal of the Wall Street firm of Salomon Brothers bought Grey Ledges on many surrounding acres and the big house just below it, where he lived with his family until the mid-1980s, when he crashed to his death in his private airplane in nearby Pleasantville. Rosenthal was a generous philanthropist, outstanding for his quiet beneficence in the new generation of Briarcliff multimillionaires.

15

The World Wars

World War I

NINETY-ONE MEN from the village enlisted in World War I.[1] Two were casualties. Howard Frame died at Georgia Military Station in January 1918. Ernest Lu Van Lu, 2nd Engineer, 2nd Division, U.S. Army, was killed in action in France, where he is buried in the Meuse-Argonne American Cemetery.

In All Saints Church on May 28, 1917, a memorial service was held for Edmund C. Genet, the first American to fall while fighting under the Stars and Stripes in France. Genet, twenty years old, was killed

somewhere in France on April 16, 1917, while serving with the Lafayette Escadrille. The young man's family and many of his relations were among the throng that crowded the church. There was also a delegation of the Daughters of the American Revolution, of which his mother Henrietta Genet is a member. . . . Edmund Genet was the great great grandson of "Citizen Genet," first minister from the French republic to the United States, who married a daughter of George Clinton, first governor of the State of New York.[2]

The Briarcliff Branch of the American Red Cross, then called the Briarcliff War Auxiliary, began in 1915 under the leadership of Elsie Gilman Law. When it was reorganized as the Briarcliff Branch of the Red Cross in 1926, Mrs. William Coleman was the chairman, and she held that post until 1943. The Scarborough Branch of the Red Cross was organized in 1915 with fifteen members. Marion L. Dinwiddie was the first chairman. Services of both branches were, then as now, voluntary, and included assisting at hospitals, home nursing, Civil Defense cooperation, Blood Bank assistance, preparation for first aid, and sewing and knitting for the armed forces and disabled veterans.

Because it was feared that the Germans would try to cut off New York City's water supply, troops were quartered in small camps along the Hudson River to guard the Croton Aqueduct. Marion Dinwiddie remembered that "they did find a German college man

Florence Dinwiddie

Marion Dinwiddie

somewhere along the aqueduct, disguised as a laborer." When the influenza epidemic struck the soldiers in the river camps, the Red Cross set up a hospital in the Holbrook School, which had recently closed, leaving vacant a big dormitory and several cottages. Red Cross volunteers from the neighborhood staffed the hospital until professional nurses arrived. Marion Dinwiddie remembered that they worked for three days setting up cots that had been sent up from the arsenal. She was working on the ambulances, but the night before the nurses arrived, she worked as a nurse's aide.

Dr. Clinton said to me, "I haven't been to bed for three nights, don't disturb me if you can help it, but make half-hourly rounds." They gave me two boys as orderlies . . . one lay down on the couch in the room I had as a dispensary, the other sat up by the table and both went sound asleep. If I wanted either of 'em, I shook 'em. Toward morning, around four o'clock, I heard a clump clump clump of martial feet and there entered the office a man who I think thought he was the toughest man in the American army—he may have been right—a certain Corporal Tully, and he had a large quid of tobacco in his jaw and he said, "Well, I got the guard posted and I went in the kitchen and cooked them some coffee. Woy, it was good!" I said, "It's a wonder you wouldn't give the Red Cross some coffee." "Youse want some?" I said Ise did, so he went away and brought me a mug . . . with something as black as ink in it . . . so I thanked him and took it and drank what I could of it. Two or three weeks afterward—all the Red Cross in the vicinity had sent the hospital all their surgical nightshirts and all their pyjamas, all the things they could staff it with, and we thought that possibly . . . they needed some more of those things. So Father and I drove in, I guess 'twas in my own car and I didn't have a uniform on . . . not anything but the insignia on the car and in the meantime Colonel Love had come down. He was the

commanding officer of the First Provisional Regiment that was guarding the aqueduct and the place was surrounded by guards armed to the teeth so nobody could get in there. No German could get in that place, I'll tell you, and one of them stopped me with drawn rifle and Father said, "They're not going to let you in." Just then a corporal stepped to the side of this man and said, "Let her in. She's the Red Cross." I think he still had the quid of tobacco distorting his cheek.

We had elements of the 12th Regiment, the 23rd Regiment and Troop A of Albany. . . . They were really very nice. Everybody around treated them as if they were all their children coming home for Easter vacation. They had them almost killed with kindness. And we opened in the village [Tarrytown] what was the YMCA building, we equipped it with shower baths and we always had coffee and cake, preferably stale sponge cake [to absorb any alcohol they had drunk], there and towels and things and they'd come all the way down there from as far as Poughkeepsie. . . . Apparently they didn't have any decent place to have baths in the camps. . . . On Christmas Day all the Red Crosses gathered and we ran three—one noon and one about five o'clock and one six o'clock—and we fed all the outposts . . . their Christmas dinner.[3]

World War II

Briarcliff Manor went all out in the war effort, particularly with respect to the number of people who entered the various branches of service. In September 1944, some 365 villagers from a population of little more than 1,800 were in the armed forces. Of these ninety-six were commissioned and seventy noncommissioned officers. Some fourteen women volunteered, half of them for service in the navy, others in the Army Signal Corps and Nurse Corps. The percentages of residents in the services and of officers among them were well above the national average. More than half served overseas, many in far-flung theaters of war—Africa, India, China, Burma, Norway, the Aleutians and the South Pacific—as well as in Europe. Many families had more than one member in the armed forces. Several families—the Fountains, the Burnses, the Winters, the Figarts and the Todds—had three, and the "Service News" Honor Roll for September 1944 lists four named Fitzgerald, four named Hutta and four named Mruz.

Civilian war effort in Briarcliff was correspondingly energetic. There was a Briarcliff Office of Civilian Protection, with 470 active personnel. There were Red Cross chapters in Briarcliff and Scarborough. There were War Bond, War Fund, Red Cross Fund, Blood Bank, U.S.O. Fund and Salvage drives, commercial war work, and victory gardening. In all of these the village regularly exceeded quotas and outdid most neighboring communities.

BRIARCLIFF MANOR SERVICE NEWS

The war effort and other village history from November 1942, to September 1945, is recorded in great detail in "Communique: Briarcliff Manor Service News."[4] This monthly newsletter was mailed to all villagers in the armed forces and paid for by civilian subscriptions. Each eight-page issue contained an editorial; a report on a special event or an overseas station; news of the Fire and Police departments, of Civilian Defense, of the schools, and of the American Legion. Full reports on Briarcliff High School athletic teams and events, including play-by-play accounts of particular games, were contributed by Harry Addis, police officer and assistant to Briarcliff High School coach Bill Bowers. There were social notes, "Altarations," and "Stork Club"; "Manorisms," a column of humor (broad) signed "Cliff Briar"; "Service News," excerpts from letters from service people, with editorial comments; "Honor Roll," the names, ranks, numbers, and addresses of service people (two pages); cartoons, and a sprinkling of jokes and appropriate verses. The overall tone of "Communique" is affectionate, humorous and fervently supportive. Response to the newsletter was enthusiastic. Some recipients reported that their buddies from other parts of the country enjoyed reading it almost as much as they did. It was felt that Briarcliff Manor did more for its service people than any other town in the United States.

A MAN O' WAR and TWO DESTROYERS

Albert Dawson of Valentine Road, president of the Briarcliff Hook and Ladder, first had the idea for "Communique." He got the grant from the Briarcliff Community Fund to get it started, organized the staff, wrote editorials, and did the makeup until, in January 1944, he enlisted as a lieutenant in the Naval Reserve, leaving the management of the newsletter to Elsie Kossow, who from the start had prepared the "Service News" and helped with the typing. Harry Addis was treasurer as well as sports reporter. Mrs. Albert Dawson wrote the social notes, George Baxter wrote "Town Topics," and cartoons were contributed by Hope Stanke, Al Nolan, Ed Kelly (proprietor of Tiny Tavern), Kay Courreges, Carroll Colby, and, from Camp Davis, North Carolina, Private First Class Frank Hewitt. But, as Dawson said, "The entire village is the real staff."

For the first page of the first issue of "Communique," Mayor Charles Schuman wrote seven paragraphs entitled "Where You Are," which one GI reader justly termed a poem:

You could feel the quiver coming down through the halyard from the flag snapping in the breeze. With the leaves gone it is visible now around the park from every direction, and it is brand new.

We couldn't fly a torn flag, worn every day since Pearl Harbor; no more than you could where you are.

The river could be seen from Edgewood Park and I was thinking, does it smell salty at Flood tide and are they fishing off the dock? It does, and they were, and it will be flowing out to sea again and nothing Hitler or Hirohito can do will stop it, no more than the rivers where you are.

A full stop sign was all that stopped me at Albany Post Road. Not a car in sight at two-thirty Sunday afternoon. That looks a little like keeping out of traffic court (35 mile speed limit now) and saving gasoline and rubber for where you are.

The sun streamed in through the Patrick Manahan Memorial window as alone I slipped quietly into your pew, Tom or Dick. It didn't need the organ or choir or Priest for one to be thankful that your Church stands untouched with the same message this Thanksgiving Sunday as you may have heard from your Chaplain under the trees or some place where you are.

Down the street, this morning the choir in another church finished up its anthem with "God Make Us Free." That's what it's all about, isn't it, Harry? Whether we sing it or pray it or think it. And in this fight for freedom we won't let you down, Bill. It takes a little longer to kindle a flame for more than a hundred million folks than for a few million of the pick of our manpower. But we are catching up and those ——! are catching ——! from you and one day you'll be catching a boat or a train or a plane back home from where you are.

Volunteers on the Home Front

The Briarcliff Manor Office of Civilian Protection was organized by Mayor Charles Schuman and Dr. Amos Baker. In January 1943, Theodore Gilman Law, grandson of Walter W. Law, took over as deputy director and served until April of that year, when he was commissioned lieutenant in the navy. Law was succeeded as deputy director by Oscar Barber of Central Drive, director of administration at Edgewood Park School. There were sixty-eight air-raid wardens under the direction of Brooks Bradbury; fourteen auxiliary police to turn out for alerts and blackouts; "Willie" Bevier's Fire Department; the Department of Public Works demolition and road-repair crew; the medical corps under Dr. Baker; messengers and war council workers. A staff of twenty women under Mrs. Kingsland Rood ran the Defense Office. Principal Otto Huddle was school coordinator, and John Rode was assistant deputy for Scarborough until June 1944, when he received his commission in the navy.

As wardens and other defense personnel were lost to the armed forces, their places were taken by volunteers from the high school, Edgewood Park, and Briarcliff Junior College. The airplane-spotting post on the tower of Maryknoll Seminary in Ossining was manned by volunteers around the clock.

In the third War Loan Drive, in 1943, Briarcliff and Scarborough collected subscriptions in the amount of $74,075. In the Red Cross Fund Drive of the same year, Briarcliff chairman, the Reverend R. B. Pattison, collected $2,700, an average of $700 per home, and

Scarborough chairman W. S. Kies raised $5,000. The Briarcliff committee working on the Fourth War Loan Drive in March of 1944 subscribed $75,525.

Martha Stafford of the Junior Class was top salesman and was given a medal for her contribution by Lieutenant-Commander Jack Dempsey of the U.S. Coast Guard. On the last day of the drive the Defense Stamp Committee sponsored a Treasure Hunt to dig up stamp books and get them turned in for bonds. The staff contributed two bonds to the school [drive] in honor of Lieutenant Charles Matthes, '32, and Lieutenant Sherman W. Burns, Jr., '39.

In the year ending in May 1944, 151 Red Cross volunteers worked 8,776 hours. They made 80,000 surgical dressings, as well as hospital and war-relief garments. Their workrooms in the Congregational Church were "open and humming with activity" two full days and one evening a week. In order to release doctors and trained nurses for service with the armed forces, volunteers took Red Cross courses to equip themselves to work in Grasslands, Mount Kisco and Ossining hospitals. The Red Cross Home Service dealt with any nonmilitary problems of service people and their families, providing information about furloughs, discharges, clemency, financial assistance and benefits, and obtaining information through the International Red Cross in Switzerland concerning service people and civilians in war-affected areas. The Briarcliff Home Service Committee was made up of Amos Baker, Mrs. Norman Babcock and Mrs. Barrett Clark. On the Scarborough committee were Mrs. John McPherson and Mrs. Percy Meredith Hall.

The Blood Bank, also a Red Cross activity, had Mrs. Julian Street, Jr. (Narcissa Vanderlip) as chairman for Scarborough in 1943, assisted by Lieutenant Marion Dinwiddie of the Hudson River Motor Corps, who had charge of transportation of donors.

The Briarcliff quota for salvaged waste paper in 1944 was 66,000 pounds; collection figures totaled 101,670 pounds. In ten Westchester communities, only Bronxville did better. Briarcliff made the Tin Can Salvage Honor Roll for the first six months of 1943 with twenty-five hundred pounds of tin cans collected. Sixty-eight tons of salvaged material, fifteen tons over Briarcliff's quota, were turned in by January 1943. Mrs. George Baxter was chairman of Salvage. William Noller, at his Pleasantville Road grocery store, collected waste fat from community housewives and turned the profits over to the local fire company to cover handling costs of the servicemen's cigarette fund. In "Communique's" "Manorisms" it was reported that: "A feminine caller recently asked Bill Noller for an appointment for reducing exercises. Never again will Bill advertise: Get rid of your surplus fat at Noller's."

When troops were on maneuvers in the vicinity of Briarcliff in 1943, the Canteen, chaired by Mrs. Gerald May, fed 232 soldiers, at a per capita cost of 25 cents, in the record time of sixteen minutes.

Aside from duties associated with civilian defense, few extraordinary events were noted on the Briarcliff police blotter during the war years. There were a few break-ins and car thefts by miscreants from out of town, especially juveniles escaped from Children's Village in Dobbs Ferry and other houses of correction.

Some of the wartime police news illustrates the pastoral nature of the 1940s village. Farm animals had to be rounded up as they had since before the Revolution:

Our police had a chance to play cowboy when Mrs. Alico of Tuttle Road called on April 5th and reported that a pony and a horse were gamboling on the Briar Hills Golf Course. Fred Borho, Ray Wolf and Everett Garvey drove to the Course armed with ropes and halters. The animals, however, went quietly to jail for one night. Owner James Moroney of Pleasantville blamed the wanderings of his pets on a touch of spring fever.

On April 6th four steers broke loose from their pasture on Todd Lane. Mrs. Preston Herbert found them lunching on the Herbert lawn [the Reuben Whitson House]. After looking twice at her ration books and the thousands of red points [for meat] on the hoof, she called the Police Department and Patrolmen Borho and Garvey again responded with lassoes. It took four hours of hard work to finally corral the steers. At times it was rather doubtful as to who was chasing who, and some tree-climbing brought cheers from passing motorists on the Taconic Parkway. But the job was completed and former Mayor Henry Ingham has his steers back in the pasture.

Cow hunt on August 17th—a Jersey belonging to the Whiting Estate broke away and police helped in the two-day search. Cow finally found in with the Lukacovic herd of cows [Long Hill and Aspinwall roads].

Judge Charles Robinson reported in "Communique" on the Police Justice Court:

By reason of the extensive parkways in the Village, and its size geographically, most of the cases are those of Traffic Violations. In the general run of such cases, there is little of spice or diversion . . . although some of the alibis offered are amusing. The stock one has been the necessity to speedily transport a passenger who has suddenly become ill.

Of interest is the amount of money regularly collected in fines for traffic violations on Briarcliff roads. Month after month it was reported in the service newsletter that one hundred or more summonses had been issued by Briarcliff police officers enforcing speed bans. In August of 1943, for example, police collected $1,080 in fines. The speed limit was 40 miles an hour on parkway straightaways during the war, and it remained exceptionally low for years, long after the need for gas rationing. All through the 1940s and 1950s Briarcliff was a famous "speed trap."

In "Manorisms," his column of humor in "Communique," "Cliff Briar" appealed to Bill Boyle, the head of rationing for the village: "Please don't confiscate the gasoline ration books of any of the younger set found 'working at woo' on Long Hill Road or any other depots of deviltry. You will recall, Bill, that when we were in our tingling teens this was considered VERY essential driving."

Who was "Cliff Briar?" His identity was not revealed until August 1945, the last issue of "Communique" in a cartoon by Carroll Colby. He was Milton Bennett, third baseman and leading hitter of the 1942 Briarcliff baseball team. Inducted December 18, 1942, he never missed an issue of "Communique" with his column. He wrote them in England, in France and in the South Pacific. In August 1943, he wrote,

Every time I think of old Briarcliff I get the "wonder-ifs" . . . if a fire is still a village reunion . . . if 2 A.M. "over-the-fence and into the pool" escapades continue—if Ike Hotaling still tries out his real estate sales talks on Julius, the barber—if the swimming pool is still the first place where old wolves notice when a girl changes from an adolescent into a doll—if the old gang still tip-toe into Tiny Tavern and Briar Oaks and tipsy out again.

Julia C. Stimson, who lived on Horsechestnut Road in Briarcliff Manor after World War II until her death in 1948, was the first woman to hold an officer's rank in the Army Nurse

"ALL THIS TIME I THOUGHT "CLIFF BRIAR" WAS *YOU* BUT HE ISN'T, HE'S *CAPT. MILTON I. BENNETT!"

~ ANY TWO BRIARCLIFFIANS ~

"3-A", "4-H", "3A(H)", "IA(H)", "2A(H)", "4-A", AND NOW, Colby.

Corps. She was designated a major in 1920 and elevated to colonel in 1948, after her retirement. A graduate of Vassar College and the New York Hospital School of Nursing, Stimson was superintendent of nurses at Harlem Hospital in New York and director of the School of Nursing in St. Louis. When the United States entered World War I, "she volunteered at once and, in dark blue dress and long cape, sailed . . . for France to become chief nurse of Base Hospital 21,"[5] and was soon directing the activities of ten thousand American Red Cross Nurses in France. From 1919 until 1937 she was superintendent of the Army Nurse Corps. In this post, and from 1938 to 1944 as president of the American Nurses Association, she worked for higher professional standards and improvement of the status of nurses. During World War II, Stimson was chairman of the Nursing Council on Defense until, in 1942, she was recalled to active duty in the Army Nurse Corps and assigned to recruiting more nurses from all over the country.

For her services in World War I, Colonel Stimson received the Distinguished Service Medal, the Florence Nightingale Medal of the International Red Cross, and British and French awards, and was cited by General John J. Pershing for "exceptionally meritorious and conspicuous service." She was the author of *War Letters*, published in 1918, a volume based on her experiences in France, and *The Nurses' Handbook of Drugs and Solutions*, published in 1910.

Marion and Florence Dinwiddie, by parental decree, could undertake only volunteer work. However, Marion, in World War II, was made a lieutenant in the American Red Cross. Among other activities, the two sisters took part in many large troop feedings. The Red Cross would be notified that certain regiments were coming through from Albany. "The bakeries would open and make bread and the shops would open . . . so we'd get stuff to feed them" in the YMCA building in Tarrytown. Florence remembered, "One of those years we had terrible ice storms and the Post Road had ruts just so far apart and if you got in a rut with one wheel you had to get out and dig yourself out . . . at forty-five below zero (*sic*). We slid down Holbrook Road very often." Toward the end of the war the Hudson Unit of the Red Cross covered Camp Shanks, "right across the river, back of Piermont." Marion went on, "The troop ships coming back would dock at half past six. . . . The milk detail would have to be over there at half past four, the Canteen at half past five and the rest at half past six . . . so it meant you had to be at Sheffield [dairy] in Yonkers at two o'clock in the morning to get in the milk and the ice . . . so we started at one." Marian wished she had a picture of a time she "stopped at a place in Dobbs Ferry where the head of the Canteen was and she [the head of the Canteen] and her husband had been making great big milk cans of soup—puree Mongole, pea soup and tomato soup put together—and I was carrying one end of this enormous milk can and he in his pyjamas and night robe was carrying the other . . . out to the ambulance."

Every spring for years after the war, the First Provisional Regiment was given lunch at Saint Mary's Church.

They came to us the nearest Sunday to Decoration Day and they went to the plot they had in Sleepy Hollow Cemetery which William Rockefeller gave them . . . and then they came to Saint Mary's Church and we furnished lunch and that lunch *had to be* chicken salad, apple pie a la mode and coffee and rolls. Once we tried to give them cold cuts and it wasn't popular at all and we didn't dare change. The Beckers and Florence and I made all the chicken salad for the regiment in this house the night before. We had a huge ice box . . . and the day after the most horrible thing was all the chicken soup you had. We cut up innumerable chickens until suddenly we had a bright idea—we said why not make chicken salad out of turkey because you can cut up six turkeys much better than you can three dozen chickens.[6]

Some Briarcliff residents worked in defense industries outside the community. Others worked in a small plant on the Vanderlip estate in Scarborough. John Vanderlip, Scarborough School class of 1933, his classmate Charles Wagner of Irvington and Fred Baker, a shop work instructor in a New York City school, turned a hobby and one or two small machines into a constructive war effort. They first set up shop in the basement of an Irvington drugstore that belonged to Wagner's father. There they received their first contract, which took several months to fill, to produce two thousand aircraft control cable terminals. Increase in their production was gradual but so steady that the shop was moved to larger quarters, first, in August 1942, to the garage of Navy Lieutenant Dudley Schoales (John Vanderlip's brother-in-law) on River Road in Scarborough, then, less than a year later, to the building on the corner of the Post Road and Scarborough Station Road, behind the Vanderlip garage. By January 1944, the shop was turning out more than two thousand terminals a week. It was equipped with three Logan Turret lathes, two bench lathes adapted to turret lathe work, two drill presses, a Universal tool and cutter grinder, and a high-precision threading machine. Wagner left to join the navy, but Vanderlip and Baker soon increased the shop's personnel to five daytime employees and a swing shift of three Sing Sing prison guards, who worked six hours every night.

"Making aircraft control cable terminals is mighty fussy work," wrote John Rode in "Communique." "Most of the terminals . . . find their way into bombers, anywhere from 200 to 400 going into a single plane. . . . We in Briarcliff like to think, and we hope you'll feel the same way, that every time a bomber is seen winging overhead, you can feel that part of it at least may have originated in Scarborough."[7]

"Boys, you should see the Victory Gardens! I'll bet about now the plough horses are more tired and discouraged than Hitler and Mussolini!" wrote Mayor Schuman in "Communique."[8] "Believe it or not, fellows, the gals are right out there digging like a Yank in a fox hole, and do they make the dirt and the weeds fly. Did you ever hear of a canned radish or a preserved scallion? Neither did I, but from what I observe a lot of vegetables and fruits are going into glass jars for tomorrow or next week or for when you get back from where you are!"

In September 1943, and again in 1944, village fairs were held, as Althea May reported in "Communique,"

at the "Crossways"—that very beautiful spot, quite level, with great elm trees spreading their branches in a natural canopy . . . for three hours the folk of Briarcliff brought their Victory Garden vegetables, their expertly canned fruits, jams and jellies, delicious looking cakes and pies, and the beautiful flowers to display them on long tables arranged for the occasion. Just beyond . . . could be seen the cages containing the ducks and fowl supervised by Mr. Charles Matthes. . . . In the show ring at the southwest corner near the Congregational Church . . . the Pet show took place. . . . Promptly at noon the judges started their journey down past the loaded tables, tasting, examining and judging.

Shortly after three o'clock the appearance of a high-wheeled Tally-ho, painted yellow and decorated with cornstalks and garden vegetables, drawn by two jet black Frisian Stallions and followed by a parade of beautiful horses, provided a dramatic climax to an already wonderful day. Mr. Van Leer, owner of the Van Leer stables in Briarcliff and the Holland Classical Circus, had very generously offered his trained animals for exhibition. . . . Several of these Lippizaners are very valuable and known to be the only ones of their breed in this country.

The afternoon's performance was finally concluded by Mr. Van Leer himself, who rode one of the Lippizaners which in turn did the Conga and the waltz. As a special event, several Fair Exhibitors were awarded rides through the Village in the Tally-ho and several of the boys and girls were given rides on the pony around the ring. These winners were selected from numbers of entries listed and were picked by the Baroness De Luze.

Almost a thousand people attended the fair.

The following spring, in April 1945, shortly before V-E day, Van Leer's Classical Circus performed again, for the benefit of the Briarcliff Ambulance Fund, under the auspices of the three fire companies. An enthusiastic audience of more than fourteen hundred adults and children crowded the section roped off at The Crossways. George Baxter, accompanied by the audience, sang the national anthem, Mayor Schuman spoke about the need for an ambulance in the village, and a variety of acts followed: "Miss Lucille and her High School horse 'Jimmy'"; Van Leer's famous Lippizaners and Frisians; "a tumbling act by ten of Briarcliff High's super athletes under the direction of coach Bill Bowers; clever slight (sic) of hand tricks by the 'Magic Arnolds'; a comical lion act of the 7th and 8th grade students dressed as lions; a horizontal bar and trapeze act from New York . . . ; 'Frankie' [Sinatra], impersonated by Jack Fountain with bow tie, swooning girls and all, rendered several hit

The Crossways Tea House, Pleasantville and South State Roads. Originally the Joseph Whitson house, the Crossways was the site of the village fairs held in September 1943 and 1944.

tunes. . . . Father Kelly read a prayer and gave a eulogy for our late President [Roosevelt], followed by the firing of a volley of three rounds by members of the American Legion. Gerald May played taps and Father Schwalenberg read the Benediction."

Briarcliff military combatants earned many honors and decorations. Air medals were awarded: to Lieutenant Edmund Quincy, Jr., pilot of a B 24 Liberator in the 13th A.A.F.'s "Lone Rangers" in the Southwest Pacific; to Lieutenant John H. Lewis, who was also awarded the Distinguished Flying Cross for air raids over Germany in his Flying Fortress "Peck's Bad Boy"; to Captain Lawrence Durrell, for fighter missions with General C. L. Chennault's "Flying Tigers" over China; to Major John Hall, for "service in air raids over Germany and occupied territory"; to Lieutenant Charles Matthes, "for service in raids over Germany" and "for exceptional meritorious achievement." Bronze Stars were awarded to Lieutenant-Commander Fred C. Myers, Lieutenant Paul Barr Zuydhoek, sergeants Mervin L. Potts, Charles Bouton and R. J. Daggett, and corporals Robert E. Johnson and Edward A. Winter. The Silver Star was awarded posthumously to Lieutenant Paul Zuydhoek. Purple Hearts were awarded to Captain Durrell, Staff Sergeant Herbert George, Sergeant Daggett, Sergeant Benjamin C. Dunn, Corporal David Doyle and Corporal S. V. Mendrick. Private Sanford Duncombe was awarded the African Star, given by the King of England to members of the British Eighth Army and the American Field Service who participated in the African Campaign. Lieutenant-Colonel Paul Hazelton, U.S. Army Air Force, was honored with a marble tablet hung in St. Louis City Hall commemorating him and nine others killed in a glider demonstration flight at Lambert-St. Louis Airfield in August 1943. It was said that techniques developed during investigations following the crash resulted in the saving of hundreds of lives.

Four writers who lived in Briarcliff served as war correspondents. Carroll B. Colby of Pine Road and Albert Q. Maisel of Sleepy Hollow Road were residents for many years. John Hersey lived in Briarcliff as a boy, and E. J. Kahn, Jr. lived in Scarborough for more than twenty years, after the war.

Maisel went to the Pacific in 1943 and wrote an article entitled "The Wounded Come Back." In 1944 he took part in the D-Day invasion of Normandy, crossing the English Channel on an L.S.T. with the invasion forces to evacuate the wounded from the beachheads. About this experience he wrote an article entitled "Blood, Sweat and Plasma." Maisel's best-known contribution to the literature of World War II is *Miracles of Military Medicine*.

Colby wrote a series of stories on aviation in the sub-Arctic and on the work of the Air Transport Command in Newfoundland, for *Popular Science* magazine. From Newfoundland he wrote to "Communique" in May 1945: "I flew over most of the country, rode in everything from dogsleds to crash boats and met a mighty grand bunch of Americans doing a magnificent job under, at times, almost impossible conditions." Colby was an airplane pilot but "the highest rating in [his] log book was for 130 h.p." until January 1945, on an inspection trip to the Bell Plant in Marietta, Georgia, when he took the controls of a Boeing B 29 Superfortress. "The Major asked me if I would like to log a little 8800 h.p. time. . . . When again able to speak coherently, I said that I certainly would . . . and he walked off and left me with the blamed thing with the copilot sitting across the aisle reading a copy of *Popular Science* (free plug). The plane handles as easily as a light plane. It gives . . . the impression of flying the Briarcliff High School by moving a dinner plate back and forth."

Mrs. Grace Hersey with her family in backyard on Valentine Road. Adults, from left (standing): Roscoe, Jr., Arthur, and John; (seated): Frances Ann (Mrs. John), Mrs. Hersey holding youngest grandchild, Anita (Mrs. Arthur), and Peggy (Mrs. Roscoe).

John Hersey was a correspondent for *Life* magazine. His parents, Roscoe M. and Grace Baird Hersey, lived first on Poplar and then on Valentine Road, and although John's residence was in New York City during the war years, he returned to Briarcliff to visit and several times spoke before local audiences. Mrs. Hersey was then, and for many years thereafter, village librarian. Hersey's first two books, *Men on Bataan* and *Into the Valley*, were about Marines in the Pacific. His first novel, *A Bell for Adano*, about Italy under the allied military occupation, published early in 1944, was very well received and widely read. Hersey's most important work of nonfiction is *Hiroshima*, a report written the year after a United States Air Force plane dropped the first atom bomb on that Japanese city.

In February 1945, this note appeared in "Communique":

Two best sellers involving Briarcliff people have made the bright lights of Broadway. As previously reported, John Hersey's play, "A Bell for Adano" starring Frederick March is a smash hit at the Cortland Theatre.

"Roughly Speaking," a picture based on the book of the same name has just recently opened at the Hollywood Theatre and stars Rosalind Russell and Jack Carson. This very humorous comedy was written by Mrs. Harold Pierson and depicts the hectic life of the author and her family, much of which took place in Ossining, Scarborough and Briarcliff. Mrs. Pierson's husband is a brother of Mr. Paul Pierson of Poplar Road.

Eleven men of the village of Briarcliff Manor were killed in World War II.★

Second Lieutenant W. Sherman Burns, Jr., U.S. Marine Aviation Corps, was killed July 23, 1943, when his plane crashed during a training flight in California. Lieutenant Burns enlisted in the Naval Air Corps in September 1942, received his commission and wings

★Regrettably, photographs of only four of the eleven were available for inclusion here.

Second Lieutenant
W. Sherman Burns, Jr.

in Pensacola, Florida, transferred to the Marine Air Corps in June, and, following his marriage, in Briarcliff, to Elsie Dineson of Ossining, reported to California.

Besides his parents, Mr. and Mrs. W. Sherman Burns, and his widow, Burns left two brothers, Captain Ashley J. Burns, U.S. Marine Corps, and Aviation Cadet Bruce Burns, U.S. Army Air Corps. He was a grandson of the celebrated detective William J. Burns. (See Chapter 14.)

In his column, "Cheering Section," Harry Addis wrote of the death of "Bunny" Burns: "I am sure his tragic passing has been the same shock to you as it has to me. All who ever knew him on the field of sports knew him for the fine competitor and able athlete that he was. To us the loss is more than the loss of a soldier, it is the loss of a real friend and gentleman."

In August 1943, Mr. and Mrs. Charles Matthes received word that their son Second Lieutenant Charles H. Matthes had been missing in action since July 26. Lieutenant Matthes, a navigator with the United States Air Force, had been stationed in England since the early part of June and was reported missing following an attack on Hanover, Germany.

Mayor Schuman wrote in the 1943 Christmas issue of "Communique":

The barberry bushes loaded with red berries against a dark green background of rhododendrons made a Christmas-like picture before the home on North State Road. Parade! A figure dribbling the ball down the floor for a shot—no, he's passing to Squee [Garvey]—to Harry—there it goes, clean basket. Team work that does it. On a bomber it's the same only more so, and a lot of kids here and yonder go on playing basketball because of that bomber trip taken by Charlie Matthes and his buddies.

Harry Addis listed Charles Matthes on his all-star basketball team.

On the Honor Roll of the last issue of "Communique," September 1945, Lieutenant Charles Matthes was still listed as missing in action.

Colonel Hazelton served in World War I in the aviation section of the Signal Corps. He reentered the army in December 1941 with the rank of major and served as resident representative at the Ford River Rouge Aviation Plant. Following his promotion to lieutenant-colonel in July 1942, he was transferred to St. Louis and named area supervisor of the U.S. Army Air Corps Materiel Command.

Of Colonel Hazelton, Mayor Schuman (the bard of Briarcliff) wrote in his December 1943 "On Parade":

There is a tall hemlock, a blue spruce and a giant spreading oak in the yard of the home on Parkway Drive. . . . Parade! The curtain goes up for Scarborough Players, we thrilled at the stage setting. Lumber, canvas, paint—Paul had a good pair of hands and spent hours and hours that the "Play must go on." They were going up, Paul in the last left hand rear seat of that giant new glider. There will be safer transport because of that test flight of Paul Hazelton's and his brother officers. You may come flying home in one, non-stop from Berlin or Tokyo!

Seaman First Class, U.S.N., John F. Schrade, 3rd, was killed in service May 31, 1944, in an airplane crash outside of Creeds Field, Norfolk, Virginia. An aerial gunner, Seaman Schrade entered the navy in January 1943, at the age of nineteen. He was the son of Mr. and Mrs. John Schrade, Jr., of Crest Drive, the eldest of six brothers and sisters and a graduate of Briarcliff High School.

Lieutenant Percy Meredith Hall, Jr., U.S. Marine Corps fighter pilot serving in the South Pacific, was reported missing in action in July 1944. His death on May 22, 1944, was not confirmed until after V-J Day in 1945. Lieutenant Hall was the son of Mr. and Mrs. Percy Meredith Hall of River Road, Scarborough. His brother, Major John O. Hall, was a prisoner of war in Germany from June 1943, until after V-J Day. A third brother, Lieutenant Franklin Hall, served in the U.S. Army Air Force.

Lieutenant Percy Meredith Hall, Jr.

Lieutenant George T. ("Tommy") Fountain was killed in action in Aachen, Germany, on September 17, 1944. Lieutenant Fountain, who was serving as a member of the 26th Infantry in General Hodges's First Army at the time of his death, had completed his second year at law school when he enlisted in the army in February 1942. Besides his parents, Petty Officer First Class George O. Fountain and Mrs. Fountain of State Road, he left a wife and young son and two brothers—Orill, who served in the Navy, and Jack, a student in the Briarcliff High School at the time.

Lieutenant Fountain's father was postmaster of Scarborough for many years both before and after World War II. With his two older sons in the armed forces, he enlisted in the navy, for service in postal work. "Communique" called the family "the Fighting Fountains. . . . The old homestead displays three stars on its service flag in tribute to George and his sons Tommy and Orill. What is more, even Orill's Great Dane Duke was one of the first dogs from this area to join 'Dogs for Defense.'"

In his "Cheering Section" for August 1944, Harry Addis had written:

Have two from Tom Fountain written from a foxhole in Normandy where he reports the going plenty rough and that all the teeth-chattering is not from the cold. We have seen Tom play a lot of baseball, basketball and football, and have played a bit with him and have always found that he did O.K. when the going was rough. Always a pepper pot and a holler guy, Tom would fight like hell to come from behind. His only weakness outside of swinging at bad balls seemed to be his temper, but if that's all he loses before we see him again, it is alright with us.

Lieutenant Paul Barr Zuydhoek was killed in action in Germany on September 25, 1944. He was a veteran of many major campaigns in the European theater and a member of the First Army Field Artillery. Following his induction early in 1941, Lieutenant Zuydhoek received his basic training at Fort Bragg, North Carolina. After Pearl Harbor he was sent to Hawaii and later returned for officer training to Fort Sill, Oklahoma, where he was commissioned a second lieutenant. After D-Day he received his first lieutenancy in the field in France. He was awarded the Silver Star posthumously for gallantry in action July 30, 1943, and the Bronze Star for heroic action June 6, 1944.

Lieutenant Paul Barr Zuydhoek

Lieutenant Zuydhoek's father, Ernst Zuydhoek of Poplar Road, was a long-time employee of Walter Law's enterprises. He closed the books of the Briarcliff Lodge in the 1930s. Lieutenant Zuydhoek was survived by his father, a sister, Mrs. Holbert Allison, and two brothers, Ernest and William.

Paul Zuydhoek was a gifted musician, a pianist and organist. He attended the Curtis Institute in Philadelphia as a scholarship student and won the Bok Memorial Scholarship to study in Italy. Before his induction into the army he was organist and choir director of Christ Church in South Amboy, New Jersey.

Harry Addis led off his "Cheering Section" in the November 1944, "Communique":

It would be impossible for us to convey . . . how much of a shock it was to receive the news that Tom Fountain and Paul Zuydhoek had been killed in Germany or how much it saddened the entire village. Paul, who played both baseball and basketball at B.H.S. in the late twenties, and Tom, who was a three letter man during the late thirties, were both teammates of a great many of you boys. We all feel sure that both Tom and Paul went down fighting in the same spirited manner which we remember so well.

Sergeant Benjamin C. Dunn was killed in action February 13, 1945, on the island of Luzon in the Philippines. Sergeant Dunn was born in Briarcliff, the son of Mr. and Mrs. Benjamin F. Dunn of North State Road. He attended Briarcliff High School and then worked as a mechanic in his father's garage on Saw Mill River Road until he entered the Coast Artillery on December 26, 1942. After completing his basic training in Virginia, he was selected to take a course at an army mechanics' school in North Carolina, where he received his sergeant's rating. He was sent to Camp Hahn, California, and put in charge of a fleet of army trucks. Before going overseas in August 1944, he was transferred to the Infantry. He was awarded the Purple Heart posthumously.

Sergeant Dunn was survived by his parents, his wife, the former Gladys Crisfield of Ossining, four sisters, and one brother, Vincent J. Dunn, a seaman first class in the Seabees.

Sergeant Arthur J. Quinn, Jr., was killed in action March 27, 1945, in Germany while serving with the 180th Infantry, 45th Division, of General Patch's Seventh Army. Sergeant Quinn was the son of Mr. and Mrs. Arthur Quinn of South State Road. He graduated in 1936 from Briarcliff High School, where he took an active part in all sports. He was a member of the Westchester Firemen's Association and a lieutenant in the Briarcliff Fire Company, in which he served as secretary. He was a licensed insurance broker employed by the Hanover Fire Insurance Company in New York City until he entered the service in November 1943.

Sergeant Arthur J. Quinn, Jr.

A veteran of both the Italian and French campaigns, Sergeant Quinn had been overseas since July 1944, and had just recently been promoted in the field from private first class to sergeant.

Two servicemen whose names are not listed or mentioned in "Communique" are listed in the Ossining Historical Society's Memorial Booklet as casualties from Briarcliff Manor. The first of these, U.S. Navy Lieutenant Daniel Fletcher Currier, of Scarborough, was listed as missing in action, then confirmed as dead in October 1943. Edward Currier was first private secretary and later assistant to Frank Vanderlip throughout Vanderlip's tenure at the National City Bank. He is frequently mentioned in Vanderlip's autobiography *From Farmboy to Financier* and, like so many of Vanderlip's associates, lived in Scarborough. It is likely that Lieutenant Currier was Edward Currier's son and likely also that he no longer actually lived in Scarborough during World War II, and so would not have been included on the lists or in the news of "Communique." A story is told that he was a naval officer who dove under his ship to save a sailor, and was never found.

Corporal Edward White, Jr., of the 26th Marines, 5th Division, enlisted in December 1942 and was killed in action March 6, 1945. He was born on Oak Road, and his parents were among the founders of Saint Theresa's Church.

PART IV

LOTS, PLATS
AND CONDOMINIUMS

Townhouses on the Beechwood property

16

Postwar Development

THE VILLAGE of Briarcliff Manor during World War II was still an extraordinarily close-knit, small community, as a reading of "Communique," the war service newsletter, nearly fifty years later, vividly illustrates. In 1942, the population and square mileage had more than quadrupled since the village was incorporated in 1902, but several of the original residents were still key figures in the government. Alfred Pearson, who had come from Scotland as a boy to work for Walter Law, was village clerk. Mayor Charles Schuman and Fire Department Chief Paul Schuman had lived in the village since 1906. Fire Commissioner Isaac Hotaling had been one of the first village trustees. Irving Manahan, commissioner of public works, was the son of Patrick Manahan, first superintendent of the Village Water Department. The Law family in 1943 was still represented by Walter Law's grandson Theodore Gilman Law as deputy county director of civilian protection. John Rode, of River Road, village trustee and commissioner of the Water and Sewage departments, was a comparative newcomer, having resided in the village since 1923. Bill Bowers, who coached the first Bear (Briarcliff High School) teams in 1928, was still coaching in the 1970s. The rate of change accelerated after the war.

In 1945 Edward Harden sold Brandywine, the estate on Sleepy Hollow Road, to Centro Laboratory, a manufacturer of battleship paint. (The sale price was $25,000.) Centro applied for a variance in the zoning law to permit the reconversion of the estate to a research laboratory. In July of 1945, the Zoning Board denied the application for legal reasons and recommended that changes in the zoning laws be made by the Briarcliff Board of Trustees so that such a reconversion would be possible. George Baxter reported in the August "Communique" on two meetings of the Board of Trustees that attracted so many residents they filled the Fire Department room in the Municipal Building: "Mayor Schuman opened one of the meetings by calling it a family gathering and it turned out to be just that, with a few squabbles, personal remarks and a lot of speeches. . . . Father Kelly . . . urged Briarcliff to expand and provide more homes for the young married couples (each to have six or seven children), and Miss Katherine Courreges . . . spoke of the need for new low-priced homes for returning servicemen as well as necessary employment, in which Centro Laboratory might

Briarcliff business center,
Pleasantville Road, 1952

Briarcliff village fair hayride,
September 1, 1945

Putting green in Law Park

figure to some extent." After the general meeting was adjourned on August 3, the Board of Trustees passed an amendment to the zoning laws allowing "the use of a plot of five acres or more for Institutions devoted to Research, providing the application is approved in each individual case by the Zoning Board of Appeals."

Centro Laboratory moved out—perhaps because there was no longer much demand for battleship paint—and the Spiegelberg-Barksdale mansion became the Brandywine Nursing Home. No other office and research facilities were established in residential zones until the 1960s, except by special permit, as in the case of Leland Rosemond's Otarion Listener (see Chapter 13) and later the Combined Book Exhibit in the Kingsland house on Route 9. But the tremendous need for new residential building immediately attracted developers. Among these was the late David Swope, of Ossining, who in 1949 built sixteen ranch- and Cape-Cod-style houses on Dalmeny Road, next to the six houses Walter Law had built for his workers just before the incorporation of the village. Swope had been in the business of development since the 1930s, when he built houses along the riverbank in Tarrytown on land that had been part of the estate of the Duchess of Talleyrand (Anna Gould). Later he acquired the Jacques Halle mansion and surrounding acres on Tappan Hill, originally part of the four hundred-acre Benedict estate, and built houses all across the crest of the hill. The mansion became an elegant restaurant.

David Bogdanoff, working with the construction company of his father, Morris Bogdanoff, builder of apartment houses in Manhattan and the Bronx, was the first to build in Tarrytown after the war. Tarrytown Village authorities were anxious to keep prices down, and with their assistance the Bogdanoffs and David Swope were able to build 149 single-family houses that sold for $14,000 to a high of $22,000. After the Crest, between Benedict and Union Avenues, was developed, they could find no land in Tarrytown where they could do this over again.

In the 1950s, land was still available in Briarcliff and the village was pleased to cooperate with developers. The Bogdanoffs bought land above North State Road east of Route 9A around what had been the "Rock Tee" of the Briarcliff Golf Links. They built the eighty-four houses known as the Crossroads, keeping prices down to levels the returning veterans could meet, beginning at $16,000 and climbing to $25,000 toward the end of their work there in 1952. They did so, David Bogdanoff has said, "Not because we were social benefactors but because we wanted to sell the houses. The fact that in the course of that these lovely young families moved in was just an added bonus."

When the Crossroads was completed, around 1952, Bogdanoff moved farther north in the Town of Ossining and developed the neighborhood called Torbank around Saint Paul's on the Hill.

Between 1955 and 1957, Bogdanoff returned to Briarcliff and built the two sections of the Briar Hill apartments, some eighty one- and two-bedroom units on land adjacent to the Crossroads on North State Road. Members of the village planning board, fearful of overloading the schools, were against multifamily housing, but Bogdanoff was able to convince them that the apartments would not attract many families with children. Bogdanoff went on to develop land at the top of Long Hill Road East. Cedar Drive East and Cedar Drive West and adjoining roads were laid out. But Bogdanoff built only a few houses, leaving construction of the other fifty-odd in the area to Yonkers-based developer Emanuel Steindl of Crestmont Homes. Costs had more than doubled, and from $30,000 some of these houses went as high as $60,000. The buyers were comparatively wealthy, although, as Bogdanoff put it, "not quite so wealthy as they are now" (in the 1980s), and building for the wealthy was "not his cup of tea." He had geared himself, since he first went into construction, to "a continuity of work," so that his workers could be assured of regular employment, and "when that continuity became dependent on sitting around a table discussing just how a lady's kitchen would be laid out" the operation was no longer efficient. Conditions for building in Briarcliff—land, community opinion and facilities—were never again comparable to those he had found when building the Crossroads. Looking for an area of greater need, another big project, took him further north. But he chose to settle with his family in Briarcliff, in one of his own Cedar Drive houses.

Richard Doty developed Hall Road at Sleepy Hollow Road in the early 1950s, building seven houses that sold for around $20,000 each.

In the mid–1950s Elias Heller built seventeen brick houses between Pleasantville and Old Briarcliff roads. On adjacent Hickory, Locust and Willow roads, the Syracuse brothers built fifty-seven houses in the early 1960s. When all the houses were sold, for around $50,000 each, the company bookkeeper pocketed the profits and flew off to Florida. Fortunately, insurance covered the Syracuse losses, and the thief was caught.

In 1958, development started just south of Chappaqua Road on Fuller and Whitson roads. Zoning was for half-acre lots, and by 1960, when Burns Place was developed, more than fifty comparatively substantial houses were built, which began by selling for $60,000 to $70,000.

Under the auspices of the Macy family, Chilmark was extensively developed between 1955 and 1960.

The Vanderlip family's Scarborough Properties resumed the development in the vicinity of River Road and Revolutionary Road which had started in the 1920s and 1930s under the direction of the corporation's vice-president Harry Benedict.

In 1946, George V. Comfort, a New York City realtor, had bought the 40-acre Titlar farm at Long Hill Road East and Sleepy Hollow Road. (The price was around $30,000.) On some of that land, which Comfort had put up for sale, Arthur Radice, in 1959, developed Butternut Road and Alder Drive, just west of Elm Road. He built thirty houses, which sold for $37,000 to $42,000. The cost of the development, putting the roads through and so forth, as Mrs. Florence Radice remembers, was so high that it was not profitable.

In the 1960s, Baltic Estates developed Hawthorne Place and Balsam Road off Long Hill Road, east of Tuttle Road, building about twenty-two houses. Baltic also extended Quinn Road and built seven houses on it.

David Swope bought the Speyer estate and sold lots to E. J. Kahn, Jr., *New Yorker* magazine staff writer, architects Don and Gwen Reiman, CBS News producer Burton Benjamin and others. In one of the existing houses of the estate, at 94 Holbrook Road, David Swope's brother John, a photographer, and his wife, Dorothy Maguire, actress of stage and screen, lived for a while. That house was later sold to Bonnie Cashin, dress designer. The Ginnells raised Labrador retrievers and pheasants on the property. In the spring you still may see a pair of pheasants bowing and dancing on the lawns of Philips Laboratories.

Steve McQueeny, a long-time Briarcliff resident, wrote of the 1950s: "Houses were being built everywhere . . . new houses went up at the rate of one or two per week. This was quite a change for a village that had a static population for decades." The population, from 1,830 in 1940, had increased to 5,105 in 1960. But, McQueeny remembered, there was still, "a feeling of home . . . despite all that building the village remained very small, very manage-

The new municipal building at 1111 Pleasantville Road, dedicated in 1964

able. It seemed you knew everyone, even the newcomers."[1]

As the village grew, the municipal building became inadequate. In 1964 village offices and the growing fire department moved into a new building at 1111 Pleasantville Road. Offices in the old building at 1133 Pleasantville Road were rented, and the ground floor housed Whigg's, purveyors of clothing, principally for young women. After Briarcliff College closed, Whigg's moved away and the space was used by a succession of restaurants.

After the establishment in 1960 of the "floating zone" for office and laboratory use of land parcels of ten or more acres, several businesses built facilities in the village. The first of these was Philips Laboratories, a division of North American Philips Corporation. This land sale was so vigorously contested by neighbors on Scarborough Road, especially Hubert Rogers, owner of the large property opposite the Philips site, that building was delayed for almost a year. Rogers, who was around ninety years old at the time, soon died. The Philips property was elegantly landscaped and carefully maintained around buildings that were scarcely visible from the road.

The next business building was American Airlines' modern offices, on Route 9 across from Saint Mary's Church. The building was later sold to NBC Television for a computer facility.

Burns International Detective Agency established headquarters at 320 Old Briarcliff Road. In 1985, the plant and land were sold to Great Lakes Carbon Corporation.

The estate of Dr. Arthur O'Connor (originally of Dr. Rufus Johnston), on Pleasantville Road was rezoned and sold to Cognitronics, a manufacturer of learning aids, then sold again to Frank B. Hall and Company, an insurance firm.

In the late 1960s, the Rosemond's residence (the birthplace of Admiral Worden, demolished in 1990) was rezoned for Roy Anthony's Marketing Innovation Company.

Philips Laboratories, Scarborough Road, on the site of the former Speyer estate

November 21, 1952, marked the fiftieth anniversary of the incorporation of the village. Mayor John A. Riegel designated October 10, 11, and 12, 1952, for the celebration of the Semi-Centennial. All residents were urged to participate and former residents invited to return during the celebration. The Historical Committee had prepared and published a ninety-five-page history, *Our Village: Briarcliff Manor, N.Y., 1902 to 1952*: "To promote a larger and better Briarcliff Manor; to cause every resident of today to feel the importance of our Village of tomorrow." Hundreds of hours had been devoted to research, sorting material, selecting pictures and writing the history. Members of the committee were Robert Heim, Mrs. Roscoe Hersey, Fritz Heynen, Lyman McBride, Robert B. Pattison (author of a history published in 1939), Alfred Pearson, Charles Schuman, Fred Sergenian and R. Everett Whitson.

Fifteen writers contributed to the text, including Edward Andrews, on the Scarborough School; Lillian Ellis, on Edgewood Park School; Robert Heim, on the Public Schools; Percy Knight, Jr., on the American Legion; Stanley MacKenzie, on the Planning Board; and Mrs. Hersey, on the public library. E. J. Kahn, Jr., contributed "Early Days," about native Americans of the region and about Philipsburgh Manor. Marc Rose wrote "Briarcliff Cultural." The Reverend Pattison contributed several articles, including "Old Houses," "Early Schools," "For God and Country," "Notable People" and "Briarcliff Out-of-Doors." Alfred Pearson contributed a short biography of Walter W. Law, a sketch of the village in 1902, and articles about Briarcliff Farms, village government and village growth.

Mrs. Ordway Tead sketched the history of Briarcliff Junior College from its beginning as Mrs. Mary E. Dow's School in 1903. Mrs. Tead, A.B., L.L.D. Smith College, had assumed the presidency of the college after the retirement of Miss Doris Flick in 1942, when the college had barely survived with an enrollment of only 42 students. By 1951–1952 the enrollment had advanced to 220 students from all parts of the United States and from Eu-

rope, Central and South America, and Asia. The curriculum had been much enlarged and fully accredited.

The history ends with "The Future Briarcliff Manor: A Vision," by Charles Schuman, closing with an address to readers: "At this dawn of a new half century! Ask your-self . . . :'Briarcliff! What has it already done *for* me? What will it continue to do *for* me?' And then spontaneously and joyfully amend that question to: 'Briarcliff! What will it do *through* me?'"

Steve McQueeny's reminiscence about Briarcliff in the 1950s continues:

Trains ran right through the middle of Briarcliff then on the one-track line of the Putnam Division. They stopped at what is now the library, or at the freight station on the spur track across from the passenger station. It was a lazy line. Mrs. Duncombe would take her kindergarten class out to see the last of the big steam engines. The engineer would let the children put pennies on the track and see them flattened by the weight of the big engine. They were powered by steam . . . then by diesel . . . then not at all.

Barclay's Bank

There were no dials on the phones until 1959. The operator got your number and Pleasantville was a long distance call.

The village was smaller then. Barclay's bank was the first of the "new" buildings, the post office was in Kipp's. (I wonder if the pony express shield is still under the wood facade?) [Kipp's Pharmacy in 1980 was replaced by the Images art gallery.]

At noon you could get a wedge at Joe's [Weldon], a comic book from Pete's and sit on the sidewalk to have lunch—some things never change.

In the early 1950s everyone was in one school—it was a good feeling as a child to know personally the football "stars" and "big kids." Todd came along in the mid-1950s. Mt. Pleasant put more students through Briarcliff High School than Briarcliff. You got to know kids from North White Plains, Valhalla and Hawthorne. (See Chapter 17.)

The railroad station as the Briarcliff Free Library

The coaches, Bill "Bongo" Bowers and Bob "Bullet" O'Keefe were special guys.

The cops were tough, but you knew them all. They all lived in town. Chief Johnson was the most feared man in the village (or was it the world?) and Harry Addis the most respected.

Police Chief Arthur Johnson

The "world," in the persons of unwary motorists passing through Briarcliff, learned to fear Police Chief Arthur Johnson. Under his direction all speed limits, as low as 35 to 40 miles per hour on Routes 9 and 9A, were strictly enforced. As Ed Dorsey put it, "He really held the line!" As a boy, Dorsey lived in Yonkers, but his father worked at the Briar Hills Country Club as caddymaster and starter. Ed worked as a caddy there during summer vacations. Chief Johnson called all the caddies together and forbade them to go into the village center. If they were found straying beyond the borders of the golf course they would be liable to arrest. But somehow young Dorsey got to know the community well enough to decide he wanted to live there. A Briarcliff resident since 1973, Dorsey, who is a managing director for New York Telephone, served three years as village trustee and three terms as mayor of Briarcliff Manor. He was responsible for the appointment of Arthur Johnson, Jr., as chief of police in 1984.

When the Putnam Division of the New York Central Railroad was discontinued in the late 1950s, the railroad station became the fifth home of the Briarcliff Free Library, following almost a year of negotiation with the railroad and an energetic fund-raising drive. The new library building was first opened to the public on Memorial Day of 1959.

In the early 1970s, Theodore and Marjorie Malsin, who lived at Ichabod Farms on Sleepy Hollow Road, gave money to the library as a memorial to their son Donald. The building was repainted and the interior rearranged to accommodate a children's room set apart from the main reading room. When Marjorie Malsin died, Milton Harrison, her second husband, made a bequest to the library in her memory and also contributed many fine volumes to the collection of art books. In 1984, under the direction of architect Don Reiman, a mezzanine was added. The library had grown from eight thousand books and other items in 1952, when its first charter was granted, to more than twenty-five thousand volumes in 1988. Charles Farkas in 1990 was in his twenty-second year as library director, closing in on Mrs. Roscoe Hersey's record twenty-eight years in that position.

In 1956, the Briarcliff Manor Garden Club, of the Federated Garden Clubs of New York State, was formed in Lee Clark's Schrade Road living room. The first project was landscaping the "rock pile" around the new Todd School. In 1961, with seventy-three members, the club had earned a voice in all civic improvement and landscaping problems and, as a news report put it, could not be mistaken for "tea drinking sissies." Club members have planted and maintained shrub and flower borders and tubs all over the village. They provide weekly flower arrangements for the library, garden-therapy sessions at the Sleepy Hollow Adult Home (adjacent to Brandywine Nursing Home), decorations for village holidays, and the Christmas tree at Phelps Memorial Hospital in North Tarrytown. Over the years, the club has won many awards, including, in 1980 and 1981, a citation from the Federated Garden Clubs and a cash award from *Westchester* magazine for landscaping the new post office on Pleasantville Road, and for their "Beautiful Briarcliff Day, 1985," awards from the Federated Garden Clubs and the Ninth District. They raise funds with a fall luncheon and a spring plant sale, and offer a student scholarship for higher education.

The club's symbol is the Briarcliff Rose (see Chapter 5), and, in 1990, co-presidents, Jane Lind and Wanda Callihan, discovered one grower in England who could provide Briarcliff rose plants. In 1991, thirty-five of them will be planted in members' gardens.

In the 1950s and 1960s, art exhibits were regularly mounted in village schools and in the Briarcliff library. A series of exhibits was organized by the Todd School PTA Special Projects Committee, which included Myril (Mrs. Jack) Adler, Alice (Mrs. Martin) Low, and Hannah (Mrs. Alan) Berman. Subjects of these exhibits were animals in art, children in art, colonial America, the UN and many others. In most cases the works exhibited were reproductions from museums and private collections. An exhibition of the artwork of French children from nine to seventeen years of age was arranged in cooperation with the French Embassy.

Regular art exhibits held at the Scarborough School were initiated by a memorial fund for Foresta Hodgson Wood, an alumna who was killed in an airplane accident. Among these was an exhibition of sculpture in the Italian garden at Beechwood, which included works by such well-known artists as Jose de Creeft, Jason Seley and Richard Stankiewicz.

For several years, beginning in 1963, exhibitions of twenty-five to thirty selected prints by well-known printmakers were mounted monthly in the Briarcliff Library. Sponsored and hosted by the Friends of the Library, the exhibitions were arranged by Myril Adler in cooperation with the Pratt Graphic Art Center, an extension of the Pratt Institute in Brooklyn. At a time when limited-edition prints—etchings, lithographs, serigraphs and woodcuts—as distinct from paintings, sculpture and drawings, were not yet generally understood and appreciated, these exhibitions offered an acquaintance with the whole range of graphics, including every kind of traditional and experimental medium. Besides the work of many individual artists, who attended their openings and talked about their work, there were exhibitions of "100 Years of Printing Processes," "Prints from Around the World," and "A Celebration of the 700th Anniversary of Dante's Birth," featuring Jack Zajac's mez-

Art by Fritz Eichenberg for exhibit at Briarcliff Free Library, April 1964

An Exhibition of
prints, drawings
& watercolors
by Michael Biddle

Public Library,
Briarcliffe Manor, N.Y.
Reception:
Sunday, Feb.5,1967

zotint etching illustrations for the deluxe edition of *The Ante-Purgatorio* printed in Italy for the Racolin Press of Mr. and Mrs. Alexander Racolin of Old Briarcliff Road. Some of the many artists whose work was shown in more than five years of regular exhibitions were well-known at the time, and others went on to reap honors and awards. Most of the prints shown were for sale, for $12 and up.

On February 5, 1967, after the devastating floods in Florence of the previous autumn, an exhibition and sale called "Art for Art's Sake," to benefit the Committee to Rescue Italian Art, was held in the Parish House of the Briarcliff Congregational Church. The project was organized by Myril Adler with Marilyn (Mrs. Joseph) Bowler and Shirley (Mrs. Murray) Neitlich. They had planned a local show of about fifty works by artists in and around Briarcliff, but the generous response of the whole community and of many artists more than tripled their expectations. The exhibition included one hundred and sixty works of art, drawings, paintings, sculpture, ceramics and prints of all kinds, contributed by almost a hundred artists from all over the metropolitan area. Briarcliff artists who contributed work were Myril Adler, Hannah Berman, Joseph Bowler, Perf Coxeter, Janet Gleeson, Jacqueline Hammer, Katherine McCormack, Rayna Schwartz, Patricia Sloan, Jean Stark and Walter Yovaish. The Congregational Church contributed the use of the parish house and janitorial services, and the mayor and village board provided storage space in the municipal building. Artist Alan E. Cober of Ossining provided a striking drawing of the Florence Duomo for the posters, which were paid for and distributed by volunteers. Robert Crandall of Briarcliff paid the premium for the insurance arranged by the William Yates office. Rhett Austell of Time, Inc. and Thomas McLaughlin of the Combined Book Exhibit contributed art books at a discount. Matting, framing and hardware were contributed by James Scalzo of the Art Shelf. Barbara (Mrs. Edward) Walker of Ossining designed and hand-lettered the parchment which was signed by the two thousand visitors to the exhibit and sent with a letter from Mayor Emile Munier of Briarcliff Manor to the mayor of Florence. The works were sold at one-third below gallery prices. Entrance contributions were a dollar for adults, 50 cents for students and 25 cents for children under twelve. In the five hours of the afternoon of February 5, the exhibition netted $4,024.85 for the Committee to Rescue Italian Art. Thomas McLaughlin, director of the Combined Book Exhibit in Scarborough, on a business trip to Italy, served as community-to-community ambassador. He carried the letter and parchment wrapped in gold paper to Florence, where he was received and entertained with great warmth and ceremony.[2]

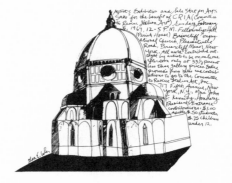

Poster for Committee to Rescue Italian Art, by Alan E. Cober

17

The Schools

AS THE VILLAGE grew, so did the school population. By 1950, grades 1 through 12 no longer fit comfortably into the combined buildings (built in 1909 and 1928) on Pleasantville Road. In 1950, some of the high school rooms had to be turned over to the grade school. Voters approved the purchase of the site of the Todd School on Ingham Road and voted approximately half a million dollars to construct a school of eight rooms for kindergarten through grade 6. The year it opened another two rooms were added, and three years later it had to be doubled in size, with three wings consisting of nine new classrooms, the gym and the library. As the elementary school population moved up it became clear that the high school buildings would soon be overcrowded. At the time they served not only Briarcliff residents in grades 7 through 12 but also, on a tuition basis, high school students from unincorporated areas of the Town of Mt. Pleasant, including Hawthorne, Valhalla and North White Plains.

In 1957 the State Education Department disclosed a new master plan calling for the reorganization of all small districts. Briarcliff was slated for merger with Pleasantville, Armonk, Bear Ridge and Middle Patent. Building aid would be denied to districts that refused to reorganize as stipulated. While a citizens' study group of more than a hundred residents investigated alternatives for the future of the district, three of the other districts merged to form Byram Hills. The citizens' group then recommended a merger with Pleasantville, but before this could be accomplished, the state again intervened with school aid legislation that made merger financially unattractive for Pleasantville. Meanwhile the Pleasantville Road buildings were filling up and the Todd School was overcrowded again, even after the second grade had moved to rented rooms in the new (1957) parish house of the Congregational Church. State building aid was available for Todd, and an addition was built of nine more classrooms, and the art room and music suite. Although the Board of Education made many trips to Albany to find a solution to the increased crowding of the Pleasantville Road buildings, plans for a new high school could not be made until the 1960s, when the state legislature finally passed a revision of the aid formula.

In 1965, the Board of Education appointed a site committee composed of local architects, engineers and real estate agents. The committee recommended acquisition of a portion of

Architects rendering of Todd School, 1952

the Choate estate on Pleasantville Road as the only suitable property available that would meet the state's new requirement for building aid. In January 1966, a public referendum authorized the district to buy fifty acres of the property. But while the referendum was taking place, Pace University bought the whole Choate estate. The Board of Education took the case to court and won a favorable decision a year later. Pace sold Briarcliff thirty-five acres, and the site was completed in 1968 with the purchase of an additional eight acres of an adjoining property, formerly the estate of the Baroness De Luze, on Pleasantville Road. In May 1968, the district voted for the new building, and two and a half years later, during winter vacation in 1971, grades 9 through 12 moved into the new building.[1]

In the late 1970s and early 1980s, as school enrollment shrank and costs spiraled, the Junior High School was moved into the High School building and the Middle School (previously also the High School) buildings were leased to Pace University until 1992, with an option for Pace to renew until 1995. The buildings were renamed Pace University Village Center.

The Briarcliff Manor school district, with a total enrollment of 972 students in the school year 1987-1988, was one of the smallest in northern Westchester. The state's Comprehensive Assessment Reports for that year, summarizing standardized test results and demographic information, rated Briarcliff schools next to best of six small districts in the pupil evaluation program and best (most students passing) in the 1988 Regents exams. Expenditure per pupil was estimated at $10,762. The ratio of students to support staff, at 143:1, was the highest of the six districts, the number of students' families below poverty level the lowest, at 2 percent.[2] Students were 87.4 percent white, 1.4 percent black, 1.4 percent Hispanic and 9.7 percent others. There were no black teachers.[3] "We're definitely a strong college preparatory school," high school principal Joseph Troy told a *New York Times* report-

er. The high school offered eleven advanced placement courses, as well as a writing course
in conjunction with Syracuse University that could earn a student six college credits. Ninety
percent of the graduates went on to higher education. To graduate, a student was required
to complete 120 hours of volunteer community service. "Even with the academic empha-
sis," Troy said, "seventy percent of the students participated in interscholastic sports."[4]

In the 1988–1989 school year, student enrollment in the Briarcliff district had increased
to 1,024, and further growth was anticipated. A twenty-one-member committee of district residents, aided by administrators and teachers, prepared a facilities report outlining
a number of renovations to increase classroom space and some building projects. "It's the
culmination of a lot of hard work and a lot of input from the audiences at several public
meetings," Joan Austin, school board president, said of the report. "I think it gives us a
road map to work from." In 1988 the district had held twenty-seven events in the cafete-
ria, the gymnasium and the Pace Village Center, none of which were large enough to accommodate all the junior-high and high school students.[5] The facilities report, approved
by the school board early in 1989, recommended building an auditorium as well as an additional playing field at the high school.

In May 1990, the Briarcliff school board adopted a budget of $12.7 million.

The opening of the new high school in 1971 generated in many villagers increased interest and ambition to enhance the position of the schools as the center of an expanding
community. A large advisory committee was formed, a meeting ground for a variety of
Briarcliff residents, "wonderful people who believed and gave." Among these were Harold
Mandelbaum, Martin Low, Jerome Harris, Jean (Mrs. Lowell) Harper and School Superintendent Gardner Dunnan. Jean Harper took on the job of directing COED, the continuing

education program, and "put everything . . . [she] had into it" for ten years. From an initial offering of half a dozen, courses increased to more than fifty, including special events, seminars, and lectures, by Burton Benjamin, Sol Stein and many others in the neighborhood who had some particular knowledge and experience they were willing to share. There were courses in Chinese, print-making, painting, calligraphy, piano and guitar, as well as quilting, carpentry, cooking, yoga and the dance. Enrollment increased from 125, mostly Briarcliff and Mount Pleasant residents, in the first semester to 5,000, from all over Westchester County, before Jean Harper stopped directing the program in 1984. In the corridor there were always coffee and hot water for tea in huge urns, and often, the sound of music, and delicious smells, issuing from Jean Harper's own Chinese cooking classes. In the mid-1980s, JoAnne Dornfield, an employee of Westchester Community College, took over the direction of COED, which then became part of the state educational establishment. Shortly thereafter the Briarcliff School Board, citing the high cost of insurance, and reflecting a change in community sentiment, requested that the program be conducted elsewhere. In 1990 COED continues in Pleasantville, Westlake and Valhalla high schools. Almost as many courses are offered, but their range has narrowed, mostly to subjects that are calculated to improve students' chances of success in business careers.

The Briarcliff Nursery School, Incorporated, began August 21, 1947, under the direction of Dr. and Mrs. Charles Churchill, with Mrs. John Akin as first president. After a short stay in rooms of the recreation building of the time (now Thalle Construction Corporation), it moved to the old Law mansion, and then to the Kingsland-Farr house on Route 9 (after 1988 the Tetko site). After 1955 the school owned its own building on two-and-a-half well-equipped acres on Morningside Drive.

Marietta (Mrs. William) Zuydhoek served as director from 1953 to 1968, followed by Barbara (Mrs. T.) Scopes. Michelle (Mrs. Alan) Grant became director in 1980. At that time sixty-five children came to the school five mornings a week. Afternoon sessions were added gradually, and in 1985, were held five afternoons a week. The number of children enrolled

had increased to 105 in 1989. The nursery-school building, not originally intended for a school, was found to be insulated with asbestos. Mrs. Grant, although told that the danger to the children from the asbestos was probably minimal, arranged to have it removed. Mrs. Grant retired as director in 1988 and was followed by Mrs. Eva Levine.

The increase in population in the 1950s caused the growing congregation of Saint Theresa's to feel the need for a school. Accordingly, when the initial mortgage on the church was paid off in 1956, a new fund-raising campaign was begun, and in 1962 four acres were purchased between Dalmeny Road and Central Drive. The site included the remains of the Briarcliff Farms Barn A, converted into a house, which became the convent. The school, for kindergarten through eighth grade, opened in the parish house of the Congregational Church in 1965 and moved into the new building, designed by architect Burke Weigel, one year later.

Since then parents of the 120 students (in 1989) have held countless fund raisers. Parents also volunteered in the lunch program, cooking and serving food daily, to save on labor costs. The school's principal, Sister Barbara Ann Mueller, told Gannett Westchester-Rockland Newspapers reporter Pamela Brisson that the high-technology equipment used at Saint Theresa's should not be attributed to the affluence of the community. "Where Briarcliff's affluence comes into play," she said, "is in the high expectations of the parents. . . . But such standards should be commonplace in Catholic schools . . . and are especially vital in areas with quality public schools, so pupils do not suffer academically to get a religious education." The school's collection of teaching tools, envied by a delegation of teachers from a national Roman Catholic conference, included programmable robots, laser video discs and an inflatable planetarium, as well as a computerized library card system. Students in the upper grades spent 90 to 135 minutes a week working on computers. The cost of the portable laboratory would have been $14,000, but the school rented it for a few hundred dollars. None of the science program's cost had come out of the school's regular budget.[6]

In 1978, the Scarborough School closed, after sixty-five years of service to young people from many parts of the county. "Scarborough School has been a force in the community educationally for many years," alumna Mary Maue, president of the Maue Oil Company of Ossining, told a Gannett Newspapers reporter. "It's been a very good school, an innovative one. When I attended it [in the 1930s] it was considered quite progressive. There were no grades. The students worked along at their own speed, and I didn't feel ill-prepared when I got to college. But they stopped that program a few years after I graduated. . . . The teachers developed creativeness in the children to a great degree." Ann Schoales Thom, then living in Pound Ridge, said, "It is a shame the school has to close. My grandfather founded the school, and I think in the past it has served the community well. . . . I have fond memories of Miss Lulu Ailes using the brook, which traverses the campus, to teach us about the Hudson River. We built bridges and towns along the brook."[7] The last member of the Vanderlip family in the community, Dudley Schoales, Jr., who lived with his family in the White Cottage on River Road, had moved to Connecticut.

The distinguished old buildings of the school stood empty until 1980, when they were purchased by The Clear View School as a day treatment center sponsored by the Association for Mentally Ill Children of Westchester, known as AMIC. AMIC, a pioneer in special education, was incorporated in 1959, and in 1961 conducted the first classes in the county for severely emotionally disturbed children. The first school was a rambling wood-frame building in Pelham Manor of which no one approved except parents who wanted to keep their children at home to avoid the forced confinement of state hospitals. Twelve years later, when the school moved to buildings rented from the Children's Village in Dobbs Ferry, enrollment had more than doubled. A nursery and a summer school had been added, the upper age limit had been raised to eighteen years (later twenty-one), and an after-care program was started to help school graduates. Services for the children's families were expanded to involve them fully in the therapy program and to provide a twenty-four-hour crisis intervention system. In 1977, because of its own growing needs, the Children's Village asked AMIC to relocate the school. In September of 1981, after years of search, negotiation and major renovations, the Clear View School opened in the buildings of the former Scarborough School. The school's first years in this new location were financially difficult, with mortgage payments, rising energy costs and a " 'battle of the budget' waged with government agencies that seem intent . . . upon saving tax dollars by reducing real services even while maintaining the full flower and vigor of their own bureaucratic activity."[8] After 1984, financial problems had moderated. In 1988, 85 to 90 children from 25 different school districts in the county were enrolled in the day school, 3 to 6 children, with their mothers, attended the nursery school, and 82 to 90 attended the summer school. The crisis intervention service was broadened to include calls of less-than-crisis proportions, and thirty-six children received speech and language therapy. Case management services provided Clear View families with help, such as homemakers, dentists, doctors, lawyers and hospitals, from other agencies. Twenty-five children, with their families, were using the after-care service, and transportation was provided by two school vehicles.

AMIC's honorary chairman was the actress Julie Harris, and the officers were: president, Courtland Herbert; vice-presidents, Norman Feinberg, Barbara Frees, Patrick Grasso, Dominick Leone, Morton Meyer, and the Honorable Alvin M. Suchin. The secretary was the Reverend Robert W. Hare, pastor of the Scarborough Presbyterian Church.

Julie Harris Theater at The Clear View School

The Beechwood Theater, within the main building of the Scarborough School, had also stood empty for some years, and AMIC and local theater groups cooperated to raise money and renovate it. In 1983, members and supporters of the Greater Ossining Area Community Theater (GOACT) did what they could to restore the theater. Ossining artist Jean Stern repainted the interior, working with the original stencils. Briarcliff pianist Mary Ann Scialdo performed a benefit concert in May, and GOACT staged *The Andersonville Trial* in December of the same year. On March 17, 1984, The Clear View School presented Julie Harris, in a one-woman performance of *Currer Bell, Esquire*, based on the life of Charlotte Bronte, by William Luce. Marc Statler, executive director of GOACT, and his colleagues assisted in the production of the sold-out, $100-a-ticket benefit. The theater was then rededicated the Julie Harris Theater.

In subsequent years several theater companies, including GOACT, renamed the Acting Company of Westchester but still directed by Marc Statler, the Little Community Theater, and the River Front Acting Company, produced, among others, works by Noel Coward, Dickens, Steinbeck, Chekhov, and Woody Allen, in the Julie Harris Theater.

18

The League of Women Voters

THE LEAGUE OF Women Voters of Briarcliff Manor, one of the first local leagues in the region, was organized in 1926. Long before that there had been a group of twenty-five members in Briarcliff who together contributed $100 a year to the County League and subscribed to the League bulletin. This early development was probably influenced by the presence in the village of two founders of the League, Narcissa Vanderlip in Scarborough and Carrie Chapman Catt, who lived on North State Road in the 1920s. Neither Mrs. Vanderlip nor Mrs. Catt served on the local League board, but Margaret (Mrs. Allan) Coggeshall, of Pleasantville, also a pioneer in women's suffrage and League work, was an active member of the Briarcliff League. Miss Margaret Parsons was the first chairman, Mrs. David Duncombe, secretary, and Mrs. N. K. Thompson, treasurer.[1]

From its early days, the Briarcliff League drew members from neighboring Pleasantville and Ossining and later from Chappaqua and Hawthorne. Members of the Briarcliff League, wherever they lived, could study and act on the village level only in Briarcliff. Many active members lived in Ossining, including Mrs. Louis Brennan, president in 1961, but the League was not reorganized as the Briarcliff-Ossining League of Women Voters until 1963. The paid membership in 1950 jumped from 100 to 141 in three months and slowly but steadily increased throughout the decade to 190 members in 1961. The budget, always comparatively small, increased from $385 in 1945 to $1,315 in 1956 and to $2,235 in 1961.

One of the several items on the League's local agenda was a study of the future needs of the rapidly expanding village—schools, a library building, a new municipal building, improved roads, parking, sewers and water supplies. A master plan was recommended to create public interest in these needs and save money for taxpayers by planned financing of development. League members distributed questionnaires and held many meetings to present and discuss such a plan. In the spring of 1956 funds were made available for the master plan.

In June of 1958, a League workshop reported on zoning changes proposed by the master plan: amended residential zoning to limit rapid growth; amended office and laboratory zoning whereby regulations would be written into the ordinance but specific locations would

161

Narcissa Vanderlip

Carrie Chapman Catt

not be designated on the zoning map. This "Floating Zone Ordinance" was intended to attract businesses to Briarcliff to help balance the tax structure.

On the county level, the League worked toward the establishment of permanent personal registration, a simplification of voting procedures, and in October 1956, P. P. R., as they called it, was approved for Westchester by the Board of Supervisors.

On the League's national agenda in the early 1950s, one of several items was a study of individual liberty, "toward an evaluation of Federal loyalty-security programs with recognition of the needs for safeguarding national security and individual liberty." This study reflected the widespread concern about the Communist threat exemplified by United States Senator Joseph McCarthy's investigation of "unAmerican activities." An evening workshop on the Bill of Rights held at the Tulip Road home of Mrs. Arthur Spear, 1953–1955 League president, was interrupted by the sudden appearance at the front door of an official of the Briarcliff American Legion with a stalwart companion. These Legionnaires hoped to protect Briarcliff, and the nation, by breaking up what they took to be a meeting of a Communist cell. Stella Spear graciously invited them to join the discussion, but they declined.

The Briarcliff League played a part in village life beyond their invaluable voters' services, making use of a range of members' talents. In 1954, under the direction of Mrs. Jerome Schulman, some members contributed a song-and-dance act to the village variety show, an annual event sponsored by the Briarcliff Civic Association to raise money for various causes. The score and lyrics of that number have been lost, but League records include the lyrics, by Maxine Randall, sung at a 1957 membership tea to the tune of "You Can Bet That He's Doin' It for Some Doll," from *Guys and Dolls*:

> When a busy mom
> can debate with aplomb
> certain measures still pending in Albany
> it's a cinch that this knowledge
> isn't something she got in college.
> You can bet that she's gettin' it from the League.
> When our spouses grouse

that the meals at our house
when we're busy are not what they call cuisine
We can't blame the poor sinners.
They're sick of those T.V. dinners
but they're sports 'cause
we're doin' it for the League.[2]

Four women who were active members of the board of the Briarcliff-Ossining League of Women Voters in the 1960s and 1970s have gone on to work in local government. Natalie (Mrs. David) Mackintosh was chairman of the Environmental Advisory Council of the Town of Ossining, then a director of community development and most recently assistant to the Ossining village manager. Sandra (Mrs. Steven) Galef, who was co-president with Natalie Mackintosh of the Briarcliff-Ossining League in the 1970s, announced in May of 1989 that she would run for a sixth term as representative of the Town of Ossining on the County Board of Legislators. She was then minority leader of the board, working "full-time . . . to correct problems of high taxes, effects of drug use and lack of affordable housing" that were attacking the quality of life in Westchester. Patricia Knapp, League president from 1983 to 1985, served as a trustee of Briarcliff Village. Florence (Mrs. Martin) Dexter became chairman of the Conservation Advisory Council of Briarcliff Village.

Sandra Galef

These women agree that their League work was excellent training for public office. The shift for some of them from volunteer work to regular employment away from home was part of a general movement. As more and more women took regular jobs in business and the professions in the 1970s and 1980s it became difficult to schedule meetings. Most younger women, with both jobs and families to care for, were too busy, and League work was carried on by a few energetic retired women. Every year there were new members, but others dropped out. In 1986, membership had dropped to 68, from a high of 200 in the late 1960s, and the Croton-Cortlandt League, with a membership of 60, joined the Briarcliff-Ossining League. The budget in 1967–1968 was $3,310. Twenty years later it was over $6,000, of which more than half went to put out the Voters' Guide.

Natalie Mackintosh

19

God Answers Prayers

T HE SIGN "God Answers Prayers" has stood for thirty-five years by the roadside just over the village line, reminding travellers on Route 9A of the power of faith and letting villagers know that they are home again. This landmark has often inspired curiosity as well as faith, and since it was erected in 1954 many people have dropped by to ask about it, including Sam McGarrity, an associate editor of *Guideposts* magazine. When he knocked on the door of the big white farmhouse on the little hill behind the sign,

Joseph Woyden, a man of 80, looking dapper in a tweed sports jacket, seemed pleased that I had come to ask. Soon he ushered me inside a spacious study, where he brought out a tray of tea and cinnamon biscuits. As I leaned back in a huge Queen Anne chair, Mr. Woyden told me how he had run away from home at age sixteen and had worked his way up in life from a hotel mail clerk to owner of a flour brokerage business. His business took him down sixty-five thousand miles of highway each year . . . and . . . whenever there was a road emergency . . . he would always turn them over to God. And God always kept him safe.

Then, in 1953, his wife was hit by a car. He was told she wouldn't live. "All I could do," he said, "was pray, and that's what I did. Constantly." Mrs. Woyden lived, but when, "after lying in traction for two-and-a-half months in her hospital bed she was brought home . . . it was said that she would never walk again." Mr. Woyden retired from business to take care of his wife and he prayed, through the summer and into the fall. . . . "This time . . . I asked God to heal her—completely." After almost three months in bed at home, she stood up, with help, announced she was going to walk across the room, and did. A month later she had "returned to her routine of horseback riding, golfing, swimming and walking with Mr. Woyden and their brood of poodles." Mr. Woyden designed the sign, had it made and put it up to declare "his strong, proven conviction that GOD ANSWERS PRAYERS."[1]

Woyden told *Citizen Register* reporter Geoff Walden that he first had the sign made out of wood, and, "Some, I guess, Communist, crossed over the little creek there and chopped it down." Next he steelbolted it, but the bolts were cut and it was stolen. Finally, he welded it onto an iron pipe embedded in concrete. A friend and former neighbor, who has maintained the sign for Woyden, called it a fitting tribute to a selfless man who regularly helped motorists stranded on 9A. "He was eighty years old and he'd go out on 9A and help them."

Mrs. Woyden died in 1985 and three years later Woyden sold the estate to developer Thomas Daly of Ossining and moved upstate. The sign is away from the planned house lots, and Daly has promised to leave it standing.

From the turn of the century, when it was the farm of the Sidney Bayliss family, until Route 9A went through in 1928, the Woyden property extended to South State Road.

Church of Saint Theresa, Pleasantville Road

Church Of Saint Theresa

The Golden Anniversary of Saint Theresa's Church was celebrated in 1976. In fifty years, seven pastors served the parish, from the Reverend James F. Kelly (a chaplain in World War I), who served from 1926 to 1946, to the Reverend Robert T. Dunn, called to Saint Theresa's in 1975 and still serving in 1990.

Throughout the '20s and '30s, the parish struggled to survive. In 1940, Father Kelly reported that there were 134 families with 141 children on the parish roles. However, after World War II, building began in earnest in Briarcliff Manor, and attendance grew steadily. The parish register for 1990 has 1,220 families.

Since the inception of the parish, its members have been totally involved in serving their church. According to the Golden Anniversary Book, three of the ushers, John DeAngelis, Edward Fitzgerald (deceased) and Irving Manahan (deceased) had performed their duties at 6,240 masses! John DeAngelis is still an active usher. Other parish members serve as lectors, eucharistic ministers, CCD teachers, in the Altar Society and on the Parish Council. They collect food for the Ossining Food Pantry and assemble clothing and food for the needy families in New York's inner-city parishes. On one Sunday each month, some of the members visit patients in the Veterans Hospital at Montrose.

The Confraternity of Christian Doctrine (CCD) was established in the parish before World War II. Today, approximately 350 children from both Briarcliff Manor and Ossining public schools take part in its program every year, meeting in the church library, the school and in private homes. More than fifty parishioners serve as teachers for the various age groups.

An extraordinary ecumenical service was conducted in Saint Theresa's Church in January 1973. Reporting on the ceremony, the Parish Bulletin said: "There is a lot of good will in the Briarcliff community, and it shows at a mass where Rabbi Philip Schnairson of the Congregation Sons of Israel and the Reverend William Arnold, rector of All Saints, acted as lectors, and the Reverend Eugene Meyer of the Briarcliff Congregational Church gave the sermon." (Father O'Connor was the celebrant.)

In that same spirit of ecumenism, the Briarcliff Manor-Scarborough Historical Society, in May 1986, requested that the Ossining Ministerial Association hold a service in the Briarcliff Congregational Church as part of the village observance of Memorial Day. The society planned the weekend to include "A Salute to the Statue of Liberty" on her 100th birthday. Clergy from all seven houses of worship participated, and Morehead Kennedy, a career diplomat and one of the recently released Iran hostages, spoke at the service.

During Saint Theresa's first ecumenical mass, the Reverend Eugene Meyer said, "if we are drawn together and work together, the dark and cold in today's world will dwindle in the light of God and the warmth of His Spirit."

The Congregation Sons of Israel

The Sons of Israel of Ossining was organized as a mutual-aid society in 1891. For some years before that, there had been a group of Ossining residents who valued their Jewish heritage and wanted their children to be educated as good American Jews. They hired a Jewish teacher, but his earnings as a teacher were so meager that he added to them by the time-consuming business of selling kosher food, which he bought in New York City, travelling there from Ossining by ferry at 25 cents a trip.[2]

The Jewish cemetery between Havell Street and Dale Avenue, still in use in the 1990s, was purchased in 1900, and the Congregation was officially organized in the spring of 1901. Before that a *minyan*, the ten men required to conduct a complete service, could not always be counted on. There were eleven founders of the Congregation. Eight of them served as the first officers: Abraham Feinberg, president; H. B. Myers, vice-president; Daniel Levy, recording secretary; Abraham Altman, financial secretary; Michael Hyams, treasurer; Myer Myers, Harry Macy, and Nachman Hart, trustees. A. L. Myers donated the first Torah.

Services were held in private homes and vacant stores until 1902, when the membership of twenty-three families bought a building on Durston Avenue (later Hunter Street). Each family contributed materials and labor, and it is told that one of the founders carried lumber on his back to save the cost of carting. In the new building, services were held upstairs, and the first rabbi lived downstairs. The rabbi also served as cantor and teacher and, as the first teacher had done, supplemented his very small salary by selling groceries.

In 1910 the Jewish women of Ossining formed the Congregation's first Hebrew Sisterhood.

When the membership had increased to about forty-five families, in 1920, enough money was raised to start the school with Rabbi Wolenchick as teacher. However, the synagogue was now crowded, particularly on the high holy days. At a farewell banquet for Trustee Morris Finkelstein, who was leaving for Europe, President Morris Schleifer made an appeal for a building fund. The Sisterhood promised to buy the land, and pledges were made amounting to $7,000. H. B. Myers pledged to build the foundation, and Isaac Kamm gave a team of horses to be raffled off for the benefit of the building fund, after they were used to excavate the foundation. In 1922, in a candle-light procession, the Torah was carried to the new synagogue on Waller Avenue.

As younger members took over the leadership of the congregation in the 1930s, there was a movement to modernize services while retaining the ideals of Orthodox Judaism. The rabbi started to preach in English as well as Yiddish. Older members were much distressed, but membership and attendance slowly increased.

Change continued, in the nature of the congregation as well as the conduct of services. Samuel Puner, Congregation president in the 1960s, remembers how things were in the early 1940s, when he first joined the Congregation of some fifty or sixty families. The women sat on one side during services, the men sat on the other side. The men's side was crowded, especially on high holy days, while the women's side was not crowded. Weekly meetings of the Congregation, to pass on all expenditures, were big social occasions, and after they broke up, the men played poker. Twenty-five cents out of every pot was given to the Congregation. The women sat apart and chatted or played other card games. The tradition of daily *minyans* was held to. When a *minyan* failed to gather, somebody just walked up Main Street and asked people to close their shops for half an hour to make one up. Not one member of the Congregation lived in Briarcliff, and Puner was for years the only commuter.

In 1950, Rabbi Mortimer Rubin, who was a graduate of the Jewish Theological Seminary, favored breaking away from Orthodoxy and joining the Conservative movement. The Board of Trustees voted for the change and submitted it to the Congregation for approval. The whole Congregation turned out in a very emotional meeting. There were people in tears, and people screaming. Ultimately the Orthodox group marched out of the meet-

Congregation Sons of Israel,
Pleasantville Road

Newsclip from "Ossining Citi-
zen Register," May 21, 1960

ing and the vote was taken. Since then services, following the practice of the Conservative movement, have been held in both English and Hebrew.

As the Jewish community continued to grow, the Waller Avenue facilities became inadequate. The decision to build a new synagogue was not unanimous; older members had grown attached to the synagogue they had built and were opposed to leaving it. There were many meetings and discussions before compromises were reached, and eventually everyone joined forces in the enterprise. Eight acres of the Mead Farm on Pleasantville Road were purchased (for $35,000) and the cornerstone laid in 1959. The Mead property had been the estate of relatives of W. W. Fuller of Haymont, the estate on nearby Chappaqua Road, and included a fine old mansion in such disrepair that to salvage it would have been too costly. The cornerstone of the new synagogue was laid in 1959. The Waller Avenue synagogue was sold to the Veterans of Foreign Wars.

In the early fall of 1960, just before the high holy days, for the second time in the history of the Congregation, the Torah was carried in a candle-light procession up Croton Avenue and around the corner to the new sanctuary on Pleasantville Road. The new synagogue and school were soon dedicated.[3]

In the early 1970s, the Rabbinical Assembly of the Conservative movement passed a resolution to grant women rights equal to those of men, to sit with the men and take part in the services, this change to be made at the discretion of individual congregations. The president at the time called a special meeting of the Congregation the day after he heard of the assembly's vote. The Congregation voted to accept the resolution, and all women achieved full religious rights. The Congregation Sons of Israel was one of the first of the eight or ten Conservative congregations in Westchester County to make this change.

The school, for decades staffed by volunteers, in the 1980s, had a staff of seven or more professional educators. Classes from kindergarten through tenth grade met three afternoons a week to study Jewish history and religion.

The tradition of daily services continued into the 1970s, but became too difficult as more and more commuters joined the growing Congregation. Complete services are now held on Monday and Thursday mornings as well as on the Sabbath. The Congregation, in 1960 composed of some 150 families, by 1990 had tripled in size. Most of the congregants are markedly different, in way of life, income and place of residence, from the original group of Ossining villagers. A 1988 membership list shows that more Congregation families live in Briarcliff Manor than in any other village. Since 1989, a $2.5 million fund-raising drive has been underway for renovation and expansion of the synagogue.

The Robert W. Searles

Dr. Robert Wyckoff Searle believed that religion should be above differences in race or creed. One of Scarborough's most distinguished residents after World War II, he was an energetic advocate of better understanding among religious groups. From 1946 until his death in 1967 he was the executive director of the Home Advisory and Service Council of New York, a social service auxiliary to the Home Term Court. He helped to organize the local branch of the Mental Hygiene Association, and served as first president of its board.

Born in New Brunswick, New Jersey, in 1894, Searle earned his A.B. at Rutgers University in 1915 and his B.D. at New Brunswick Theological Seminary in 1921. In 1917, he served in the U.S. Ambulance Service, then joined the Field Artillery and was stationed in France, advancing in rank from private to sergeant major. After pastorates in New York City and Albany, New York, he became a member of the Presbytery of New York and from 1930 to 1934 served as associate minister of the Madison Avenue Presbyterian Church in New York City. From 1934 until 1941 he was general secretary of the Greater New York Federation of Churches, and his "tenure was marked by improved working relation-

Robert W. Searle, 1965

Helen Menzies Searle, 1950

ships between various faiths, particularly in regard to the battle against slums and the fight for better lower-class housing."[4] He was a founder and the director of community relations of the Protestant Council of the City of New York until 1946, when he became executive director of the Home Advisory and Service Council of New York, associated with the Home Term Court. That court handled cases caused by family conflicts that had previously been heard in a criminal court and aimed to resolve the conflicts rather than punish the offenders. It was Searle's idea to recruit volunteers, particularly mature women, to counsel the troubled families. The volunteers, who underwent intensive training, worked in the same building with the court and provided a day nursery, a marriage-counseling service, a training school for social workers and probation officers and a clinic for alcoholics, the only one in the country operated as an adjunct to a court. The Home Term Court was reorganized as the family offenses part of Family Court in New York City, which the Home Advisory Council continued to serve.

Searle was a guest lecturer at many colleges, and taught philosophy of religion at Briarcliff College for some years after 1950. He preached from time to time in churches of sixteen different denominations, was a founder of the National Conference of Christians and Jews and a delegate to many religious conferences. He wrote numerous articles and three books: *City Shadows* (1938), *Author of Liberty* (1941), and *Tell It to the Padre* (1943).

Helen Menzies Searle, like her husband, was an outstanding member of the community. She was tall with a graceful carriage and very handsome into her eighties, when she died. She taught drama at Briarcliff College for many years and wrote and produced the play, *Highlights from Fifty Years in the Manor*, presented at the 50th Anniversary celebration in October of 1952. It was she who helped to define the difference between Scarborough and Briarcliff with the often-quoted remarks, "Scarborough is a state of mind," and "I reside in Briarcliff Manor; I live in Scarborough."

Faith Lutheran Brethren Church

The congregation of Faith Lutheran Church came to Briarcliff in 1965, when they bought (for $15,000) two acres on Pleasantville Road, adjacent, on the side toward Briarcliff Village, to the houses that had been the Baroness De Luze's Luthany. Before that, since September of 1959, the congregation had met and held services in a small rented chapel on Central Avenue in Scarsdale. Charles Winters drew the plans for the new church and groundbreaking ceremonies were held on June 12, 1966. The congregation was composed of only twelve families, but there were builders among them, and they built their church in a little more than a year. The official opening day service was held on October 8, 1967.

In 1972, Mrs. Joan Ruud started the Little School, a Christ-centered nursery school to serve the community. Begun as a three-day program with a handful of children, the school continues in 1990 with more than eighty children as a two-, three-, and five-day program.

Pastor John Kilde, the first minister in Briarcliff, left in July 1973 to teach Greek at the Lutheran Brethren Seminary in Minnesota. In August 1973, the Reverend Harold Peeders, with Mrs. Peeders and their two sons, began his ministry. Within a year the congregation, again with all-volunteer labor, had built a parsonage for the family, at 40 Burns Place. In 1977, the Reverend Peeders, with his family, left Briarcliff for Portland, Oregon, to become pastor of the Rose of Sharon Church, a smaller, but socially and economically more heterogeneous congregation. Mrs. Peeders was an Oregon girl and their first son, who had been born there, considered it his home.

Faith Lutheran Brethren Church, Pleasantville Road

"God has blessed us as a community, and a nation," the Reverend Peeders told Beth Smith, life-styles editor of the *Citizen Register*.[5] "The people should enjoy the fruits of their labor . . . but I hope they remain conscious . . . that, 'by their fruits ye shall know them.' . . . As a minister perhaps I am too idealistic, but I see in my study people who are caught hopelessly in the competition of today's society." The result, he felt, was broken marriages, alcoholism, and the like. He and his wife, he added, had made friends in Briarcliff and taken part in various activities. He made friends with local clergymen, but generally avoided ecumenical services because his church represents a conservative, evangelical position. "Faith Lutheran does not mean to be exclusive," he said, "but rather wishes to worship in a specific way."

Groundbreaking ceremony, Faith Lutheran Church. From left: Tom Sandnes, Dr. Robert Cook (past president of King's College), Pastor Bergstad, Fred Kossow (deputy mayor of Briarcliff at the time), and Astor Stave.

Congregation members building Faith Lutheran Church

Robert Duncanson, recently returned from missionary work in Africa, served as interim minister until August 1979, when the Reverend Joel Egge was installed. Reverend Egge had been a pastor in Pasadena, California, and Marysville, Washington, and is a member of the Board of Home Missions for his denomination.[6]

Faith Lutheran Brethren Church is the center of a friendly, very active community of families and singles, which has grown tremendously over twenty-five years in Briarcliff. From the charter membership of 28 adults and 22 children, the average attendance at Sunday worship in 1989 ran over 250. Since 1983 there has been an assistant pastor, and in 1985, the first full-time office secretary was hired. In June 1985, 3.1 acres adjoining the church property were purchased for $53,000, and negotiations for the acquisition of property to the south of the church are under way (in 1990).

There are weekly Bible study meetings for community women, weekly meetings of Young Ambassadors (grades 3–6), two confirmation classes (junior and senior), teens (called Senior Youth), college and career adults, and a learning center for adults, who meet every Sunday morning before the regular services. Each of these groups has a social gathering once a month. Young-adult Bible studies are held twice a month in parishioners' homes. Sunday school classes are held for children three years old and up. Just inside the front door of the church, to the left of the entryway, there is a nursery for infants, staffed by volunteers. There are also nurseries for toddlers and for two and three-year-olds.

The King's College

The Edgewood Park School moved away from Briarcliff in 1953. The buildings stood empty for more than a year while the village considered prospective buyers. An offer was made by a hotel chain and another by the King's College, a private four-year coeducational Christian liberal arts college offering programs of study leading to baccalaureate and associate degrees. There was some controversy in the community about the sale. Some villagers deplored the occupation of some forty acres of prime real estate by a tax-free institution. Others feared that a hotel on Scarborough Road would spoil the atmosphere of peace and privacy. The latter viewpoint prevailed, and in 1955 the King's College bought the property and moved into one of the finest Christian college campuses in the country.

The King's College, started in 1938 with sixty-seven students on the Marconi estate in Belmar, New Jersey, had moved to New Castle, Delaware in 1941. The first president was evangelist and youth leader Dr. Percy B. Crawford, who led the college for twenty-two years, until his death in 1960.

In Briarcliff, the college grew and prospered. In 1960 it was accredited by the State Board of Regents and since then has granted the degrees of Bachelor of Arts, Bachelor of Science, Associate in Arts and Associate in Applied Science. In 1968 the college was fully accredited by the Middle States Association of Schools and Colleges. To the original Briarcliff Lodge buildings, King's College has added Squire Hall, a gymnasium, Miller Circle, a dormitory for two hundred students, and a $2,000,000 academic/science building, completed in 1979. In 1970, the college purchased the stone house on Scarborough Road that had been the residence of Walter Law, for use as a men's dormitory. Also in the 1970s the college owned part of the former Stroock estate on Cedar Lane in Ossining, calling it the "Tarryhill Campus" and busing students back and forth for various activities. This property was sold to a developer in the 1980s. The Golden Anniversary campaign was launched in 1983 to raise $6 million to renovate the main men's dormitory and build a chapel/auditorium.

The enrollment of the King's College increased from 285 students in 1955 to 862 in 1980, but the decreasing pool of college-age students in the 1980s moved the college administrators to concentrate on marketing strategies to attract qualified applicants. In 1986, President Friedhelm K. Radandt affirmed that the outlook for maintaining and even increasing enrollment was excellent, "because I know we have something positive to offer . . . a quality education which is Christ-centered."[7]

The King's College offers a range of courses in the humanities and science and in newer fields such as computer science and medical technology. The curriculum emphasizes elementary education (teacher and missionary training), business administration and economics. There are pre-professional programs for medicine, law and theology. The ratio of teachers to students is approximately one to thirteen. All students, including transfers, are required to take one Bible course each semester, up to a total of sixteen semester hours of credit, or graduation, whichever is reached first. Courses of study in many fields include required seminars designed to relate the subjects to a Christian world view. In the college catalog is a "statement of doctrine . . . adopted by the Board of Trustees," spelled out from the divine inspiration of the Bible to "the bodily resurrection of the just and the unjust—the just going to everlasting blessedness in heaven with God, the unjust to everlasting punishment in hell." This is followed by six columns on the Christian philosophy of the college and goals for the student, who "should be characterized by a personal faith in Jesus Christ." However, the "Introductory Information" section states that, "admission is open to all men and women—regardless of race, creed and national origin—who meet the admissions requirements and who believe they can profit from study at King's."[8]

The cost for a full-time resident student at the King's College in 1986 was $3,915 per semester, which covered tuition, room, board, and most fees. For nonresident students, tu-

ition and fees came to $2,765, but they could live outside the college only with close relatives in the vicinity. Many scholarships, grants and awards are available to students as well as a variety of low-interest and long-term loans. Many students take part-time off-campus jobs, and requests for childcare and yardwork in the neighborhood usually exceed the number of students available. The Field Experience internship program offers juniors and seniors the chance to work in New York City and Westchester County business and nonprofit organizations to gain career experience as well as academic credit. Interns have been placed in Pan Am, AT&T, Marriott, the County Medical Center, Brooklyn Botanical Gardens, Revlon Health Care, General Motors and General Foods.

No college housing is available for married students, and men and women may not enter each other's residence halls. All members of the college community, teachers, students and administrators, are required to refrain from the use of alcoholic beverages, tobacco, narcotics and "traditional" playing cards. They may not participate in oath-bound secret societies or social dancing of any kind and must exercise "Christian discretion" in their choice of entertainment, including the performing arts, radio, television, recordings and "various forms of literature."[9]

In the autumn of 1989, student enrollment at King's College had fallen to 515 from a high of 870 in 1979–1980. Faced with the high costs of living in Westchester and of maintaining the rambling old Briarcliff Lodge buildings, the trustees voted to study the possibility of moving the college from Briarcliff to another site in the New York metropolitan region. President Friedhelm Radandt told Gannett Westchester Newspapers[10] reporter Carole Tanzer Miller that "Remaining in Briarcliff . . . would mean launching a major renovation and building program. The college needs a larger library, a performing arts center, new gymnasium, chapel, student center and room to start a communications program aimed at attracting students to offset a decade-long enrollment plunge." Radandt told staff and students that he did not, however, expect any moves for the next two years. Village Manager Lynn McCrum said, "they're a good neighbor and it would be a loss to the village if they move." He estimated that about thirty-eight homes could be built on the property, or under the "floating zone ordinance" it could be used for an office or research plant.

The Episcopal Churches

On September 30, 1989, Saint Mary's Episcopal Church celebrated its 150th anniversary. During its first century the parish had only six rectors. In all it has had ten (eleven with Dr. Hillary Bercovici, who came to the parish in 1989), with an average tenure of ten years. As Marion Dinwiddie remembered, when expressing her regret at the 1904 resignation of the Reverend Thomas R. Harris, B.D., to accept another call, "We're the kind of church where they stayed—and stayed and stayed, and we like to have them stay." For the first forty-three years the parish was presided over by the founder, Dr. William Creighton, and his two sons-in-law, Dr. Mead and General Morell. They were followed in 1882 to 1895 by the Reverend Abraham Gesner, in 1895 by the Reverend Harris and in 1904 by the Reverend Berry Oakley Baldwin, B.D. When Baldwin contracted tuberculosis, his brother, the Reverend Charles Warren Baldwin, "who had been in Tiffany's Studios and had joined the church as a minister out of devotion to his brother," came up and took a great many of the services while Oakley (as Marion Dinwiddie called him) was ill. When Oakley died "the entire congregation unanimously called for Charley," and he was the rector for thirty-seven years, followed in 1951 by the Reverend Leland Boyd Henry, D.D., who resigned, on doctor's orders, in 1965.[11]

In the meantime the church property grew. The parish house and cloister were built in 1897, the gift of Mr. and Mrs. William Kingsland, in memory of their son, Cornelius. The present rectory was built in 1931. The first bell, given by Commodore Perry, hung in a bell tower, as Marion Dinwiddie remembered, and was replaced, when it cracked, by a new bell, given by August Belmont. The bell tower was taken down and replaced in 1937 by the peal of bells, given in memory of Mason B. Starring by his two sons. In 1956 and 1957, the church was completely restored and the walls of all the buildings repointed and waterproofed. In 1960 an addition to the parish house was built, containing a sacristy, a room and facilities for the kindergarten and other church school classes, vestment cupboards and rest rooms. In the windows of the addition are four stained-glass medallions from the V. Everit Macy mansion, given by the Ossining Historical Society. The architect was Paul L. Wood of Scarborough. In 1956–1957 and again in 1985–1989, the priceless Bolton windows were removed, section by section, releaded and restored. Land was obtained from the Sleepy Hollow Country Club for a parking lot, and a memorial garden was created. An office building was built in 1988. Paul Moore, Jr., Bishop of the Diocese of New York, attended the groundbreaking ceremony for this latest addition. He spent the day performing worship services and confirmations for both children and adults.

When the Reverend Paul Zahl became rector of Saint Mary's in June of 1982 there were 110 members of the church. In March 1988, at a time of nationwide decline in the membership of Episcopal churches, the congregation had more than quadrupled, to 450 members. State figures in a report issued by the Episcopal Diocese of New York indicate membership at 76,969 in 1977 and 64,486 in 1986.[12] But, as Saint Mary's senior warden John Nolan put it, "Last year we reached the choke point and began turning people away in the parking lot and in the pews. . . . When you walk through those doors you get the message of personal redemption through forgiveness. That simple message communicated by Reverend Zahl effectively is what packs the pews." Even with the assistance of the Reverend Nancy Hannah, starting in 1986, and committees of the laity, the Reverend Zahl's schedule was exhausting. Trying "to build a parish into a family of people" included attendance with his charming wife at forty cocktail parties during their second Christmas in Scarborough, as well as at innumerable parent-teacher functions, and social and community events throughout the year. Zahl also made it a habit to respond promptly to phone calls and to visit the homes of members and nonmembers alike, including sick people, elderly people, single-parent families, people suffering grief or hardship and people in need of spiritual comfort. In the fall of 1988, the Reverend Zahl announced his resignation. The Reverend Nancy Hannah served as interim rector during the nine-month search for the new rector, the Reverend Hillary Bercovici.

The building of All Saints Church was completed in 1854 and services were held there by visiting clergymen. However, the parish was not regularly established and recognized as part of the Episcopal Diocese of New York until 1869, when title to the church property was conveyed to the church corporation by the widow and heirs of the founder, Dr. John D. Ogilby. The first rector after incorporation was the Reverend J. Breckenridge Gibson, followed by Abraham H. Gesner, who left All Saints to become rector of Saint Mary's in 1882.

Drawing of south transcept window, Saint Mary's Church

Throughout the years between 1869 and 1887, most activities of the church were motivated by the related families of Brinckerhoff and McFarlan, who were also related by marriage to the Ogilby family. The first rectory, on Old Briarcliff Road opposite a tennis court (later on the property of Charles Samson, and more recently of Mr. and Mrs. Alexander Racolin), was given to the church in 1879 by Harriett McFarlan. The present rectory, on Scarborough Road, was built during the rectorship of A. F. Tenney, 1882–1884, on two acres given by Robert Oliver, with the help of $1,025 from the sale of the first rectory. The Sunday school conducted by the J. Warren Rogers family in the Long Hill schoolhouse became a mission of All Saints Church, "thus adding sixteen children to the Sunday School." Miss McFarlan presented the church with a new organ, and the family of Henry Brinckerhoff, vestryman for many years, established a memorial fund. Another fund, "in memory of the little girl we have lost," was given by Mr. and Mrs. Charles W. Woolsey, who lived on forty-six acres just east of the All Saints property. (The Woolsey estate, including the stone mansion later called the Manor House, was purchased by Walter Law in 1891.)[13]

After 1887 attendance at All Saints diminished and deficits increased to such an extent that "the vestry questioned the expediency of separate corporate existence." In 1900 "the parish was indebted to the rector [the Reverend H. L. Myrick] for salary accumulated over a period of seven years." The Brinckerhoff Fund was used to meet the obligation, and services were conducted by clergymen on a temporary basis until 1902, when the Reverend Thomas R. Hazzard was called as rector. Under his leadership the parish grew, and with the increased revenues much-needed repairs were made to the church building. Around 1905 the women of the parish constructed a small fieldstone parish house behind the Scarborough Road rectory. Under the supervision of the Reverend Hazzard, the women, in par-

ticular Elizabeth, Emily, Bertha, and Helen Becker, did all the building by hand, except for placing the roof. In 1906 Fanny E. Rogers started the Auxiliary Women's Guild with seven members. In 1910 the congregation, now including guests from the Briarcliff Lodge and students from Mrs. Dow's School, had outgrown the church. Boys from the Holbrook School sat outside on the stone wall during services because there was no room inside. The vestry voted to enlarge the church and, with funds pledged by the congregation, architect William Henry Deacy designed the extension, using the existing building as nave and adding transepts and chancel to create the present cruciform fieldstone church. A bell tower was erected over the crossing. Miss Brinckerhoff, Mrs. Mortimer Flagg and other members of the congregation donated stone for the walls from their estates, and Charles A. Fowler donated a pipe organ. The remodeling was completed in the summer of 1911, at a cost of $7,000.

The years of the Depression and World War II brought hard times again to the parish of All Saints. The Lodge closed and some large estates were broken up. There was a fire in the rectory in 1934 and a fire in the church basement in 1943. The Reverend George F. Bratt, rector of St. Paul's Church in Ossining, served All Saints as priest-in-charge for over thirteen years. On Sunday mornings he conducted four services, shuttling back and forth between Ossining and Briarcliff. Sometimes, he said, only angels attended the early services at All Saints.[14] Under the hearty leadership of the Reverend Bratt, the small but devoted congregation managed through the lean years and when, toward the end of World War II, it appeared that the church population would soon increase, a .6-acre plot of land surrounding the church was purchased. Funds for the purchase were provided by James Cooley and Mrs. Frederick Hilton, widow of a former vestryman, who lived in the house

All Saints Church in 1911 after the addition of the transcept and chancel

called Treetop, across Scarborough Road from the church. William Deacy, who had designed the 1910 addition to the church, designed a new parish hall, the required $25,000 was raised, and the building was completed and dedicated in January 1950. In 1948, the Reverend Bratt was appointed archdeacon of the New York Diocese, and the Reverend Constant Southworth became rector of All Saints. In 1952 Southworth resigned and the Reverend William E. Arnold, who had been a vicar in Massachusetts and a chaplain in the United States Army during World War II, became rector, a position he held until 1981, the third longest rectorship in the village. As the Venerable George Bratt had foreseen in 1944, the church population steadily increased through the 1950s and 1960s. More than an acre of land in two parcels across Kidderminster Way were given by parishioners, including Hubert Rogers and Harold Rose (who lived in Edith Law Brockelman's Mount Vernon on Scarborough Road). After the Reverend Arnold resigned, the parish underwent another difficult period until the Reverend Steven Yagerman was called as rector in 1984.

Rev. William E. Arnold, rector of All Saints Church, 1952–1981

How have two Episcopal churches survived in a village as small as Briarcliff Manor when there were (and are) two Episcopal churches, Trinity and St. Paul's, in nearby Ossining and, until 1953, two in the Tarrytowns? Both of Briarcliff's Episcopal churches were founded by particular families to serve close neighbors in the middle of the nineteenth century, when travel on the unpaved roads could be difficult. Since then the two churches have at times competed for the loyalty of important parishioners. A Miss Brinkerhoff, troubled by the unwanted attentions of a young rector at All Saints, as Marion Dinwiddie recalled, went down to Saint Mary's "with the whole lot" of her friends.[15] Bertha Becker, who, with her three sisters, built the first All Saints parish house in 1905, shortly thereafter taught sewing and chair-caning at Saint Mary's Church school. How have these churches maintained their

All Saints Church choir, 1925.
The second boy is Don Hotaling,
the third is Harry Addis; the first
girl is Ruth Hotaling, and the last
is Harriet Finne

separate identities through so many years (some of them very lean years for at least one of the parishes)? The answer seems to be in the quality of the various rectors, many of whom subsisted, in affluent Briarcliff, on salaries ranging from ten to twenty-five thousand dollars a year. The key to the survival of these churches has been the "hearty and inspiring leadership" of the Reverends Thomas Hazzard, George Bratt and Steven Yagerman at All Saints, the popularity of Charles Baldwin and "the personal piety, warmth and urgency" of Paul Zahl at Saint Mary's. "God answers prayers!"

20

Briarcliff College

UNDER THE energetic direction of President Clara Tead, Briarcliff Junior College grew and prospered from 1942 to 1961. Mrs. Tead was well qualified for the job. In New York City she had been executive secretary of the Consumers' League, executive director of the Women's City Club, dean of Katherine Gibbs School, and, from 1935 to 1942, dean of Finch Junior College. During World War II she also served as director of the women's branch in the office of the Chief of Ordnance.

Mrs. Tead and Dr. Ordway Tead, her distinguished husband, lived on campus in the stucco house which became the college library after her retirement. Dr. Tead taught social science at the college and served as chairman of the Board of Trustees. He was also professor of industrial relations at Columbia University, editor of books on economics for the McGraw-Hill Book Company and Harper & Brothers, chairman of the Board of Higher Education for New York City, a member of the President's Commission on Higher Education, and the author of many books, including *Character Building and Higher Education* and *Trustees, Teachers, Students—Their Role in Higher Education.*

The Teads enlisted for the college a lively and accomplished group of trustees—men and women, neighbors, friends and colleagues. Among them were Carl Carmer, author; Norman Cousins, author and editor; Barrett Clark, author (and neighbor); and Thomas K. Finletter, lawyer and diplomat. Three noted educators and authors, Esther McDonald Lloyd-Jones, Eduard Lindeman and Lyman Bryson, were on the board, along with the artist William Zorach, whose monumental sculpture of a nude female figure, "Spirit of the Dance," commissioned for Radio City Music Hall in the 1930s, had been a subject of controversy.

The college steadily improved in academic scope and standing. In 1944 the curriculum was registered by the State Education Department of the University of the State of New York and accredited by the Middle States Association of Colleges and Secondary Schools. In 1951 the State Board of Regents authorized the college to grant degrees of Associate in Arts and Associate in Applied Science. In 1952 the U.S. Army Map Service selected Briarcliff as the only junior college in the country to give professional training in cartography and map-making techniques. The library, 5,500 volumes in 1942, contained 20,000 volumes in 1960.

Science and art buildings, Briarcliff College

Shelton House, across Elm Road, was purchased for dormitory space in 1944, a new classroom-and-office wing was dedicated in 1951, and a new dormitory, Howard Johnson Hall, was built in 1955. Howard Johnson, the ice-cream and restaurant tycoon, joined the Board of Trustees.

Of the college under President Tead, Helen (Mrs. Robert) Searle, who taught theater arts there for many years, said "It was a vivid and exciting place to work." Eileen O'Connor Weber told a *Citizen Register* reporter that Clara Tead "was goodlooking, vibrant and darkhaired with a twinkle. She just sparked up the whole town." The college was sometimes denigrated as merely a residence for debutantes between dates with men from nearby Ivy League colleges. Some students did make their debuts at New York social ceremonies, but many did not. A very few kept their own saddle horses at nearby stables. There were scholarships and a variety of foreign students. In 1957, the "Junior" was dropped from the name of the college. Kay McKemy, who taught English composition there in 1960–1961, described the students as "highly literate . . . products of exclusive girls' schools and the best public schools. They knew how to read, speak, study, listen and take notes. They had seen plays in the three Stratfords, been to the Louvre and eaten at the 21 Club."[1]

Before her retirement in 1960, President Tead chose as her successor Charles Adkins, then vice-president for development and public relations at Wheaton College in Massachusetts. In 1962 the college bought the former residence of the Roger Wallach family, next door to Shelton House, for the president and his family.

Postwar prosperity and the population growth, which had started to crowd the Briarcliff public schools in the 1950s, resulted in an unprecedented growth in college enrollments in the 1960s. Housing Authority loans at interest rates as low as 3 percent were readily available for college building. Starting with a $3.6 million building loan in 1963, Briarcliff College expanded rapidly. Two new dormitories were built, Hillside House in 1962 and Valley House in 1964. To these were added in 1965: the fine arts and humanities building,

Dormitory, Briarcliff College

with an art gallery and studios as well as classrooms and faculty offices; the Woodward Science Building, with laboratories, an auditorium and a day nursery; and the three-story dining hall with sit-down meal facilities for six hundred. Gray Taylor, of the firm of Sherwood, Mills and Smith, was the architect in charge of all this building. Peter Fazzolare, hired in 1956 by President Tead as the college's first business manager, continued to manage prudently the increasingly complex finances. The newly converted library, with a thirty thousand-volume capacity, was dedicated in the fall of 1964.

Harper Woodward, a director of Eastern Air Lines and other corporations and a trustee of the college since 1957, became chairman of the Board of Trustees in 1965. President Adkins recruited as trustees Charles Shain, president of Connecticut College and William Dietel, who had been professor of humanities at Amherst and was from 1967 to 1970 principal of the Emma Willard School in Troy, New York, to represent the academic community on the increasingly business-oriented board.

In 1964, the New York State Board of Regents amended the college's charter to offer four-year courses leading to the Bachelor of Arts and Bachelor of Science degrees. Eight major courses of study were offered, including child development, geography-cartography, history, urban studies and English. The Center for Hudson Valley Archeology and Prehistory, under the direction of Louis Brennan, was opened at the college in 1964. Student enrollment, just over three hundred in 1960, had increased to over five hundred in 1964. Faculty members, most of them full-time, numbered around sixty. Burnham Carter, Jr., a Princeton graduate with advanced degrees in English literature, came from the English Department of Purdue University to supervise the enlarged curriculum. Kenneth Skelton, who had been dean of the college for twelve years, retired to become director of a new liberal arts program at New Paltz.

In the fall of 1967, enrollment had climbed to 623, including nearly 240 freshmen. In June of the same year the first bachelors' degrees were given to 46 women. A fourth large

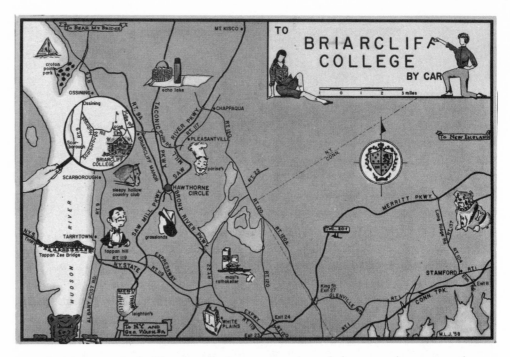

new dormitory was built. The education boom was at its peak, but great changes were brewing. The civil-rights movement, the women's movement and organized opposition to the war in Vietnam aroused college students all over the country. The ideals of gentility and service of the young ladies of Mrs. Dow's and Mrs. Tead's schools were no longer embraced by many Briarcliff students. The college was dispelling "its former image as an exclusive college for rich women . . . not smart enough to go to Smith or Vassar and who wanted to marry Protestant lawyers. While still heavily Waspish (about 60 to 65 percent . . . compared with 90 percent two decades ago), the college now gets between 70 and 75 percent of its new admissions from public high schools."[2] Fraternity parties and debutante balls were out of style. Briarcliff women, with the men they saw at Yale, Columbia and elsewhere, were talking about political issues and action.

After the retirement of Helen Searle, Charles Newman, a young graduate student in experimental drama, had been hired to assist Professor Mary Douglas Dirks in theater arts. Under his direction drama students presented a lively revue climaxed with a mock-solemn reading from the college handbook, such passages as "a student . . . is expected to behave in a manner appropriate to a young lady, at all times." As she read, the young actress led the cast up the aisle and appeared to be tearing pages from the handbook and throwing them around the auditorium. Administrators of the college and some students, especially those who had worked on the handbook, were offended.

A group of students marched around the campus holding lighted candles and signs protesting the war in Vietnam and the invasion of Cambodia. A few of their teachers joined them. Briarcliff's trustees, like many college administrators at the time, were thoroughly alarmed. Differences of opinion among them seemed irreconcilable. President Adkins and some trustees resigned. James E. Stewart, head of an engineering firm in Pittsburgh, took on the difficult job of interim president.

In the early spring of 1969, following an evening lecture by Mark Rudd, president of the Columbia Chapter of Students for Democratic Action, a group of twelve Briarcliff students seized the college mimeograph machines and ran off a list of nine demands to present to the administration. These students were led by Edie Cullen, former president of students, and Susie Huggins, president of the Briarcliff chapter of Students for a Democratic Society. The next day, after the demands were presented to all (or most) of the students, almost fifty students took part in a sit-in in the lobby of Dow Hall. One of the nine demands was for an immediate explanation in writing of the contract terminations of three teachers, another was that those three teachers be rehired. Other demands were for immediate student evaluation of faculty; equal representation for students on a committee dealing with faculty employment; formation of a committee of students, faculty and administration to search for a new president; immediate student representation on the educational policy committee; more scholarships for black and Puerto Rican students; and absolute control by students of their social activities. "We will no longer tolerate rules that restrict our abilities, our fantasies and our sexual lives to the fixed roles of housewives and mothers," Edie Cullen told *Citizen Register* reporters. "We are ready to act in our own interests and fight against the administration and the forces behind them."[3]

The sit-in went on for some forty-eight hours. A sympathetic young teacher and his wife spent nights with the demonstrating students to advise and support them. When it was all over the students hired a crew to clean up the lobby. No material damage had been done, except to the rug.

The students were told that their demands would be considered, but the end result of the sit-in was to harden the resolve of disciplinarians in the administration and deepen the disenchantment of many students. Thomas E. Baker, dean of men at Case Northwestern in Cleveland, was chosen (without consulting the students), to be president of Briarcliff College in 1970. In September of 1970, Dean Carter was dismissed without the one-year notice that is customary for deans.

President Baker kept faculty meetings to a minimum, discouraging any discussion of educational policy. Within a year he had terminated the contracts of twelve of the faculty, including the college psychiatrist and the head of the Language Department. Two tenured members of the English Department and the dean of students resigned in protest.

Students generally were showing a preference for coeducational schools, and to remain competitive as enrollments decreased, several women's colleges had started to admit men. In the summer of 1969, Dr. Leo Rockas of the English Department and Dean Carter were given the job of investigating the possibilities of coeducation at Briarcliff. After careful study, they reported that although the costs in additional staff, instructors and security personnel would be considerable, the change might be desirable. Dean Carter told Betsy Brown, reporting for the *Patent Trader*,[4] that he was "dedicated to women's education—but it's like the midi [long alternative to the fashionable mini-skirt]: 18-year-old girls won't buy it. I am more flexible about it; I'm not for coeducation, but for survival."

Faculty opinion was sharply divided on a variety of issues, including coeducation. When Dr. Rockas became eligible for tenure in 1970, the committee, which included opponents of coeducation, voted against granting him tenure. President Baker was free to terminate his contract. Dr. Rockas, backed by a committee of sympathizers, sued the college for $100,000. The case he presented against the college, President Baker, and two members of the tenure committee listed fifteen causes for action, including denial of academic freedom, violation of work law and employment rights, and charges that the tenure denial was made in violation of college rules.[5]

Several hundred Briarcliff students walked off campus to protest the firing of eight professors who said they had been given notice because they supported Dr. Rockas. Later, at an angry, crowded meeting called by the students, Dr. Baker said the dismissals were part of an economy drive. The students replied that while the English and Theatre-Arts departments had been "destroyed," the Psychology Department, largest in the college, headed by Dr. Myrtle McGraw, and the Physical Education Department had been expanded. Dr. McGraw told the students that the college "must determine what it can do best [her own Psychology Department] and we may lose some students but we will get others, perhaps more dedicated students." "Baby lab!" one student called out "and physical education— that's what you're giving us!" "Most of the students," Betsy Brown reported, "appeared to support the fired professors, and they gave a standing ovation when Dr. Mary Dirks . . . charged that 'if this isn't repression and reprisal, I don't know what is.'"

Spokespersons for Briarcliff College let it be known that the college had decided against coeducation "because . . . it would cost too much to set up the new programs needed to attract men. Then, like many other women's colleges [they] watched in horror as freshman enrollment tumbled to 71—down from a 1967 high of 260."[6] The Board of Trustees in 1973 replaced President Baker with Josiah Bunting III, a personable, well-spoken young army officer and Rhodes scholar, who had taught at West Point and at the Naval War College in Newport. Bunting had published two novels, one, *The Lionheads*, drawn from his experience as an officer in the Vietnam War. His account of the West Point cheating scandals in a national magazine had made headlines in *The New York Times*. President Bunting was well covered by the press. He did his best to put Briarcliff College on the map by inviting, at considerable expense, New York City literary celebrities to the college to take part in seminars, which were open to the public and very well attended. Enrollment continued to decline although several excellent teachers had replaced those who had been fired. In 1974, Bunting named Peter Fazzolare senior vice-president of the college. Hillside Dormitory was leased to New York Medical College of Valhalla. Pace University rented space in two Briarcliff dormitories, paying $960 for accommodations for each of 115 Pace students. But the budget excess ($3 million in 1969) that Fazzolare had hoarded over the years was slowly dissipated. Bunting's fund raising fell short of what was needed. The remaining Briarcliff students, down to 350 in 1977, enjoyed luxurious half-empty dormitories. Some were annoyed by young men who moved in when the administration granted twenty-four-hour parietals (visiting rights) in an attempt to pacify militant students. And they worried about the status of their credits if the college closed.

Mergers—with Bennett College in Millbrook, New York, with New York University and with Pace—were considered, but Bennett closed, and agreements were not arrived at with NYU or with Pace. In April of 1977 the assets of Briarcliff College, nine buildings on fifty acres, were sold to Pace University for $5.2. Peter Fazzolare served as chief administrative officer of Pace in Briarcliff, succeeding Bunting, who resigned in protest at the takeover. None of the faculty was retained, and no attempt made to preserve the identity of the college.

For lack of funds, Dr. Rockas' lawsuit was eventually dropped. Most of the teachers who had been fired in 1970 and 1971 were teaching elsewhere within a year or two. Dr. Rockas went to Hartford University, where he was soon tenured and promoted to a full professorship. When one young instructor was forced to leave Dr. McGraw's Psychology Department at Briarcliff College (her salary was discontinued), she started the Hudson Community School, which in its second year became an open-classroom school for third through sixth grades, in the Congregational Church. After three years the school moved to the Asbury Methodist Church in Croton. The teachers who were trained in this school all started schools of their own elsewhere, including one in Chappaqua which was still going strong in 1990.

Because enrollments were shrinking in most liberal-arts colleges, the transition for some of the unemployed teachers was difficult, to say the least. They consoled and amused themselves by composing broadsides, which they mimeographed and distributed in quantity around the campus. This excerpt from one of them is densely allusive and suitably literary: *Briarcliff Broadside*, Vol III, no 1., "The Wilful Wasteland":

> What are these thorns that prick, what good can grow
> Out of this sere cliff? Son of a gun,
> You cannot say. I met a traveler from an antique land
> Who saw a vast and trunkless caryatid.[7]
> Stand in the desert. Come in -
> The water's fine if you like dust baths.
> I can show you pain in that handful.
>> Bye Cadet Bunting
>> Soon to go a-hunting.
>> Academe's a winding sheet
>> To wrap the brave young bunting in.

"Caryatid" cover by Megan Mitchell, class of 1971

Pace University

Pace University, founded in 1906 as a one-room business school for accountants, in 1980 had become a university of twenty-six thousand students in eight schools in New York City and Westchester County. Under Edward J. Mortola, who became president of the university in 1960, Pace recognized the potential student market in the suburbs and in 1963 opened a 175-acre campus in Pleasantville on the former Choate-Coggeshall estate. In 1975, Pace purchased the financially troubled College of White Plains, retaining the faculty and preserving the college's identity. The White Plains campus became the site of Pace's new law school.

In the early 1980s, when the Briarcliff Middle School moved into the new High School building, Pace University leased from the village the former Middle and High School building, adjacent to Law Park. (See Chapter 17.) The building was renamed the Pace University Village Center, and Pace generously allowed the community use of the auditorium, for special events, and also provided space for the Briarcliff Manor-Scarborough Historical Society and the Village Youth Center.

The Hastings Center

The Hastings Center, started in Hastings-on-Hudson in 1969, moved to the former Tead Library building on the campus of Pace in Briarcliff in 1988. An independent organization of physicians and scientists, lawyers and professors, corporate executives and government officials, the center addresses moral problems raised by advances in biomedical science and the professions. Willard Gaylin is the president and Daniel Callahan the director. There are a board of twenty-four directors, a staff of thirty, and 130 fellows. The center's annual budget

in 1988 was over a million dollars, one-third of which came from private and government grants and two-thirds from individual and corporate contributions and income from membership and educational programs. The bimonthly *Hastings Center Report* is received by thousands of individuals and institutions. Many books and monographs on ethical issues originating at the center are published by the Indiana University, Plenum and Humana presses. Center staff members have assisted in drafting legislation, served on state and federal commissions, given lectures and taken part in public discussions all over the country.

Among ethical issues the center devoted research and educational efforts to in 1989 were those associated with care of AIDS patients, care of the elderly, termination of life-sustaining treatment, new reproductive technologies, maternal-fetal relations, genetic screening, skilled nursing homes and civic education.

21

The Wars in Asia

The Korean War

THE COLD WAR sent one very small ripple into the living room of the Arthur Spear family in the heart of Briarcliff village, when a League of Women Voters study group was mistaken for a Communist cell. (See Chapter 16.) The Korean War was not so benign. Lieutenant John K. Koelsch, navy helicopter pilot, died July 3, 1951, in a prison camp in North Korea after three months of captivity. He had been an ensign in the navy in World War II, one of three members of the Koelsch family listed on the "Communique" Honor Roll in 1945. The son of Mr. and Mrs. Henry Koelsch, who lived at Brae View on Central Drive, he had attended Scarborough School, Westminster School in London, and was a graduate of Princeton. He was awarded the Congressional Medal of Honor posthumously, the first helicopter pilot ever to receive that medal.[1]

The Vietnam War

Three men from Briarcliff Manor were killed in Vietnam in the armed services of the United States. A fourth, Anthony Shine, in 1989 was still listed as missing in action.

Kenneth L. Hirst, Jr., corporal, was the first Briarcliff casualty of the war. On May 12, 1967, three days after his twenty-second birthday, he was killed in action in Quang Tri Province, South Vietnam, while serving in the First Battalion, 9th Regiment of the United States Marines. He was twenty-two years and three days old.

Randall Breward Purdy, corporal, enlisted July 1, 1966, in the United States Marines. He was assigned to the post of Forward Observer and killed near Con Thein, December 19, 1967. He was twenty-one years old.

Jonathan Shine, first lieutenant, who had graduated nineteenth in the West Point class of 1969, was killed in action with the 25th Infantry Division near Cu Chi on October 15, 1970.[2] His brother Alexander, a third son of Mr. and Mrs. George Shine, also served and was wounded in Vietnam.

22

Government and Politics

"IT'S A GREAT little village, served now as from the beginning by dedicated people," community development Director Anthony Turiano said of Briarcliff Manor in 1986. Officials and employees were no longer, as in the 1940s, mostly members of a few families who had lived in the village since the turn of the century, yet several worked for the village for many years. Turiano, building inspector and assessor for thirty-four years—including ten years as assistant to Max Vogel, Briarcliff engineer and first village administrator—was one of seven employees awarded trophies in 1989 for more than twenty-five years' service to the village. Also honored were police Chief Arthur Johnson, Jr., who had worked for the village since 1946, Patrolman Fremont Stafford, and three maintenance workers. In 1990 Lynn McCrum was in his nineteenth year of administrative work for the village. He was appointed village manager, an office newly established by local law, in 1971. Also in 1989, Mayor Edward Dorsey entered his fourth term, trustee William Wetzel entered his seventh, and Arthur Sullivan started his sixteenth year as village justice.

The caucus system, which allowed any resident over the age of eighteen to run for office, kept national politics out of village elections. Candidates chosen by the caucus are usually guaranteed election. "There was no speaking," William Kossow, told a Gannett Newspapers reporter, recalling his 1940s campaign. "Your name was placed into nomination . . . you didn't run." By 1956 candidates were allowed to address the caucus, but questions had to be submitted eight days before the meeting.

Charles Rodgers, Jr., is given credit for making the caucus more democratic. When he became caucus party chairman in 1972, he considered that candidates were still hand picked and that it was his job as chairman to encourage as many as possible to run. Under his leadership, eight people ran for two open trustee positions in 1973, eliciting a record voter turnout, and the first woman candidate, Anita P. Miller, a liberal Democrat, was elected trustee. Rodgers, a marketing expert, lived in the village for thirty-one years until his death in 1981. He was very active in the affairs of the community and of Saint Theresa's Church. George Kennard, mayor of Briarcliff from 1977 to 1983, called him "the conscience of our village."

Charles Rodgers, Jr.

At the 1988 caucus nominating meeting, former Board of Education president Jean Flink surprised an audience of about thirty-five people with the impromptu nomination of Rodgers' son, Charles Rodgers III. Asked if this nomination was a message to newcomers like candidate William Stewart to stay out of local politics, Ms. Flink said, "My motive had nothing to do with another person. I learned my lesson at his [Rodgers'] father's knee that it's important to have choices in an election."[1]

Challenges to the caucus nominations have been rare. In 1928 residents of a new section of the village who were denied the right to vote at the caucus organized a write-in campaign and elected Isaac C. Hotaling trustee. In 1954 and again in 1956, Carroll Colby was elected trustee, running on his own Scribe Party ticket, after losing the caucus nomination by a narrow margin. In 1986 John Rapoport and his running mate, Susan Parker, challenged the nominating petitions of the caucus candidates, Kathryn Pacchiana and Robert Cerrone. The County Board of Elections ruled the incumbents' petitions faulty because 89 of the 109 signatures on them were found to be invalid, most of them because they were not dated. Four former Briarcliff mayors, George Kennard, Emile Munier, Howard Holmes and Robert Plumb, wrote and mailed a letter to village residents urging them to defeat the two candidates and write in the names of the incumbents. A record turnout of twelve hundred voters elected the incumbents by a nearly 2:1 ratio. Mayor Dorsey said the election should be viewed as a mandate for the current system: "The people had a chance to say what they thought about our system and it was upheld." Rapoport criticized the caucus as a closed system that encouraged voter apathy. Mrs. Parker called the caucus committee "a club that doesn't want any new players." The newly reelected trustee Robert Cerrone replied that Rapoport and Parker, comparative newcomers, had been very little involved in village affairs before the election.[2]

Whether or not it encouraged voter apathy, the nonpartisan caucus system made it possible for two liberal Democrats, Anita Miller and Patricia Knapp, to serve as trustees in a community where Democrats sometimes felt like aliens. Traditionally, Briarcliff residents have voted Republican in out-of-village elections. There have been notable exceptions. Caroline (Mrs. Martin) Parker, a long-time village resident, has been County Democratic Committee Woman for the 27th district since 1956. In 1956, Martin Low, of Sleepy Hollow Road, ran for the same office in another district, got six votes, and was elected. In the 1960s and early 1970s, the 15th and 27th districts became Democratic in terms of actual party enrollments, making the village as a whole about half and half, Democrats and Republicans. In 1948, while Jonathan Bingham, son of a Connecticut senator, his wife, June, and their children were living in Scarborough, Bingham ran for the state senate on the Democratic ticket. He influenced another Briarcliff Democrat, the writer Albert Q. Maisel, who had worked on the Committee to Reelect Roosevelt during World War II, to run for the State Assembly. In 1948, Maisel was covering the investigation of the Veterans' Administration by a group of U.S. senators. Concerned as always with the social consequences of the public malfeasance he scrutinized, Maisel was persuaded that he might work effectively for reform in the state assembly. His candidacy was endorsed by the Progressive Labor Party. Neither Bingham nor Maisel were elected. Bingham, some years later, represented another constituency in the United States Congress.

23

"The Flavor of the Community"

VILLAGE TRUSTEE Freda Delton, running for a fourth term in 1989, said, "I think growth and variety of housing will be the two most important issues. I would like to continue to try and keep the flavor of the community in spite of growth." Mayor Dorsey said he would work to maintain Briarcliff's "rural look."

Development continued through the 1970s, but did not seem to threaten the rural look of the village until the surge of building in the 1980s. In the early 1970s the firm of Robert Martin Associates proposed to build attached town houses on the east bank of the Pocantico River, eight on Ash Road and nine on Jackson Road. When the Planning Board refused them a building permit, the developers took the case to court and won. But under the watchful eyes of village engineers the buildings were set on piles, and water problems in the apartments were minimal in spite of the low ground.

In 1974, developer Reynaud Gheduzzi laid out the segment of Law Road nearest to Long Hill Road West and built, on Law Road and Nichols Place, eleven houses that sold for around $100,000.

In 1972, Thomas Shearman bought the 110-acre Whiting estate off Scarborough Road, and with his family took up residence at Ashridge. Shearman extended Law Road and laid out forty building lots. Some of these he sold but some he still held in 1990. Also in 1974, he sold to Mrs. Vincent Astor twenty acres adjacent to her estate, which she had purchased some ten years earlier from the heirs of Hubert Rogers.

In 1987, a neighbor who had been a schoolmate and friend of Mrs. Whiting's daughter, Ann, wrote of the two most recent Ashridge residents:

I saw Mrs. Whiting once since we've lived here. She was at the Briarcliff hairdressers. I spoke to her and she was very gracious, spoke of Anne, etc. I said that she looked exactly the same—which she did—and she made a tell-tale gesture to her temple. I remember Anne talking about her face lifts and—[another friend] said that every summer she went to some spa in Germany to take a tuck.

The Whiting house certainly had a renaissance when the Shearman family moved in. They had been in the community for several years and had four children in the schools. Tom and Martha were very active in the community, and entertained a great deal. Martha, who was loved by everyone, redecorated the place in her own excellent taste; more people saw the house than ever before.

Sounds idyllic, doesn't it? But the darker side was that for more than fifteen years Martha fought an agonizing battle with cancer, which she lost in 1986. The annual Christmas party for all their friends and neighbors had had to be given up because it became so well known there were more crashers, or as many, as invited guests. Gone the way of Mrs. Vanderlip's dance class and New Year's party. The community has become too big and people don't know each other in the same way.

After this letter was written, Shearman remarried, and with his wife, Pam, again offers the hospitality of Ashridge to the community on many occasions.

In March 1974 the Board of Trustees of Briarcliff Manor appointed a committee of twelve to plan the celebration of the seventy-fifth anniversary of the village. The committee, which included Stephen McQueeny, chairman, Margaret Pearson Finne, Thomas Vincent, Andrew B. Vosler, William and Audrey Sharman, Edwin C. Walton, Thomas B. Shearman, and Eileen O'Connor Weber, began by establishing the Briarcliff Manor-Scarborough Historical Society "so that the past of the village could be preserved for future generations," and set about composing a detailed, fully illustrated history of the village. *Briarcliff Manor, A Village between Two Rivers* was published in the anniversary year of 1977. The ninety-seven-page history, now a collector's item, opens with a biography of Walter W. Law, written by William and Audrey Sharman. Next, several pages of pre-Law history, including six (with pictures) about Scarborough, precede detailed accounts of Law's Briarcliff Farms and Briarcliff Lodge. Accounts of the 1905, 1934 and 1935 Briarcliff automobile road races were written by Claire McQueeny. Margaret Finne contributed information about private schools in the village and Midge Bosak and Helene Mandelbaum wrote the history of the public schools. Carroll Colby researched the history of the Briarcliff Library, Stephen McQueeny reviewed seventy-five years of Village Board minutes for the section on village government, and Ed Dorsey compiled the Fire Department's colorful history. Histories of the churches were contributed by Cathy Caltagirone, Karin Mueller and Dick Murray. The list of acknowledgments ends with thanks to "Irv Manahan, Arthur Osterhoudt and Emile Brown for their outstanding memory of Briarcliff through the years; and Eileen O'Connor Weber for being 'Eileen.'" The history concludes with "Growing Up in Briarcliff," reminiscences written by Eileen Weber, Donald Armstrong, Cynthia Purdy, Joy Ozzello and Steve McQueeny. (These last have been freely quoted in this later history.) The last pictures in the book are of Coach Bill Bowers, who "for more than forty years . . . served his village—as teacher, coach, fireman, and special friend"— and of the parade in 1965 to honor him, which was followed by a picnic, a presentation of "This Is Your Life, Bill Bowers," and a dance. "The day culminated," the caption adds, "with the presentation by a grateful community of an automobile and boat to the man who gave so much of himself to the village he loved." The compiling of the 1977 history was "a job well done" as Mayor George Kennard wrote, and he thanked the Historical Society on behalf of the board and the village.

Bill Bowers

The Briarcliff Manor-Scarborough Historical Society grew in membership, and collected historical documents and memorabilia, establishing headquarters first in the Briarcliff Middle School, then moving to the second floor of Weber-Tufts, Incorporated, realtors, on Pleasantville Road, and then back to the Pace University Village Center (the former middle school), always with the hope of finding a permanent home. Among the many programs the Society has presented are an annual bus tour of the village, a tour of historic village houses, a

tour of village churches, and a cruise up the Hudson River. Fund raisers have included a square dance in the Saint Theresa School gymnasium, a formal dance at Rosecliff (the former Harden estate), an antique car exhibit, and day-long trips to Hyde Park and Winterthur. Between 1974 and 1990, the Society has had ten presidents, including William Sharman, Edith Bronson, Audrey Sharman, Joyce Pandolfi, Eileen Weber, Barbara Dollard, Arthur K. Myers, Harriet Olden, Rosemary Cook and Maureen Crowley. Many other members have served as officers and on committees responsible for the numerous functions and events.

In the early 1970s moderately priced new housing was already in short supply. Government housing subsidies were available for old people who did not require nursing-home care. William Wetzel had studied the matter and visited such projects in Newburgh and elsewhere. He knew the state was interested in proving the idea feasible and would do everything possible to make a Briarcliff project work. But the whole subject of low-income, government-subsidized housing was controversial in the village.

Conservative residents imagined that the tenants would be large welfare-supported families. Their vigorous opposition to the project made the 1974 election one of the most hotly contested in village history. For two places on the Board of Trustees there were three candidates—Wetzel and Stephen McQueeny, who favored the senior-citizen housing project, and George Kennard, who had not taken a position on the subject. At the last minute, on the very day of the caucus meeting, Albert Goudvis, who was opposed to the project, announced that he would run. Goudvis and Kennard were elected. After the election the caucus party hosted a debate at a public meeting. The middle school auditorium was jammed. Wetzel, Robert Marville and Richard Murray argued in favor of the housing project, Goudvis, Robert Gale and Ed Scott, a magazine publisher who lived in the village at the time, spoke against it. Once the facts of the matter were presented and the rumors dispelled, Wetzel remembered, "Everyone thought it was a wonderful idea. It was sliced bread!" At a public hearing later held by a state agency, ninety-two people spoke in favor of the project and two against it.

Construction of the North Hill Apartments for senior citizens on North State Road was completed in 1977. The project operated very well for the independent elderly and had no negative impact on the village. There would not be another like it unless and until housing subsidies were resumed. Tenants paid 25 percent of their income, whatever it was, in rent, and the government paid the remainder. People who had lived in the village or had relatives living in the village were preferred on the list of applicants. The waiting list for the apartments, restricted to fifty names, had been closed for four years in 1989.

The Briarcliff Manor Seniors' Association, established in January 1973, holds weekly Wednesday meetings and sponsors trips and recreational activities, as well as monthly blood-pressure testing by a registered nurse. In 1989 the village acquired a van that transports seniors to supermarkets and other shops, doctors' appointments, movie matinees, and the like. From a nucleus of ten people, the Association has mushroomed to a mailing list of over two hundred for the bi-monthly bulletin and the senior van schedule.

Briarcliff Manor has been a leader in municipal recycling in the county. Barbara Mackintosh, a fifteen-year-old Briarcliff High School sophomore, was responsible for the first push in 1970 toward a recycling program in the village. Barbara had become concerned about the environment while studying earth science at school. "I immediately knew that I—as an individual—had to do something about it, but I didn't know just what," she told a Gannett Newspapers reporter.[1] "Then, one day on my way to school I thought of a newspaper recycling program." That same day she wrote a letter to the Briarcliff Board of Trustees suggesting that the village become involved in recycling. The board answered with an invitation to a meeting, at which the trustees listened to Barbara's proposal and decided it had merit. The Youth Council, an official village group of adults and teenagers, agreed to sponsor the project and selected Barbara (who was not a council member) to be coordinator. Barbara found a firm that would buy newspapers for recycling, hired a truck to cart the papers and helped to direct a publicity program about the project. Twelve tons of newspapers were collected on the first weekend and seventeen on the second. The Youth Council received $10 a ton for the papers and netted $170. Asked what the council would do with the money, Barbara said it would be put toward another program to better the environment, possibly a water-monitoring kit. With such a kit, she explained, students working under the direction of the Board of Cooperative Services could monitor streams in Westchester to spot pollution problems. Barbara's parents, David and Natalie Mackintosh, were among the volunteers who went around picking up newspapers from people who couldn't get them to the truck. Twelve-year-old Billy Mackintosh checked out firms that might take bottles for recycling and wrote a letter to the village board suggesting bottle recycling as a possible next step in the village program. Nine-year-old Ginny Mackintosh represented the paper drive at the Todd School.

Briarcliff village officials set about analyzing the costs of running a municipal recycling program. There were no statistics available from any community that broke down the costs of recycling in money and man hours. These costs in the first four-station system in Briarcliff were high. But in the fall of 1971, Village Administrator N. Michael Markl worked out a plan to lease truck bodies, station these at one point (behind the new post office), and hire a private carter to come in with a truck chassis and transport the glass to a glass-manufacturing plant in Orangeburg, Rockland County. Village Public Works employees would continue to haul newspapers to a paper plant in Peekskill, tin cans to a plant in Elizabeth, New Jersey, and aluminum to buyers nearer home. It was hoped that the costs of the program would be offset by the sale of the materials and savings on dumping fees at the Croton landfill.[2] A study in 1985 by Ben Larkey, county recycling coordinator, showed forty-three communities engaged in some recycling, if only of leaves and newspapers, but Briarcliff was one of only fifteen that recycled glass and even fewer that recycled metals. Larkey estimated that Briarcliff at that time recycled 60 percent of its glass and 68 percent of its newspapers.[3] Briarcliff had demonstrated that neat and almost complete recycling could be accomplished at a reasonable cost. At the first annual Westchester recycling awards meeting in September 1985, Briarcliff's rate of participation in recycling was cited as highest in the county.[4]

Since the spring of 1989, the village of Briarcliff has furnished plastic baskets to each homeowner, and collects glass, tin and aluminum cans, and foil containers, as well as newspapers, twice monthly.

The Mackintosh children

24

A Briarcliff Family, 1962–1982

THE FLAVOR of a community is determined by the people in it, especially the families, as much as by the architecture and the size and cost of residential lots.

Many families have been raised in Briarcliff, each one unique but most with some common elements and concerns. Marilyn Slater wrote this account of her family's first twenty years at 72 Poplar Road:

On a golden Saturday in late summer, we burned our mortgage. We invited to join us the neighbors of old, most of whom had moved away, as well as the attractive young couples who had replaced them. Our extended family was also on hand to help us celebrate. For we were to end a major financial obligation and it seemed important to gather around us the people who had filled these years with fun, support, companionship and love.

During our twenty years in the modest frame and shingle house, inventively termed "Village Colonial" by the real estate people, many things had happened to us, some wonderful, some we could have done without. We had raised our four children here and somehow managed to get them through the vicissitudes of childhood and adolescence, and now the youngest had almost finished college. There was a time when it seemed this last would require a financial miracle.

In July of 1962, when we took possession of this house "with considerable potential," the grass was knee deep, dark green wallpaper with violet flowers adorned the walls of the small living and dining rooms and a baby grand piano, legs removed and covered with a tarpaulin, lay on the side lawn. My dad told us later that when he first saw our home he had to go out onto the porch till his stomach stopped turning.

The piano in the grass had been abandoned by the previous owner. Neighbors, disturbed by such wanton waste, covered it against the rain and later traded their indoor upright for it. Our outdoor baby grand was a benefit for all of us.

That summer we spent every spare moment scraping, painting, wallpapering and refurbishing. We made some mistakes. One morning, called to their room, we found our boys covered with long strips of wallpaper which we had put up with the wrong kind of paste. By fall we thought the basic work of making our eyesore a home was accomplished. One Saturday afternoon we refilled the hot water heating system, which had been drained for repair, and as the water level rose slowly

in the pipes a chorus of "Dad, there's water pouring through the ceiling!" came from all corners of the house. The system had not been drained when the oil burner was turned off. The water had frozen, expanded and burst all the radiators!

Not all our early memories of 72 Poplar Road are negative. There were fourteen children living in four houses in a row on our seldom quiet side of the street, and during the summers they regaled us with backyard shows. They sang, danced and did terrible comedy routines. On one occasion they invited their parents to a "church" service, complete with a sermon and, of course, a collection.

These same adjacent backyards were the setting for weekend get-togethers of the thespians' parents. We served each other drinks and snacks and had lively exchanges of ideas. Among the issues we argued was whether or not Briarcliff High School should merge with Pleasantville. Indoors in the fall and winter we continued to share our weekly news and the world's. We spent New Years' Eves together too, drinking a bit too much and making resolutions and predictions which we checked out each subsequent year. Our good fellowship was born largely of similar values and concerns, which, of course, made our child-rearing infinitely easier than going it alone.

Along with the usual childhood diseases we had more than our share of orthopedic problems. Our older daughter developed Perthes Disease, a softening of the hip joint bones which kept her on crutches from the ages of seven to nine. Still vivid memories of those years include the sight of her sitting under a large maple tree waiting until her crutches, pressed into service as machine guns by neighborhood children, were returned to her. A memory that still can move me to tears is of the sight of her hurrying to catch the school bus on a rainy morning in her blue and white checked raincoat and hat, slipping and falling near the road. Books, crutches, lunch and child all spilled out in different directions.

Our second oldest tore the ligaments in his knee one evening when we were busy with dinner guests. He went out to ski with non-release bindings on the golf course behind our yard. We spent the next spring and summer going for hydro-therapy at a nearby hospital to repair the damage from his fall that night.

During subsequent summers I watched these same children, healed and tanned, going off each morning to the recreation program in our village, first as campers, later as counsellors and life guards. In fall and winter, the school bus stopped at our driveway and when it was especially cold or snowy, the group would wait on our porch or in our front hall. The picture of this wool-hatted and mittened group clutching brown bag lunches, oak tag art projects, cellos, gym bags, cleats and even a stringed bass return to me easily still.

In later years we watched a procession of young people go off nervously in caps and gowns and prom dress, uncomfortable at being photographed before departure.

And so this summer afternoon we gathered to recall and celebrate some very good years. The young lawyers, salesmen, social workers, mechanics and students found it surprisingly easy to renew old ties, while their parents enjoyed the reunion, promising to repeat it often.

Burning the mortgage at 72 Poplar Road

25

Development and Planning in the 1980s

IN 1980, construction started on the remaining thirty-four acres of the Beechwood property in Scarborough, on thirty-four town houses and three two-story apartments in the renovated, forty-room Vanderlip mansion. The prices ranged from $285,000 to $350,000 for the town houses, and from $475,000 to $650,000 for the units within the mansion. The $10 million redevelopment was a joint effort of MTS Associates of New York and the Vector Real Estate Corporation, under the corporate name of Beechwood Associates. Sean Scully, an architect and principal of MTS Associates, told *New York Times* reporter Lee Daniels that the key to adapting such estates as Beechwood for modern residential living lies in "valuing the landscape and character of the old estate above all. . . . In effect, redeveloping the property becomes an act of stewardship." Robert Marville, head of the Briarcliff Manor planning board, said that the MTS-Vector plan for the property was "very intensively scrutinized" by village officials.[1] "They showed far more sensitivity than anything we had yet seen," he said, "and the widespread feeling is that it has worked out very well." Frank Vanderlip, Jr., gives MTS Associates "credit for saving Beechwood from the bulldozer . . . Beechwood was divided into three very fine condominiums, and the library converted into a ballroom for the use of all the families of the development. This was done carefully, retaining everything of architectural merit. . . . The garden is beautifully preserved in its strong design."

In 1986, 110 building permits were issued, 83 percent more than the year before and the greatest increase in 30 years. The rise was attributed to three projects then under construction: Briamor Associates was building Rosecliff, 116 detached houses off Sleepy Hollow Road on the former Harden estate; the Willoughby development on North State Road would be 24 semi-attached single-family houses on 2.5 acres; Richard Albert and Ellis Lasberg were building the Briarcliff Commons, 40 attached single-family housing units on five acres off Route 9A behind the shops on Pleasantville Road. Before the permit was issued for this project the village engineer saw to it that borings were taken to make sure the ground was solid. The prices of the Commons condominiums were comparatively low, starting at less than $200,000. However, they soon went up.

Twelve houses on Peach Tree Lane off Sleepy Hollow Road were built by Joseph Mar-

And this is only the backyard!

Now imagine it in one of Westchester's most exclusive settings…in an enclave of distinctively designed, single-family homes…each on lovely one-third to one-acre lots!

Think of it…untamed woodland views…sunken living rooms, huge master suites, sunlit breakfast rooms, skylit baths…large customized decks, brick-paved walkways, special landscaping, 2-car garages …and endlessly more…with a staff attending to all exterior maintenance.

Mansion clubhouse, pool, all-weather tennis courts, health club, nature trails and more are all yours to enjoy in a great Westchester location…just 45 minutes from mid-Manhattan…15 minutes from White Plains… near some of the finest schools in the County.

The Estates at Rosecliff. If we were confident enough to show only the backyard, just imagine what the rest is like! Please call (914) 762-3200 for an appointment to tour the grounds and model homes, open daily 10 A.M. to 6 P.M.

THE ESTATES
at Rosecliff

The Manor on Wilderness-Way, Briarcliff Manor, New York 10510 • (914) 762-3200
Sponsor: Briamor Associates • Exclusive Marketing & Sales Agent: RAMS Marketing, Inc.
The complete offering terms for the Homeowner's Association are in an Offering Plan available from Sponsor

DIRECTIONS FROM NYC: Saw Mill or Sprain Pkwy to Taconic Pkwy. Exit immed at Rte 117. Turn left onto Rte 117. Follow until sign for Rte 9 No. Approx 2.7 miles.
Take 9 No. 1½ miles to Scarborough Rd (church on corner). Make right, then make second right onto Long Hill Rd West. Proceed approx. 1 mile to Rosecliff gatehouse on right.

Briarcliff Commons

*Copley Court plan of
two-bedroom apartment*

tino. Nineteen building permits were granted for houses in a development named Cherry Hill Estates on the slope behind Dalmeny Road. In 1988, after five years, five different proposals, and a court action, the Briarcliff Board of Trustees approved a plan for 87 condominium units to be clustered on 10 of the 145 acres of the Briar Hall Country Club to be built by the Pilot Development Corporation of Mamaroneck. The sale price of each unit would be approximately $450,000, including membership in the club. The golf course was to be retained and, with the other club facilities, rented and under new management. At the same time developer Riccardo Tedesco proposed to build Briar Vista Estates, a forty-four-lot cluster of four- and five-bedroom houses on fifty-seven acres off Sleepy Hollow Road. In 1989, one of these houses was on sale for approximately $1 million. The Savoy Development Corporation of Scarsdale was building Copley Court, off North State Road, sixty-six condominiums priced from $214,500 to $425,000, plus monthly taxes and "common charges." Alamit Properties of Purchase was building the Orchard, nineteen houses on twenty-nine acres in and around the orchard of the old Becker farm on Scarborough Road. These houses were to sell for $800,000 to $1,000,000.[2]

In 1973 Stein and Day Incorporated rented, and later bought, Hillside (Admiral Worden's birthplace), renamed Scarborough House, from Roy Anthony's marketing company. Sol Stein, author and founder of the book publishing company, and Patricia Day, his wife and partner, over fourteen years in Scarborough published a variety of works—fiction, nonfiction, and some poetry (this last more for love than for profit). The company operated on a comparatively small annual budget of about $6 million a year. In May of 1987 a creditor, R. R. Donnelley, printers, obtained a restraining order that prevented Stein and Day from publishing, even from paying staff. Stein and Day filed for protection under Chapter 11, in the hope of publishing two seasons' books that had already been catalogued and promoted to the trade, in order to earn enough to pay Donnelley's note and their other debts. The Michigan National Bank, principal mortgage holder on the Scarborough House property, did not allow Stein and Day to publish. Scarborough House on eleven-plus acres, not including land designated as parkland over the aqueduct that crossed the property, had been independently appraised at $2.6 million, but Stein and Day was finally forced to sell it for $1.5 million to Judelson Development Corporation of White Plains, after many other prospective buyers had failed to present plans acceptable to the planning board. A clause in the agreement gave Stein and Day $129,000 for each home beyond ten that Judelson might build on the property. Judelson applied to build sixteen houses. Neighboring property owners, including the president and many members of the River Road Association, supported the developer's petition, but the village planning board recommended and the village board of trustees voted to rezone the property from office-laboratory use to R-40, residential lots of 40,000 feet, which would allow for only ten houses on the property. Stein told Gannett Westchester reporter Robert Derocher[3] that he "felt betrayed. . . . I never thought the elected officials of my home town would act this way in my biggest crisis." Mayor Dorsey said, "We did the right thing for the community as a whole." Despite the efforts of the Westchester Preservation Society, the historic and beautiful Scarborough House was torn down in February 1990. Details of the sad and tangled story of the demise of Stein and Day Incorporated are told in Sol Stein's book on "the corruption in Chapter 11" called *A Feast for Lawyers*.[4]

In 1983, Tetko, Inc., a Swiss screen printing business based in Elmsford, applied for rezoning of the property on Route 9, adjacent to Marlborough Road, that had been the site of Rosemond's Otarion Listener and, until 1977, the headquarters of Thomas J. McLaughlin's Combined Book Exhibit. The William Kingsland mansion (later one of physical culturist and publisher Bernarr McFadden's schools for poor children), which had housed these businesses, had burned down in 1982. Although the decision was controversial because neighbors on Marlborough Road feared possible chemical emissions from the plant, the property was rezoned and the plant constructed.

In the early 1980s, Poly-Flex Corporation, designers, printers and suppliers of polyethylene mailing envelopes for such clients as Time, Inc., the Meredith Corporation, and *Reader's Digest*, built headquarters at 445 North State Road. Barry Neustein, head of the company, also built his home in Briarcliff, near Hardscrabble Road at the eastern edge of the village.

At around the same time, Soudronic, Ltd., a foreign-based company that manufactured welding robots, built a training facility at 465 North State Road.

In 1988, the twenty-nine-year-old master plan was revised. Frederick Wiedle of Frederick P. Clark Associates, planning consultants, wrote a fifty-two-page study proposing that portions of the land zoned for commercial development be rezoned to form a residential town-house bonus district. In these new town-house zones, developers would be able to build six units per acre instead of four if one of those units were moderately priced. Municipal employees and firefighters would have priority for the bonus town-houses, and the prices would be pegged to the median salary of village workers. Parcels considered for this town-house zone were: land to the east of Woodside Avenue between North State Road and Route 100; twenty acres on the east side of Route 9 opposite the Arcadian Shopping Center; and about thirteen acres between North State Road and Route 100, west of Chappaqua Road. In 1989 developer Richard Albert bought this last mentioned parcel for $1,400,000 and it was rezoned to a bonus town-house district.

In April 1989, Briarcliff Manor took first place in the Empire State Local Government Achievement Award Competition for encouraging moderately-priced housing in the village.

In 1988, the village noise ordinance was amended to ban frequent loud construction sounds between 7:00 P.M. and 8:00 A.M. daily and all day Sundays and holidays and any loud sounds outdoors after 11:00 P.M. Noise from stereos, television sets and other electronic equipment was limited to sixty-five decibels, as registered on sound-monitoring equipment at a neighboring property line. All audible burglar alarms were required to have an automatic ten-minute cut-off and to be registered with the village police. Fines for violations were to range from $25 to $250. A tree ordinance was proposed to protect the rural look of the landscape from environmentally unscrupulous developers. Florence Dexter of the Village Conservation Council lobbied for an ordinance like those already adopted by several northern Westchester municipalities to protect trees with trunk diameters of eight inches or more. Members of the Planning Board stated that the village did an adequate job of protecting trees without an ordinance. "We preserve as many trees as humanly possible," said board member and former mayor George Kennard. "We've altered the locations of roads and houses in order to preserve trees."

The problem of burglar alarms may be taken as a sign not only of the advent of the electronic age, but also of a change in the financial standing of residents, especially the most recent. Although there were always people of wealth in the village, especially in Scarborough, many were of middle income, comfortably and not-so-comfortably middle class. Changes in both the number and income level of Briarcliff residents were gradual after the 1950s. Transfers of families in or out, "practically unheard of" in the 1930s and 1940s that Eileen Weber wrote about, were less common in the 1980s than in the two preceding decades, because of the more cost-conscious management of large corporations. Many people moved within the community, from one house to another or from a house to a condominium after retirement. In the 1980s, people of modest means—young families, the children of long-time residents, teachers and village employees—could not afford to buy houses in Briarcliff. The 1988–1989 tax rate was $19.39 per $1,000 of assessed property value. The $6.27 million village budget, adopted in April 1989 raised taxes 4.82 percent. The owner of a median home, assessed at $70,000, would pay $1,420, an increase of $65. School taxes and taxes for the Towns of Ossining or Mount Pleasant, which most villagers paid in addition to the village tax, also increased. Recreation fees increased across the board, tennis/pool permits rising from $255 to $300 for families, although much less for children and seniors. The service fee for licensing Briarcliff's more than five hundred and forty registered dogs, excluding seeing-eye dogs, rose to $10. Fines for parking violations rose to $25 for a first offense and $50 for a second within the year. The cost of a permit to park at the Scarborough train station (if obtainable at all) rose to $160. Water rates rose by 5.6 percent.

Most of the $400,000 spending increase in the village budget would go to social security, state retirement funds, and health insurance for village employees. The village also planned to purchase a new fire truck, street sweeper and police car. In June 1989 an eighteenth officer on the village police force was hired at a salary of $37,802.

The Briarcliff police force in the 1980s, as in the 1940s, was mostly occupied with accidents and traffic violations on the three major arteries that traverse the village. In the mid-1980s, a police officer on routine patrol stopped a car that went through a red light on Route 9A. Someone in the car shot at the policeman, who was wearing a bullet-proof vest and was not injured. The car got away.

Burglaries have been mostly residential and spread out geographically from Chilmark to Route 9 to Camp Edith Macy. In September 1988, Lieutenant Ronald Trainham of the Briarcliff police force told a Gannett Westchester Newspapers reporter that a man described as "a heavyset Caucasian, about 6 feet tall . . . [with] thick, wavy, shoulder-length, blond hair . . . entered the Video Shoppe at the Chilmark Shopping Center . . . pulled a black handgun from the pocket of his denim jacket . . . took . . . cash from the register . . . ordered the clerk to lock the front door and turn off the lights . . . then shoved the woman into the storage room . . . where he raped . . . her." No shots were fired. The miscreant "was last seen driving a tan car with a large number of decals on the passenger window."[5]

Cases of murder are very few in the records of the Briarcliff Manor police. In the 1940s an employee of the Edgewood Park School killed a fellow employee. That case was solved. In the late 1960s a Dr. Shapiro was murdered on his way home from the Scarborough train station. That case was never solved. In November of 1984 an employee of the Sleepy Hollow Country Club was killed in a drug-related incident. That case was solved. In the autumn of 1987, a corpse was found near Route 100. That case was not solved.

Arthur Johnson, Jr.

In the summer of 1989, Briarcliff Manor Trustee William Stewart, a Republican candidate for county legislator at the time, suggested that members of the Briarcliff police force should carry semiautomatic 9mm pistols in place of their .38 calibre, six-shot revolvers, which are, Stewart asserted, " . . . difficult to load, difficult to aim and difficult to fire." Opinion was divided within the police department on the matter, and Chief Arthur Johnson said that he had not considered it. "Village officials could not say when an officer last had to fire his gun in the line of duty."[6]

In January 1990, Police Chief Arthur Johnson, Jr., announced that he would retire in March, at the age of sixty-seven, after forty-four years of service in the department. The village board voted unanimously to appoint as Johnson's successor Lieutenant Ronald Trainham, who had been with the Briarcliff police for eighteen years. Trainham served in the United States Army from 1965 to 1967, studied criminal justice at Westchester Community College, and graduated from the FBI National Academy after an eleven-week management training course in 1986. He told a Gannett Westchester Newspapers reporter, "Being a police officer is one of the most interesting jobs in the world." His salary as lieutenant was $53,950. Chief Johnson's salary was $60,420.[7]

In March 1990, Carolyn Miller, the first female officer on the force, joined the Police Department.

The Briarcliff Fire Department continued to grow, from 1970 to 1990. The Scarborough Engine Company, established in 1972, moved into the newly built fire station on Scarborough Road in January 1975. The first women, Rachel Higgins and Debra Ann Connachio, were admitted to the department in September 1982 and first helped to fight a fire in the same month. Also in 1982, the new engine 94 and the new ladder 40 were put into service.

In the 1970s and 1980s, the department fought several major fires, including a fire at 211 Central Drive in August 1979; the Ossining Car Wash fire on Route 9 in May 1978; the fire that gutted some shops on Pleasantville Road in January 1982; the Combined Book Exhibit (formerly the William Kingsland mansion) fire in April 1982; and two fires, in February 1981, and January 1985, at 162 Old Briarcliff Road. In April 1990, firefighters saved millions of dollars worth of artworks from a fire in the Racolin house on Old Briarcliff Road.

In April 1990, Lawrence I. Reilly, Jr., a third-generation Briarcliff firefighter, was elected chief of the department. His father was a charter life member of Hook & Ladder, and his grandfather was a Briarcliff Village fireman. Reilly's brother, Timothy J. Reilly, was elected first assistant chief, also in April 1990.

The Ladies' Auxiliary of the fire department, since it was formed in 1932, has been at the scene of every fire to serve refreshments. The ladies of the auxiliary march in all the parades with the firemen, and every year hold a penny sale to raise funds and finish the year with a dinner.

In 1959, there were some 103 acres of parkland in the village: Law Park, 7 acres given by the Law family; Pocantico Park, 57 acres beside Pocantico Lake on the border of the Town of Mount Pleasant; Pine Road Park, between Pine and Long Hill East, then 37 acres; and Scarborough Park, 6 acres adjacent to the Scarborough railroad station. The recreation budget was $19,000, and planning of programs and activities was left to volunteers and part-time help. A group of residents lead by Myril (Mrs. Jack) Adler with coach Bill

Bowers, Marilyn (Mrs. Joseph) Bowler and Trustee George Dillon solicited a study of village recreation services by the Westchester County Recreation Commission. The commission's report recommended a full-time, year-round recreation supervisor for the Briarcliff school district to correct the lack of program continuity and planning and as plain good business practice. The village trustees responded by appointing a Recreation Commission of seven (volunteer) residents with a rotating chairmanship. In 1966, Edward Ghiazza was appointed the first full-time director of recreation. By 1980, when the village purchased the Chilmark Club, on 11 acres, as the recreation center, three more parks had been established: the 5-acre Neighborhood Park at Fuller Road; the 4.7-acre Jackson Road Park; and the 3.8 steep acres of Nichols Park. Pocantico Park had been enlarged to seventy acres, and Pine Road Park to sixty-six. Five of the village parks in the 1980s were "active," with facilities such as playgrounds, and tennis and basketball courts. The bicycle path between South State Road and Route 9A was put through on county parkland.

In 1989, the operating budget of the Recreation Department was $540,000. The staff of the department had increased to six full-time, two part-time, and several seasonal employees: the trained and civil-service-tested director and two recreation supervisors, the parks foreman, the parks groundsman and two secretaries—one full-time, the other part-time.[8]

Before the second recreation supervisor was hired as "youth advocate," in December 1988, a resident of Jackson Road had requested police supervision of the parks, where some of the young people were drinking and using drugs. The Village Board held a public hearing to address the problem of teenage substance abuse and responded to the concern expressed by the community by asking Recreation Director Dan McBride to design a youth program. Mayor Dorsey told Gannett Westchester Newspapers reporter Terry Lefton, "They need a place to go with recreational activities. And they need someone to go to if they are in trouble." McBride, who had been working on the project for some time, proposed a two-part program: one, to provide recreational alternatives for seven-to-twelve year-olds; and two, a youth center and a "youth advocacy," to provide crisis intervention and referral and substance abuse education. He estimated the expanded program, including hiring a youth coordinator at an annual salary of about $20,000, would cost $35,000 to $40,000 a year. The village budget adopted in the spring of 1989 included an increase of $34,000 for recreation. On June 13, 1989, the doors were opened to the "Bears' Den," as the young people named their center, which is on the third floor of the Pace University Village Center. In October 1989, Bruce Ferguson, a thirty-five-year-old coach from Duke University, became director of the youth center. By the end of his first month, nearly thirty teenagers were showing up on Friday and Saturday nights. One night in November sixty-four young people dropped in. There are video games, pool and Ping Pong tables and a lounge area with a television. There is usually a basketball or floor hockey game in the gymnasium. A monthly nightclub opened in January 1990 with a disk jockey, closed-circuit television, strobe lights and smoke effects, a small cover charge, and a cash juice bar to pay for these attractions. The rules of the center are few but clear: no drugs or alcohol; no excessive public display of affection; no throwing objects. Ferguson said, "This is a place for kids to relax, get out of the house. I and my staff are the guys that keep it a safe environment."[9]

In 1981, the Rotary Club of Briarcliff Manor was chartered. It was founded by Rotarians from Ossining and Pleasantville, including Mons Grinager of Birch Road, a past president of the Pleasantville Rotary Club. The charter president was Dr. Barry Farnham, then superintendent of schools for Briarcliff Manor, and the president-elect and program chairman was realtor Leonard Young. The first club program featured county legislator Sandra Galef. Since the chartering, the club has grown to a membership of around thirty-eight.

In 1987, following a Supreme Court ruling, the Briarcliff club became one of the first in the country to admit women as members, which previously had been prevented by the wording of the Rotary International constitution, written in 1905. The three charter female members were local realtor and Briarcliff Village Trustee, Freda Delton, Ossining Town Clerk, Marie Fuesy, and People's Westchester Savings Bank Manager Ronnie Hotz.

The Briarcliff Rotary Club donates up to $10,000 a year to such projects as the James Gaffney Community Service Award, Recreation Center improvements, the children's ward of the Westchester County Medical Center, the Ossining Food Pantry, and the Blythedale Children's Hospital, as well as supporting the Rotary Foundation, which offers outstanding undergraduate and postgraduate scholarships. The club took part in a fund-raising campaign named PolioPlus, a worldwide effort to eradicate the disease, and also studied and approved the sponsorship of Project DARE, a drug-awareness program for sixth-grade students that features a local police officer trained to teach a seventeen-week course within the school curriculum.[10]

Roz Abrams, an anchorwoman with Channel 7's "Eyewitness News," and a journalist for almost twenty years, had lived in Briarcliff for four years in October 1989, when she addressed the weekly meeting of the Rotary Club on "the need to keep America great into the twenty-first century." She "looked a bit anxious" but "had little trouble charming the three dozen people who turned out to hear her. . . . " "I'm just a working mother who drives a little Grand Am to work in the city and has to park four blocks away and walk through the snow, rain and hail," she said, and added that she cleans her own house, takes care of her husband and sends her two teen-age daughters to Briarcliff Junior-Senior High School. As she spoke, she recognized in the audience her husband's chiropractor and a local wine merchant from whom she buys her favorite white Zinfandel. She admitted that she still gets excited about interviewing celebrities, especially women like Cher and Oprah Winfrey. "I'm just like everyone else. I'm star-struck too. But you find out that their [celebrities'] homes may not be real clean and they may have fat thighs. You see these finished products but you find there is a common history among all people."[11]

26

Briarcliff Arts and Letters

ALONG WITH the bankers of Scarborough and the millionaires of industry and retailing of Walter Law's old high Briarcliff, many artists and professionals associated with the arts have lived in the village. There have been painters, sculptors, architects, Tiffany glass designers and a leading Japanese bonsai artist; art collectors and an art gallery; journalists, novelists, writers of children's books, social and dramatic criticism, plays and poetry; publishers of books and magazines; a sports broadcaster and a television anchorwoman; actors, directors and producers of theater, film and television; musicians playing a variety of instruments, an opera singer, a folk singer and a symphony conductor. A few of the many are identified below.

Abbott Thayer's "Caritas"

In the late 1880s, the Holdens rented the family homestead, built by Dr. James Holden in 1861, to the painter Abbott Henderson Thayer. Born in Boston in 1849, Thayer studied at the Ecole des Beaux Arts in Paris. He was a contemporary and friend of Childe Hassam, Frank Benson and Winslow Homer, but his work is not classified as American Impressionism.[1] He is best known for his ideal figure pictures. In 1889 he painted the first of his winged figures, now owned by Smith College. Following this he painted the *Caritas* (reproduced here), and the *Virgin*, which hang in the Freer Gallery of the Smithsonian Institution of Washington, D.C., along with the *Virgin Enthroned* and other angel paintings. The models for the *Caritas* (Charity) were Mary Thayer, Gerold Thayer and Dr. James Holden's granddaughter, Harriet.

M. Coburn Whitmore, an artist well known for his pictures and illustrations of beautiful women on magazine covers and in stories, lived in Briarcliff from 1945 to 1965. Born in Dayton, Ohio, he came to the Charles Cooper Studios in New York City in the early 1940s. He is in the Society of Illustrators Hall of Fame, an honor rarely accorded artists who are still alive and working.

Joseph Bowler, when he was just out of art school, joined the Cooper Studios, where Whitmore was his mentor. He is most famous as a portrait painter, and so much in demand

Myril Adler with students in her printmaking studio

"Incident at Rockwood Hall," by Myril Adler

that he is booked for portraits through the 1990s.

In 1955, Jack and Myril Adler, with their young son David, came to Briarcliff to live in one of the houses built in 1949 on Dalmeny Road. Jack Adler, a psychotherapist for children and families, had come to Westchester to work at the Hawthorne Cedar-Knolls School for emotionally disturbed children, where Myril also worked as art director. Myril, who had studied at Brooklyn Museum School and the Art Students' League, had exhibited her work in Paris and in Merano, Italy, in 1950 and 1952. Within a year of the move to Briarcliff, Myril was teaching groups of children and adults, as she has continued to do for more than thirty years. She believes that "every human being is endowed with a creative potential" and provides in her studios "an environment . . . and facilities [an extensive art library as well as art materials] to nurture and promote this . . . creativity." Her teaching programs are comprehensive, including work in all media: drawing, modeling, painting in acrylic and watercolor, collage, construction, and many kinds of printmaking. Students' work has been exhibited frequently in local banks and libraries. Of the hundreds of young people Myril has taught over the years, twenty-seven have gone on to become professionals—in graphic design, illustration, photography, ceramic arts, film and theater arts, architecture, museum administration and art instruction in public schools and universities. Five of Myril's former students are presently studying various fields of art in colleges and universities.

Teaching has not hampered Myril Adler's own growth as an artist. Rather, her students "represent catalysts for new ventures of creativity."[2] Her work—illuminated embossments, intaglio etchings, monoprints, photo etchings and etchings from computer-generated images—has been exhibited in one-woman shows at galleries in New York City, Katonah, White Plains and Yonkers and in innumerable juried and travelling group exhibits in the United States, Europe, North Africa and Russia. Her work is represented in several public and many private collections and has won twenty-five awards, including five first prizes.

Jack Adler, since his retirement as director of professional training at the Jewish Child Care Association in 1984, has been able to devote more time to his sculpture and ceramics. The Adlers' daughter, Sharon, also a gifted artist, has taught art in a New York City public school and at the Metropolitan Museum of Art. The three Adlers have exhibited their work together at galleries in Katonah, Croton and Briarcliff.

In the Patterson family there have been professional artists for three successive generations. Howard Ashman Patterson, born in Philadelphia in 1891, was a well-known painter and a member of the Pennsylvania Academy of Fine Arts. His son, Robert Burns Patterson, is a painter who studied at the Pratt Institute in Brooklyn and works as a television director and producer, mostly of commercials. He has lived in Briarcliff with his family for thirty-two years. His two sons, David and Michael, are painters. Both went through the Briarcliff schools. David studied at the Silvermine College of Art in Connecticut and at Pace University in Pleasantville. Michael has studied at SUNY Purchase. While the work of both young men is primarily representational, it is markedly different. David paints landscapes, mostly in oils, with a very fine brushstroke. Michael, who is more prolific, paints in oils and watercolors and prints from woodcuts, both landscapes and cityscapes, often including human figures. Both show their work mostly at local galleries. The artists of the Patterson family enjoy and take pride in each other's work. When a particularly fine landscape of David's was shown at Images Art Gallery in the village, Mr. Patterson bought it. He explained that he wanted it to remain in its place on the wall of the family dining room, *with* the red dot on it indicating it was sold. A prospective buyer of that picture was persuaded to accept in its place another, similar painting of David's.

Brice Marden, an abstract artist who before he was forty years old had "achieved international recognition,"[3] grew up in the house at 729 Pleasantville Road, built in 1901 for the foreman of Barn E of Walter Law's Briarcliff Farms. The family—Brice's father, Nicholas B. Marden, who worked in a bank, his mother, Kate, and a sister and brother—lived in the house for almost fifty years. For the last twenty of those years the house was threatened by a plan to widen the Taconic. In 1987, it was demolished. All three children went through the Briarcliff public schools from kindergarten through high school. Brice Marden became interested in painting when he was an undergraduate at Boston University, where he majored in fine arts. He was awarded a scholarship to Yale University Art School, where he earned the Master of Fine Arts degree. Marden "first came to public attention with grayish monochrome paintings done with a mixture of beeswax and oil. Reacting against the rhetorical brushwork of second generation Abstract Expressionism, he strove for a single unified surface."[4] When he was in his thirties his work was shown at the Guggenheim Museum, and it was soon represented in the collections of the Museum of Modern Art, the Whitney Museum, the Pompidou Center in Paris, and the Stedelijk Museum in Amsterdam, as well as the Guggenheim.

Brice Marden

Several noteworthy art collections have hung in village residences. Roger Wallach possessed works by old Dutch and English masters and modern French painters. The Vanderlips' Beechwood was liberally hung with Dutch and Italian Renaissance paintings. Vanderlip was proud of "the beauty of my Van Dyck,"[5] a large painting of Andromeda robed in blue that hung in the library.

In the 1970s and early 1980s, the international art dealer Eugene V. Thaw and his wife, Claire, lived at Edgehill (also known as "the brick villa"), on Sleepy Hollow Road adjacent to the grounds of the Sleepy Hollow Country Club. Among the works in their extraordinary private collection were two Cezannes, a still life and a portrait of Madame Cezanne, and a Delacroix. The Alexander Racolins' collection of modern European and American art includes works by Braque, Modigliani and Picasso. Arthur Spear, Jr., of Tulip Road, owns several fine paintings by his father and turn-of-the-century painters who were friends and associates of his father's, as well as a great many paintings of cows by Charles Franklin Pierce.

Marie and Leonard Alpert had lived in Briarcliff for twenty-three years when they opened their art gallery, Images, in 1980. Marie was a working artist, and both she and Leonard were employed by the Sears Roebuck Company, he in data processing, she as an art consultant, buying art to cover half a million square feet of wall space in the new Sears building in New York City. When it was decided to move most of the company to Chicago, the Alperts were unwilling to move with it. They had always wanted to open an art gallery and found this a good time to explore the possibilities. They considered locations all over the county. Then Kipp's Pharmacy moved out of Briarcliff, leaving vacant the corner store at 1157 Pleasantville Road (formerly the post office). The Alperts decided to set up their gallery there because of "the quality of the town—a pleasant place to shop and people with good taste." Marie went to juried shows and developed a list of artists. She knew what she liked, but not yet what would sell. The gallery opened with a show of the work of about nineteen artists, ranging from very realistic to very abstract.

Gradually the Alperts learned to set the outer limits on what would sell. Marie learned to trust her own taste. Echoing Walt Kelly's Pogo, "We have met the enemy and he is us," she said, "I have met my customer and she is I, a person not born to great wealth, educated in art but not of New York museum curator calibre." Leonard "keeps Marie pure," supporting her inclination not to sell reproductions or posters, which are easy to find elsewhere. They are most happy that their business has turned out to be in art rather than gifts or framing. Although Marie does some framing, all the growth has been in wall art and sculpture. The gallery handles the work of about forty-five artists. Around eight of these are local—the Adlers and the Pattersons, Harvey Kidder of Pocantico Hills and Donald McKay and Eleanor Wunderlich of Ossining. Another twelve live elsewhere in the county. Their best-selling artist is Ed Parkinson of Pennsylvania. They usually keep two framed pictures by each of the artists on the wall and three or four in storage.

Architects

The big stone-and-stucco house, now 924 Pleasantville Road, originally Dysart House (see Chapter 9), in the 1930s was the residence of Mr. and Mrs. Arthur Ware and their two sons, Arthur, Jr., and Wilson Peterson Ware. Arthur Ware, Sr. studied painting and architecture at the Ecole des Beaux Arts in Paris from 1902 to 1905. He worked in his father's architectural firm in New York City until his father's death in 1918, when he and his brother, Franklin, reorganized the firm. Among that firm's works were Y.W.C.A. buildings in ten American cities from Galveston, Texas, to Stamford, Connecticut. The firm also designed the swimming pool and auditorium for the New York military academy at Cornwall, New York, the swimming pool building for Mrs. Dow's School in Briarcliff, the Ossining post office and the entrance gate and mortuary chapel for the Sleepy Hollow Cemetery. He took a particular personal interest in the complex of buildings for Marymount convent and college in Tarrytown, which were completed just before his death in 1939. As an avocation, Ware continued to paint "unusually well, particularly in water colors."[6] He designed the stained-glass window in the east transept of the Briarcliff Congregational Church. Not the least beautiful of the church's several fine windows, most of them made by the Tiffany studios, the east transept window depicts a stylized garden scene with the steeple of All Saints Church just visible in the background. The window was made in London by John Hardman's Studios. It is inscribed, "To the glory of God and in loving memory of Walter William Law, 1837–1924, and his wife Georgianna Ransom Law, 1839–1910. This window is dedicated by their children." It was unveiled March 17, 1929.

William Sharman has lived in Briarcliff since he was five years old. He has worked as an independent architect all over Westchester and surrounding counties and in Connecticut. Within the village he has designed many buildings, including the residence of Emile Munier on Pleasantville Road, the S. Amenta residence on Scarborough Road (near the site of William Burns' Shadowbrook), and the brick office building at 1250 Pleasantville Road. Among innumerable additions and conversions he has designed and supervised was the 1958–1959 conversion of the railroad station to the Briarcliff Library.

H. Burke Weigel, his wife, Mary Laura, and their children lived on Scarborough Road from the early 1950s to the late 1970s. Weigel was an architectural coordinator for the United Nations, then worked in Pakistan supervising military installations for the Pakistani government. Later he had his own firm in Stony Brook, New York, where he designed many buildings on the state university campus. He designed seminaries in Albany, New York, Boynton Beach, Florida, and, locally, Saint Theresa's Church in Briarcliff (not including the addition). The Weigels were active in the community, he as head of the Briarcliff Civic Association (now the Friends of Briarcliff), she in the Junior League of Tarrytown, and both, in many fund-raising campaigns. They lived on the corner of Scarborough Road and Becker Lane in the house Weigel described as "stripped-down General Grant—too large for American carpenter, too plain and unembellished for Victorian," with a verandah across the front and curving around to one side and long windows on the first floor with working shutters, which they restored and painted yellow. Mary Laura Weigel remembers that "the driveway was impossible in winter, the house was difficult to heat, but nothing diminished our fondness for it. . . . Our neighbors—to the north, the Dinwiddies, across the road, the Spaights, and way up on the hill to the south, Hjalmar and Claire Hertz—all of them very special and interesting people."

Claire Hertz was a sculptor and schoolteacher. Hjalmer Hertz, the president of the Singer Sewing Machine and Diehl Manufacturing Company, bought land high on the hill from the Beckers in the 1940s, and built his stone house, which commands the finest view in Scarborough.

In 1952 Don and Ginger (Gwen) Reiman started to build their house on Scarborough Road, where they raised their three children. They had both graduated from the Columbia School of Architecture shortly after World War II. Don Reiman worked in partnership with architect Arthur Malsin from offices in New York City for many years until he and Ginger established their own firm, which they moved to Pleasantville Road in Briarcliff in 1974. Locally, Don Reiman designed the residences, among others, of the Burton Benjamins on Holbrook Road and the Jerome Harrises on Sleepy Hollow Road, as well as many additions and conversions. He was the architect of the firehouse of the Archville Fire Company, built in 1966, and of the Ossining public library.

Writers

The first noteworthy local writer, James Barrett Swain was a friend and Scarborough neighbor of Dr. William Creighton. He was editor of the *Hudson River Chronicle*, a small paper published at Sing Sing (Ossining), assistant on Horace Greeley's *New York Tribune*, city editor on the fledgling (1852) *New York Times*, and then Albany correspondent of the *Times*. He is credited with the introduction of the correspondent system.[7] After his Civil War army service and some years of work as an engineer on the staff of Governor Reuben Fenton, he returned to jounalism, reviving, in 1876, the *Hudson River Chronicle*, which was for several years printed in Scarborough at the "Sunnyside Press." The *Chronicle*, a four-page weekly, was discontinued after Swain's death in 1895.

Swain's wife, Relief Davis Swain, was the organist of Saint Mary's Church. When she died, her daughter Florence, then eighteen years old, went to New York City, "where the original organ came from," as Florence Dinwiddie remembered, "and studied how to play it," and took her mother's place at the console. She was the church organist for many years.

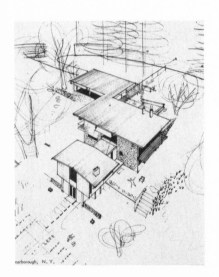

Don Reiman house, Scarborough Road. The Speyer estate brick wall is indicated in the background.

Barrett Harper Clark (See chapter 8), drama critic, author, editor, translator and teacher, studied at the University of Chicago and the University of Paris, then played the season of 1912–1913 with Mrs. Fiske's acting company, as actor and stage manager in New York and on the road. He returned to Europe and studied the theater of France, England and Germany while contributing articles to American and English magazines. A pioneer popularizer of European drama in the United States, he translated several French plays including three by Emile Augier that, in 1913, became the first book ever published by Alfred A. Knopf. He edited fifty-five titles in the World's Best Plays series for the use of amateur actors. He also lectured and occasionally taught at Chatauqua, Columbia, and Bryn Mawr. As editorial advisor of Samuel French, he helped to publicize the work of several young American playwrights. He wrote regular reviews of the New York theater for *The Drama* and other magazines and newspapers. Active in the National Council on Freedom from Censorship, he wrote two pamphlets, "Oedipus and Pollyanna" and "The Blush of Shame." In 1918–1921 he was associate director of foreign language information in Washington and New York, and spent 1922 and 1923 in France and Germany writing on the theater. He was on the Board of Directors of the Provincetown Playhouse and the Group Theater. Some of his principal works are *The Continental Drama of Today*, 1914, *The British and American Drama of Today*, 1915, *Contemporary French Dramatists*, 1915, and *European Theories of the Drama*, 1916. One of his most important books, *Eugene O'Neill: The Man and His Plays*, the first biography of O'Neill and an essential text for the serious drama student, has been translated into more than a dozen languages and is still in print. It is no wonder that H. L. Mencken called Clark "a savagely industrous man." A contemporary biographical reference work describes him as "a serious-looking, bespectacled man with stiff dark hair and lined face which expresses both forthrightness and kindliness."[8]

Barrett Harper Clark

In the 1920s John Hersey came with his family from Tientsin, China, where he was born in 1914, to live in Briarcliff. He was educated in the Briarcliff schools, at the Hotchkiss School in Connecticut and at Yale and Cambridge. For a time Hersey served as Sinclair Lewis's secretary and then worked as a journalist. After 1947 he devoted himself mainly to fiction, but also taught at Yale for more than twenty years. His books include *A Bell For Adano*, which won the Pulitzer Prize, *Hiroshima*, *The Wall*, *A Single Pebble*, and *The Call*, in which the principal character, a Y.M.C.A. missionary, ends his days in a fictional village named Thornhill, close to Ossining, New York.

In the late 1940s Jack Kahn (E. J. Kahn, Jr.), his wife, actress Virginia Rice, and their young son moved to Scarborough from New York City. Through their friends Julian and Narcissa (Vanderlip) Street, the Kahns learned that Charlotte Vanderlip had moved to Virginia with her second husband, Henry Schufeldt, and would like to rent them the house, sometimes called Beechtwig, in the corner of the Beechwood wall on Scarborough Station Road (John Vanderlip's wartime factory, remodeled). Kahn's father, the architect Ely Jacques Kahn, designed a house for the young family, and while it was being built on Holbrook Road, across from the Chilmark gatehouse, they lived at Beechtwig. Jack Kahn had started to write for *The New Yorker* in 1937, while he was still at Harvard, and after his graduation he joined the staff of that magazine. While serving in the army, from 1941 to 1945, he published books of war reporting, including *The Army Life* and *G.I. Jungle*. Before 1990 he had written and published some twenty books, including histories of Coca-Cola and Harvard, a biography of Herbert B. Swope and a memoir about *The New Yorker*. Kahn remembers that "one of the things that made the Briarcliff-Scarborough-Ossining area special in the Fifties was its capacity for creating and nurturing friendships." The three Kahn sons attended the Scarborough School, and from 1959 to 1969 Kahn was chairman of the school Board of Trustees. With his friends Don Reiman, Murray Goodwin and John Cheever, he served as a volunteer in the Scarborough Fire Company, which, with the much older Archville Fire Company, was at that time part of the Briarcliff Manor Fire Department. The Scarborough Fire Company's Diamond T truck was housed in the old Archville firehouse, the second truck in a garage behind the Presbyterian Church. "The Scarborough Fire Company members were a tight group that partied better, *thought* they were better firemen, and ate roast beef and drank India Pale Ale while the Briarcliff members ate baloney sandwiches and drank Rheingold beer."[9] The feasts of the Scarborough Fire Company were presided over and largely provided by Angelo Palumbo, estate superintendent at Beechwood. On May 7, 1956, John Cheever wrote a friend: "There was a back-porch fire in Briarcliff last night. It's the kind of fire that I like to help extinguish. I rode on the engine and nearly fell off."

Ely Jacques Kahn (Senior) also designed the house at the west corner of Ridgecrest and Long Hill Roads for Red Barber, a pioneer in play-by-play sports broadcasting, who was known as "the voice of the Brooklyn Dodgers."

John Cheever

When the Kahns moved into their new house on Holbrook Road in 1951, John Cheever, his wife, Mary, and their two small children moved out of New York City to Charlotte Schufeldt's Beechtwig, where they lived for almost ten productive years. There, at times in one of the rooms off the large living room (where John Vanderlip had manufactured aircraft control terminals), at times in a rented room over the office of the Scarborough Properties down near the station, Cheever wrote all the stories in *The Housebreaker of Shady Hill*, published in 1958, and many stories included in other collections. In that back bedroom—for some weeks in the company of a litter of Labrador retrievers—he finished writing his first novel, *The Wapshot Chronicle*. In the *Chronicle*, Moses Wapshot climbs at night to his beloved Melissa's room over the "chaos of wet roofs" of "the towers and battlements," of Clear Haven, his Cousin Justina's castle. After the novel was published, Cheever wrote to Mrs. Vanderlip to express his gratitude for the privilege and the many pleasures of living on the Beechwood estate and assured her that Cousin Justina and Clear Haven, roofs and all, were entirely fictional. Mrs. Vanderlip, gracious as always, responded that while she had some understanding of the use of facts in fiction, she did recognize the roofs of her house in his description and was astonished that he should imagine she would not know them. However, since Cheever was overcome by vertigo if he so much as mounted a stepladder, it is unlikely that he had any first-hand knowledge of the roofs of Beechwood, or any other house. *The Wapshot Chronicle* won the National Book Award for 1957, and Cheever's *Collected Stories*, many of which were written in Scarborough, won the Pulitzer Prize in 1978.

Burton Benjamin, his wife, Aline, and their two daughters came to live on Holbrook Road in 1955. They were neighbors and close friends of the Kahns, the Cheevers and the Reimans for more than thirty-five years. Bud Benjamin started his career as a journalist while still at school in Cleveland, and at the University of Michigan. Before and after his service as a lieutenant in the United States Coast Guard during World War II, he worked as a reporter for the Newspaper Enterprise Association, and in 1946 he joined RKO-Pathe as a writer-producer-director. In 1957 he joined CBS and became executive producer of documentary broadcast series such as "Twentieth Century" and "World War II" and later of CBS specials such as "The Rockefellers," as well as "CBS Reports." From 1978 to 1981, he served as vice-president, director of news, and supervisor of the development of "CBS Sunday Morning." From 1975 to 1978, he worked closely with Walter Cronkite as executive producer of the "CBS Evening News." His many awards included eight Emmys, a Champion Media Award, and the American Bar Association Silver Gavel Award. Before he retired from CBS in 1985, Benjamin investigated "The Uncounted Enemy: A Vietnam Deception," the controversial CBS documentary about the Vietnam War involving General William Westmoreland. He was asked to do so because "CBS management knew Mr. Benjamin's name would lend the inquiry instant credibility."[10] Concluding his investigation, Benjamin wrote a report finding CBS guilty of serious journalistic lapses. The report was "in its way, a heroic deed." Benjamin's profound loyalty to CBS, after twenty-nine years of professional service to the network, did not alter the conviction, which had always governed his own work, that "the essence of good journalistic practice [is] fairness, accuracy, balance."[11] After retiring from CBS, Benjamin took a fellowship at the Gannett Center for Media Studies at Columbia University and wrote *Fair Play: CBS, General Westmoreland, and How a Television Documentary Went Wrong*. The book was very favorably received. Shortly after its publication Bud Benjamin, age seventy, died of a brain tumor. Howard Stringer, president of CBS Broadcast Group, told a Gannett Westchester Newspapers reporter, "With Bud Benjamin's passing, broadcasting has lost a giant. He was, in many ways, the standard by which news judgment is measured in our industry." The Benjamins' daughter, Ann, a television producer with ABC, told a reporter that her father "loved being at home with his family more than anything else."

Burton Benjamin

Carroll B. Colby, writer and illustrator, after working as a war correspondent (See Chapter 15), went on to research and write more than a hundred books. Best known of these are the Colby Books, designed to introduce young readers to a wide variety of subjects from firearms, airplanes, ships, and space-age travel to wildlife and America's natural wonders. More than two million copies of these books have been sold. Colby was an outdoorsman, a coast-to-coast traveller, and an active participant in community affairs, who lived on Pine Road until his death in 1977.

Carroll B. Colby

Alice (Mrs. Martin Low), who has lived with her family on Sleepy Hollow Road since the early 1950s, is the author of some seventeen books for children and young adults, of poems and lyrics in books and on records, of film scripts and folk-tale adaptations for textbooks. She has compiled several anthologies and book lists. *At Jasper's House*, 1968, a collection of her short stories for young adults, was one of the New York Public Library's One Hundred Best Books of the Year. *Herbert's Treasure*, 1971, a picture book, was a Junior Literary Guild selection. *The Witch Who Was Afraid of Witches*, 1978, was a Children's Choice Book Club selection. "Each book," she has written, "is an exploration, both difficult and exhilarating."

Sol Stein, founder and president of Stein and Day, Incorporated, is the author of eight novels, including *The Magician*, a Book-of-the-Month Club selection, *Other People*, and *The*

Touch of Treason, and two produced plays, *Napoleon* (also known as *The Illegitimist*), a verse drama that won the Dramatists' Alliance prize as "the best full length play of 1953" and was performed at the ANTA Theater in New York and also in California, and *A Shadow of My Enemy*, performed on Broadway in 1957. Stein has also published computer software. His program, WritePro, was the first software selected by the Literary Guild, the Doubleday Book Club and Barnes & Noble.

Publishers

The village of Briarcliff Manor has been the home of many publishers of all sorts. Rhett Austell, a longtime resident, was group vice-president of Time-Life Books. During World War II, John Farrar of the publishing firm of Farrar & Rinehart (later Farrar, Straus & Rinehart, etc.) lived in Scarborough. He was the author of twelve works, including *Portraits*, a book of poems, *Nerves*, a play, and *The Magic Sea Shell*, a play for children. He had worked at the Yale University Press and the publishing firm of Noble & Noble.

Frederick Ungar was a publisher-translator in Austria before he fled the Nazis and established his publishing company in New York City, where over nearly fifty years, he published some two thousand titles on subjects ranging from history and philosophy to science-fiction criticism. He translated some two thousand books, among them Thomas Mann's *Reflections of a Nonpolitical Man* and Erich Fromm's *Marx's Concept of Man*, in its thirty-third printing in 1988, when Ungar, at the age of ninety, died at home in Scarborough. He "worked to the last moment he could hold a pen," his wife, Hansi, told a Gannett Westchester Newspapers reporter.

Arthur Spear, Jr., who has lived on Tulip Road in Briarcliff since 1950, was an editor of the World Book Company of Yonkers for many years before that company was taken over by the publishing firm of Harcourt Brace Jovanovich, under the direction of William Jovanovich, another longtime Briarcliff resident.

Jovanovich, born in Louisville, Colorado, of Yugoslavian descent, graduated from the University of Colorado and attended Harvard and Columbia. He joined Harcourt Brace in 1947 as editor of general and educational books, and seven years later, at the age of thirty-four, became president of the firm. "He built Harcourt from an $8 million company in 1954 to an enterprise with $1.3 billion in revenues in 1990."[12]

In 1953, Jovanovich and his wife, Martha, came to Briarcliff to live, on Horsechestnut Road and later in a large new house on Birch Road. When the major part of the publishing company moved from New York City to Orlando, Florida, and San Diego, California, around 1980, Jovanovich and Martha moved with it, followed a few years later by their son, Peter, and his family.

Among the friends that the Jovanovich family made in the village of Briarcliff Manor was William Brown, part owner with Al Schlechting, the butcher, of Noller's grocery store. Brown told Jovanovich that he was going to night school because he felt dissatisfied with his future in the grocery business. Jovanovich found him a job in warehousing with Harcourt Brace Jovanovich, and Brown sold his share of Noller's and left the East Coast to continue that work in California. The grocery store later became The Gala Buffet, the headquarters, and the chocolate works, of the Dumas family's catering business.

Sol Stein and Patricia Day not only live in the village but also for fourteen years conducted their publishing business in Scarborough. Stein and Day Incorporated was the originating publisher of works by (to name only a few): F. Lee Bailey, famous trial attorney; Elia Kazan, theater and film director; Jack Higgins and Oliver Lange, novelists; and Leslie Fiedler and William Phillips, literary critics. They were American publishers of works, among many others, by J. B. Priestley, Peter Shaffer, Barbara Woodhouse, and three heads of state, including Edward Heath, prime minister of Great Britain. Their publication of the Che Guevara diaries made a four-column headline on the front page of *The New York Times*. Among the bestsellers were *Think: A Biography of the Watsons and IBM*, *The Sovereign State of ITT*, and Kazan's *The Arrangement*, which was number one for thirty-seven consecutive weeks, the biggest selling hardcover of its decade.

Under the imprint of Racolin Press, Briarcliff Manor, Alexander and Dina Racolin published five works illustrated by leading contemporary artists. Robert Rauschenberg made ten silk screens to illustrate *Opal Gospel*, nine poems by North American Indians. The book consists of ten transparent acrylic panels, each with a poem and an illustration signed and numbered by the artist and all encased in a stainless-steel box. Andy Warhol made eleven silk screens to illustrate a text by Philip Greer, titled *Flash*, about the first three days of and after the assassination of President Kennedy. An English translation of *Oedipus Rex* is illustrated by seven etchings by Giacomo Manzu. A selection of poems by Neruda, translated into English by Ben Belitt, is illustrated by ten signed and numbered lithographs by Siquieros. The Longfellow translation of Dante's *Ante-Purgatorio* is illustrated by ten signed and numbered etchings by Jack Zajac.

Books 'N Things

In 1956, Henry and Flora Krinsky opened a bookstore in one of the smallest of the shops in the northwest block of the Chilmark shopping center on Pleasantville Road, just inside the village line. In the first years, in order to meet expenses, Flora, a professional accountant, did outside accounting jobs and Henry did some picture-framing and carpentry. It seemed doubtful that the business would survive competition with the Avalon book and record shop in Ossining village and Fox & Sutherland, the big book/stationery/toy store in Mount Kisco. The Krinskys named their shop Books 'N Things, although they had few things for sale other than books. The community soon responded to the Krinskys' prompt service and encyclopaedic knowledge of literature, and the business steadily expanded, moving in 1963 to the other side of the shopping center into a larger space, which was doubled in 1970. By that time Books 'N Things served a community that extended far beyond Briarcliff Manor and Ossining, and was thought to be one of the best, if not the very best, of the bookstores in the county, comparable to a university bookstore. When an effusive customer congratulated Henry Krinsky on the quality of the store, supposing he must be happy about all the good it was doing, he replied, with scarcely a twinkle, that he hoped it also did some harm. Charles Newman started to work at Books 'N Things in 1969, soon after he left Briarcliff College (see Chapter 21), and when the Krinskys retired in 1977, he and his wife, Diane, who had worked for the store since 1962, bought the business. Ten years later they opened a branch in Tarrytown. Newman finds that his study of literature and the liberal arts was good preparation for the book business, which, he said, "is very hard work, but the customers make it worthwhile." The success of the business is, he believes, a credit to the community.

Katherine Moran Douglas
in her Ossining studio,
circa 1960

Katherine Moran as a flower
maiden in Wagner's "Parsifal,"
circa 1903

Musicians

One of the world's foremost operatic sopranos was born in Ossining and lived in Briarcliff for more than thirty years. Katherine Moran Douglas, daughter of Michael Moran, the influential publisher of the *Democratic Register*, was trained in piano and voice at Miss Fuller's School in Ossining and later under Amalia Jaeger, a pupil of Jenny Lind. In the spring of 1903, a chance meeting brought her to the attention of Heinrich Conreid of the Metropolitan Opera Company. "The majority of artists were then imported from Europe," Kitty Douglas told a reporter, "and Mr. Conreid was about to leave for his annual trip when a family friend, who was a director at the opera, invited my parents and me to luncheon in his honor. Before the afternoon was over, I had auditioned successfully for the Metropolitan, a possibility farthest from my thoughts that morning!"[13] In December of the same year, young Kitty Moran made her official debut in the first stage performance outside of Bayreuth of Wagner's *Parsifal*. At the beginning of her second season she was chosen to go on a scholarship to Germany and Austria, where, then and later, she studied repertoire with the great conductors of the time, including Gustave Mahler. In the 1905–1906 season of the Metropolitan Opera Company she sang with Enrico Caruso in Zlotow's *Martha* and in *Hansel and Gretel*. She was selected by Puccini to sing, with Caruso and Antonio Scotti, in the first Metropolitan Opera Company performance of his *Manon Lescaut*. In the first Italian production in America of *Madame Butterfly*, she sang la Zia. She crossed the continent with the opera company three times, singing in all the major cities. In 1906 the company was staying at the Palace Hotel in San Francisco when the great earthquake struck.

With Caruso, Scotti, and other members of the company, Moran escaped from the quaking, flaming city in a coal cart commandeered by Scotti.

Moran also sang in musical comedies and on the concert stage before her marriage to James Forsythe Douglas, a British wool merchant whom she had met on an Atlantic crossing. In 1913 the Douglases settled in Briarcliff in one of the Spanish-style houses on Pine Road. After her husband's death and further study abroad, she and her daughter, Mary, moved to a smaller house up the hill on Pine Road, where she embarked on the teaching profession, assisting many singers to professional fame and influencing the lives of many more. She is remembered as a strict although gracious taskmaster, "demanding the best from her students and thoroughly grounding them in all vocal techniques." Some she helped at considerable sacrifice of her own time and money, because she believed that "youth and talent must have a chance!" In 1947 she moved from Briarcliff to the old "Captain Aitchison house" on Broadway in Ossining, close to her grandmother's former home.

Folksinger and composer Tom Glazer, known as one of the country's foremost balladeers, lived in Scarborough for almost thirty years. With his wife, Miriam (Mimi), he raised two sons in a house on Long Hill Road. At the start of his career, shortly after the great wave of "big-city" folksinging began, Glazer performed often with Burl Ives, Leadbelly, Josh White and others. His 1946 record album contained the first vocal recordings in this country of "Greensleeves" and "The Twelve Days of Christmas." Many of the records he has made for children, including *Tom Glazer's Concert for Children*, *Ballads for the Age of Science*, and *On Top of Spaghetti*, have been given the National Critics' and Parents Magazine awards. Along with innumerable concerts he has given all over the country, he has appeared on leading radio and television programs, for which he received several Peabody awards, and has composed songs and background music for television and films. He has published more than eight books of songs for children and adults and of fingerplays for children, including *Tom Glazer's Treasury of Christmas Songs*, *A Musical Mother Goose*, and *Eye Winker, Tom Tinker, Chin Chopper—50 Musical Fingerplays*. A *New York Times* reviewer wrote: "The kids vibrate like strings when Tom Glazer, that old sorcerer, sings."

Tom Glazer

Briarcliff has been the home for many years of several dedicated music teachers. Audrey (Mrs. David) Graham majored in music at Brooklyn College and studied at Juilliard and other schools. For thirty-three years she has taught piano in Briarcliff, mostly to Briarcliff children—over the years hundreds of them—and also some adults. A number of her students, including Barbara Mort, Marina Belicka, Carol Hess and Jean Crandall, have gone on to serious careers in music. Audrey has also devoted a great deal of energy and talent to organizing and maintaining the Ossining Choral Society, which has often performed in the Pace University Village Center.

Lucy (Mrs. Arthur) Blachman, a concert pianist who trained at the Juilliard School with Rosina Lhevinne, has lived in Briarcliff since 1965. When her children were very young she cut down on concert work and did some teaching. When she resumed an active playing career, she also taught more, and trained intensively in Suzuki teaching, a modality for beginners of all ages in piano studies. After years of teaching in numerous places, Lucy Blachman has chosen to devote most of her teaching time to her Briarcliff studio, where she gives lessons and holds classes for all ages and levels. She says, "Teaching young people who may make a life in music is a pleasure, but opening the world of music and good playing to a lifetime of enhanced pleasure for the amateur is an even greater joy."

The Blachmans three sons received their early music education in Briarcliff. Two of them, Eric, who plays the saxophone and clarinet, and Neil, a violinist, have made music their careers.

In 1957, Sidney Polivnik came to the Briarcliff schools to direct the instrumental program, including the band, and he initiated the study of stringed instruments. He was an influential teacher and soon became chairman of the music department of the Briarcliff schools. Looking back on his years of teaching, he remembers that "everything seemed to be centered in the schools"; there were community nights when the whole village appeared to be involved. In 1978, Polivnik was voted Teacher of the Year in the district and one of four finalists for Teacher of the Year in the state. He retired in 1983. Students of Polivnik's who have become professional musicians are Dorothy Duncan, clarinetist; the Blachman brothers; Jennifer Graham, oboist; Barbara Mort, pianist and clarinetist; Judy Spoke, violinist; and the Hess sisters, Bonnie, flutist, and Carol, pianist and clarinetist. Many of his former students in other careers still play instruments and pursue musical interests. From time to time old students visit him, and he hears from them from all over the country, even from overseas. He is very happy when they choose to share a little of their lives with him.

Sidney Polivnik's son, Paul, became music director and conductor of the Alabama Symphony in Birmingham in 1985. Before that he conducted the Milwaukee and Indianapolis symphonies. He has been guest conductor of the Los Angeles Philharmonic and many other orchestras in this country and in Vienna, London and Seoul.

Accounts of the Beechwood Playhouse/Julie Harris Theater are in the sections dealing with Frank and Narcissa Vanderlip and The Clear View School, respectively.

Dina and Alexander E. Racolin have co-produced many Off and Off Off Broadway productions in New York, and fringe productions in London. They coproduced five plays, including *Monsieur Amilcar* and *Chekhov in Love*, at Riverwest, and four plays, including the critically well-received *Nasty Little Secrets* at the 45th Street Theatre. Their London productions include *Peter Pan*, *Holmes and the Ripper*, and, by Tom Stoppard, *Artist Descending a Staircase*. In association with the Riverwest Theatre they coproduced *Tales of Castle Nancy*, by Tom McBride, at the Schoolhouse Theatre in Croton Falls, New York.

Afterword

T HE LANDSCAPE has changed and goes on changing. In the 1890s Scarborough Road was "a country road . . . with plenty of dust," where the Dinwiddie sisters remembered "a mixed team of a horse and a cow," pulling a sleeping farmer in his wagon home to the barnyard.

In 1981, David and Caroline Boute bought the northernmost of the two Dinwiddie houses on Scarborough Road. They were a charming couple, he very tall and soft-spoken, she slender and pretty. They had been married just five days before the closing on the house. As a captain in the Marines, David had been wounded in Vietnam and spent a lot of time in hospitals before taking a position with Mobil Oil. Caroline had her Master of Arts degree from the Harvard University School of Design. They moved in at once, although the house had stood vacant for some time and was in disrepair. They set about installing new heating, plumbing and electric systems, working from the ground up to the roof, which they replaced. They had lived in the house very happily for more than five years and started a family before they added the final embellishments, a double stairway on the beautiful old oval porch at the front of the house, a brick terrace with rose planters and Chippendale railings, and a colonnade from the house to a three-car garage with an apartment above it. All this took eight years and a lot of money. Then David Boute's work required the family to leave Scarborough, which they enjoyed and still miss although they are very pleasantly located elsewhere. The house, which the Boutes bought in 1981 for less than half a million dollars, in 1989, was sold a few days after it went on the market for more than two million.

As the landscape changes, so does the population. In the 1990s, the Dinwiddie-Boute house is one of the principal ornaments of what might be called Millionaire's Row. Very big houses on very small lots on River Road and in the new developments off Sleepy Hollow and Dalmeny Roads are creating a landscape that resembles the affluent suburbs of southern Westchester more than the "charming country" of old Briarcliff. The business center, which in 1906 consisted of three stores on Pleasantville Road, in 1990 extends south with some gaps to Law Park on the corner and north across Pleasantville Road and around the corner of Poplar Road and east across 9A to the A&P and North State Road shopping centers. The Chilmark shopping center has more than doubled in size. Noller's, the neighborhood delivery grocery and butcher shop, where customers were greeted by name and waited on by Harry Appel in his "happiest relationship," has been replaced by the Dumas family's gourmet shop and catering service, which often caters as many as twenty parties on a weekend. There are, among other businesses within the village, three liquor stores, three banks, three gas stations, three pharmacies and a funeral parlor.

The "rural look" of most of Briarcliff's residential roads has been preserved, but at a cost. Living in a "strictly residential . . . all year home village," at a convenient distance from the city, yet protected from pollution, congestion and crime, is becoming too costly for any but the very rich. The community will no longer be leavened by a variety of young families like those who came to Briarcliff in the 1950s, by young writers and artists or by retired people living on small fixed incomes. There will be no more single ladies like the Misses Becker and Dinwiddie, who gave so freely of their time and talents. Housewives, who gave so much, today are working away from home in demanding careers or to help support Briarcliff households.

There is bound to be change, and not all of it is regrettable. Some of the newcomers, especially those who have children in the schools, will take an active part in village affairs. Some of the small close-knit community that grew up around the Briarcliff Congregational Church still exists, but it shares influence in the village with other groups centered in Saint Theresa's Church, the Congregation Sons of Israel and several other churches and neighborhoods. The population is ethnically much more diverse, including Hispanics, Orientals and a few middle-class African Americans. The distinction between Scarborough and Briarcliff, once so strongly felt, is blurred. They are just two of the several parts of a much larger village, now reflecting a much larger world.

APPENDICES

Notes

Chapter 1

1. Nicholas A. Shoumatoff, He Who Stands Firm, Tukswit (Wolf Clan), Eastern Oklahoma Delaware (Lenape) Tribe, Unami Division. Written and oral communication.
2. Juet, Robert, "of Limehouse," officer of Hudson's *Half Moon*. Journal. Jameson, J. Franklin, editor. *Narratives of New Netherland. 1609–1664.* New York, 1909. (Juet probably mistook striped bass for salmon, which never swam in the Hudson River.)
3. Verplanck, William E., and Collyer, Moses W. *The Sloops of the Hudson.* New York, 1908.
4. Grumet, Robert Steven, "Children of Muhheahkkunnuck: A Lower River Indian History." *Many Trails: Indians of the Lower Hudson Valley.* The Katonah Gallery, Katonah, New York, 1983, page 18.
5. Scharf, J. Thomas. *History of Westchester County.* Philadelphia, 1886. Volume 1, page 46.
6. Scharf, op. cit., I:19.
7. This claim was recently disproved by documents obtained by Philip Field Horne from Philipse's birthplace in the Netherlands.
8. *The Dictionary of American Biography.* Page 538.
9. Hall, E. H. "Philipse Manor Hall at Yonkers, New York," 1912. Ossining Historical Society.
10. Scharf, op. cit., II:10.

Chapter 2

1. Eckholm, Erick. "Early Records Shatter Image of Indians as Dupes." *The New York Times,* January 28, 1986.
2. Scharf, op. cit., I:160d.
3. Grumet, Robert Steven. *Many Trails.* Katonah, N.Y., 1983.
4. A Plan of the Manor of Philipsburgh . . . John Hill. 1785. Scharf, op. cit., I:opposite page 160f.
5. Scharf, op. cit., I:281.
6. Haight, Ada C. *Genealogy of the Washburn Family.* 1937.
7. Crandall, John. "Buckhout House Housed No Buckhouts." *Saw Mill River Record.* December 26, 1974.
8. Wright, Esmond. "Benedict Arnold and the Loyalists." *History Today.* London. October, 1986.
9. Haight, op. cit., page 247.
10. Deeds, Westchester County.
11. Mt. Pleasant Minute Book, page 39.

Chapter 3

1. Burgess, John. Letters. Greta Cornell, editor. Ossining Historical Society.
2. Scharf, op. cit., II:365.
3. Watson map, copyrighted 1891.
4. Brennan, Louis. *Literature Search for a Cultural Resource Survey of the Beechwood Project* (former Vanderlip Estate), for MTS Associates, 2315 Broadway, New York, N.Y. Typescript, 15 pages plus addenda. Ossining, 1981–82.
5. Pattison, Robert B., pastor of the First Baptist Church of Ossining. Paper read before the Ossining Historical Society, April 1, 1940.

6. Haff-Auchmuty Deed. Beechwood Archive. Briarcliff Manor-Scarborough Historical Society.
7. Lindsley, James Elliott. *This Planted Vine*, Harper & Row, New York, 1984.
8. Scharf, op. cit., II:347.
9. Scharf, op. cit., II:347.
10. Beechwood Archive.
11. Lindsley, op. cit.
12. Beechwood Archive.
13. Beechwood Archive.
14. Shonnard and Spooner, *History of Westchester County*, Harrison, New York, 1974, page 574.
15. *The American Railway.* Reprinted from 1897 edition. Benjamin Blom, Inc., New York. 1972.
16. *Dictionary of American Biography.* 1929. Volume II.
17. *Atlas of New York and Vicinity from Actual Surveys by F. W. Beers, Geo. E. Warner, etc.* New York. 1867.
18. Scharf., op. cit., II:347.
19. Shonnard and Spooner, *Westchester County: Biographical.* New York. 1900. Page 79.
20. Beechwood Archive.
21. Scharf, op. cit., II:329.
22. Knapp, Anne Holden. "The History of the Scarborough Presbyterian Church." Typescript. 1960. (Mrs. Knapp was a granddaughter of Dr. James Holden.)
23. French, Alvah P, Editor-in-Chief. *History of Westchester County, New York.* Lewis Historical Publishing Company, Inc. New York and Chicago. 1925. Volume IV, page 380.
24. Dinwiddie, Marion and Florence interviewed by Bill McClurken and Bob Davis. February 2, 1972. Audiotape.
25. *Briarcliff Manor: A Village Between Two Rivers.* Briarcliff Manor-Scarborough Historical Society. 1977.
26. Knapp, op. cit.
27. Knapp, op. cit. (Mrs. Knapp's older sisters and brothers went to the Long Hill School.)
28. *Our Village: Briarcliff Manor, N.Y., 1902–1952.* Page 46.

Chapter 4

1. Dinwiddie audiotape.
2. Shonnard, Frederick, and Spooner, W. W., *Westchester County, New York. Biographical.* New York, 1900. Pages 78–79.
3. Briarcliff Manor, New York. Honor Roll. Ossining Historical Society War Memorial Booklet. 1989.
4. Dinwiddie tape.

Chapter 5

1. *Briarcliff Manor, A Village Between Two Rivers.* Briarcliff Manor-Scarborough Historical Society. 1977. Pages 23–24. Also Pearson, Alfred H. "Forty Years Ago." *Communique.* February, 1944.
2. Auchincloss, Louis. Commentary in *Maverick in Mauve.*
3. Steele, Chauncey Depew. "Announcement." 1923.

4. Menus, programs and other material about Briarcliff Lodge and The Metropolitan Masons' Country Club courtesy of Gerard LaCroix.
5. "Briarcliff Once a Week." August 23, 1903.
6. Pattison, Robert B. "The History of the Briarcliff Congregational Church. Prepared for the Observance of the Fiftieth Anniversary of the Church—October 18 to 20, 1946."
7. *Briarcliff Manor: A Village Between Two Rivers*. Briarcliff Manor-Scarborough Historical Society. 1977.

Chapter 6

1. Auchincloss, Louis. Commentary. Sloane, Florence Adele. *Maverick in Mauve, The Diary of a Romantic Age*.
2. Shonnard, Frederic, and Spooner, W. W. *Westchester County, New York. Biographical*. The New York History Company. New York, 1900.
3. Shonnard and Spooner, op. cit. Pages 79–80.
4. Auchincloss, op. cit.
5. Knapp, Anne H. "History of the Scarborough Presbyterian Church."
6. Shonnard and Spooner, op. cit., page 78.
7. Knapp, op. cit.
8. Sanchis, Frank E. *American Architecture, Westchester County*. North River Press. 1977. Page 264.
9. Knapp, op. cit.
10. *The New York Times*. October 21, 1896.
11. Knapp, op. cit.

Chapter 7

1. Dinwiddie audiotape.

Chapter 8

1. Told by Eileen O'Connor Weber.
2. The major part of the information in these pages about the early village is taken from *Briarcliff Manor, A Village Between Two Rivers*. Briarcliff Manor-Scarborough Historical Society. 1977.
3. Briarcliff Manor-Scarborough Historical Society bus tour. Audiotape. 1980.

Chapter 9

1. *Briarcliff Manor, A Village Between Two Rivers*. Briarcliff Manor-Scarborough Historical Society. 1977.
2. Told by Eileen O'Connor Weber.
3. Told by Eileen O'Connor Weber.
4. Told by Barrett Clark, Jr.
5. "Briarcliff." The College Handbook. 1931–1932.
6. "The Residence of Dr. Rufus Johnston." *The Pleasantville Journal*. May 28, 1925. Collection of John Crandall.
7. *Briarcliff Manor, A Village Between Two Rivers*. 1977.

Chapter 10

1. Berri, William. *The Carpet and Upholstery Trade Review*, November 15, 1907.
2. Pattison, Robert B. *A History of Briarcliff Manor*. Reprinted from "The Briarcliff Weekly." 1939.

3. *Briarcliff Manor, A Village. . . .* 1977.
4. "A Brief History of Sleepy Hollow Country Club."
5. Vanderlip, F. A. *From Farmboy to Financier*.
6. *The New York Herald Tribune*, August 16, 1960.
7. "Briarcliff in the Hills of Westchester." Briarcliff Realty Company booklet. Ca. 1921.
8. "Metropolitan Masons' Country Club, Inc." Ca. 1927.
9. Told by Dudley Nevison Schoales.
10. *Our Village, Briarcliff Manor, N.Y.*, 1902–1952.
11. *Briarcliff Manor, A Village. . . .* 1977.

Chapter 11

1. Watson Map. 1891. And Brennan, Louis, "Literature Search. . . ."
2. Beechwood Archive.
3. Beechwood Archive.
4. Beechwood Archive.
5. Scharf, op. cit., II:310.
6. *The National Cyclopaedia of American Biography*. Vol. VI. New York. 1889.
7. Crouthamel, James L. *James Watson Webb: A Biography*.
8. *The National Cyclopaedia of American Biography*.
9. Record of Baptisms, Saint Mary's Church, Scarborough, N.Y.
10. Henry, Leland Boyd, D. D. "St. Mary's Church of Scarborough, N.Y." 1962.
11. *The National Cyclopaedia of American Biography*. New York, 1898. Volume I, page 532.
12. *Who Was Who In America*. 1897–1942.
13. Beechwood Archive.
14. Zukowsky, John, and Stimson, Robbe Pierce. *Hudson River Villas*. Rizzoli. New York. 1985.
15. Beechwood Archive.
16. Dinwiddie tape.
17. Vanderlip, Frank A. *From Farmboy to Financier*.
18. Beechwood Archive.
19. Beechwood Archive.
20. Wharton, Edith, and Codman, Ogden, Jr. *The Decoration of Houses. Introduction*. Scribner's. New York. 1902.
21. *Wharton/Codman*. Op. cit.
22. Lewis, R.W.B. *Edith Wharton, A Biography*. New York. 1985. Page 118.
23. Lewis. Op. cit. Page 100.

Chapter 12

1. Vanderlip, Frank A. *From Farmboy to Financier*. Page 100.
2. Vanderlip. Op. cit. Page 35.
3. Vanderlip. Op. cit. Page 24.
4. Watrous, Hilda. *Narcissa Cox Vanderlip*. Foundation for Citizen Education. 1982.
5. Vanderlip. Op. cit. Page 133.
6. *Briarcliff Manor, A Village Between Two Rivers*. 1977.
7. Told by Frank Vanderlip, Jr.
8. *McMillan Encyclopaedia of Architecture*. Volume I.
9. Vanderlip. Op. cit. Page 221.
10. Vanderlip. Op. cit. Page 225.
11. Pierson, Louise Randall. *Roughly Speaking*. Simon & Schuster. New York. 1943.

12. Armstrong, Donald. "Growing Up in Briarcliff." *Briarcliff Manor. . . .* 1977.
13. The Walter B. Mahonys lived on Scarborough Road. Walter B. Mahony, Jr. was an editor of *The Reader's Digest.*
14. Pierson. Op. cit. Page 122ff.
15. Hibbard, Shirley. "An Investigation of the Vanderlip 'Preservation' Project at Sparta, New York." Typescript. 1987.
16. Carroll, Raymond G. "All Over New York." *Public Ledger.* Philadelphia. January 21, 1921.
17. Vanderlip F. A. Letter to Geo. F. Kunz, President of the American Scenic and Historic Preservation Society. November 17, 1920. In Hibbard. Op. cit.
18. Hibbard. Op. cit.
19. *Gary Evening Post.* Gary, Indiana. Nov. 22, 1920. In Hibbard, op. cit.
20. *The New York Times.* April 26, 1927.
21. *The New York Times.* April 26, 1927.
22. *Daily Mirror.* July 3, 1927.
23. Fitch, Murrie Marden. Letter to David Grant after an ad about Beechwood appeared in *The New York Times,* Sept. 16, 1984.
24. Scarborough Properties versus Village of Briarcliff Manor. Court of Appeals of New York. July 7, 1938.

Chapter 13

1. Vanderlip, F.A. Op. cit. Page 157.
2. Vanderlip. Op. cit. Page 236.
3. Robins, Natalie, and Aronson, S.M.L. *Savage Grace.* New York. 1985.
4. Birmingham, Stephen. *Our Crowd.* Harper. New York. 1967. Pages 392ff.
5. Birmingham. Op. cit.
6. Birmingham. Op. cit.
7. Swanson, Susan Cochran, and Fuller, Eliz. Green. *Westchester County, A Pictorial History.* 1982. Page 126.
8. *The National Cyclopaedia of American Biography.* New York. 1944. Volume XXXI, page 493.
9. Told by Frank Vanderlip, Jr.
10. Vanderlip, F. A. Op. cit. Page 80ff.
11. Canning, Jeff, and Buxton, Wally. *History of the Tarrytowns.* Harrison, New York. 1975. Page 290.
12. Canning and Buxton. Op. cit. Pages 290–291.
13. Told by Kay Courreges.
14. "Cholly Knickerbocker," (pseudonym of Maury Paul), society editor of the *New York Journal American* April 26, 1927.
15. Told by Frank Vanderlip, Jr.
16. Vanderlip, F. A. Op. cit. Pages 274ff.
17. Canning and Buxton. Op. cit. Page 222.
18. Told by Frank Vanderlip, Jr.
19. Dinwiddie tape.

Chapter 14

1. D'Alvia, Mary J. *The History of the New Croton Dam.* 1976. Page 45.
2. Reif, Rita. *The New York Times,* May 2, 1972.
3. *The New York Times.* Obituaries. January, 1927.
4. Land Records, Westchester County. Liber 431, page 36.
5. Land Records, Westchester County, Liber Y, page 178.
6. Reif, Rita. *The New York Times.*
7. Reif, Rita. *The New York Times.*
8. Reif, R. *The New York Times.*
9. Caesar, Gene. *Incredible Detective.* Prentice-Hall. Englewood Cliffs, N.J. 1968. page 188.
10. Caesar. Op. cit. Page 107.
11. Caesar. Page 18.
12. Told by Joan Goldsborough, granddaughter of Burns.
13. Kunitz, Stanley, and Haycroft, editors. *Twentieth Century Authors.* New York. 1942.
14. Addis, Harry. "Cheering Section." *Communique.* August, 1942.
15. *The National Cyclopaedia of American Biography.* Volume XXI. Page 494.
16. Crandall, John. "Buckhout House Housed No Buckhouts." *Saw Mill River Record.* December 26, 1974.
17. Crandall. Op. cit.
18. Law Notebooks. Briarcliff Manor-Scarborough Historical Society.
19. Told by Ruth (Mrs. Norman) Simon.

Chapter 15

1. *Our Village, Briarcliff Manor,* 1902 to 1952.
2. *The New York Times,* May 28, 1917.
3. Dinwiddie tape.
4. Briarcliff Manor-Scarborough Historical Society.
5. *The New York Times,* October 1, 1948.
6. Dinwiddie tape.
7. "Communique." January, 1944.
8. "Communique." June, 1943.

Chapter 16

1. *Briarcliff Manor, A Village Between Two Rivers.* 1977.
2. Grinager, Virginia. Gannett Westchester Newspapers. May 29, 1967.

Chapter 17

1. This account of the public schools is condensed from *Briarcliff Manor, A Village Between Two Rivers.* Pages 51 to 58.
2. Gannett Westchester Newspapers. December 30, 1988.
3. Gannett Westchester Newspapers. May 5, 1988.
4. *The New York Times.* July 24, 1988.
5. Gannett Westchester Newspapers. March 14, 1989.
6. Gannett Westchester Newspapers. April, 1988.
7. Gannett Westchester Newspapers. August 20, 1978.
8. "About the Clear View School." Typescript. 7 pages.

Chapter 18

1. Briarcliff Manor, N.Y. League of Women Voters. Bulletin #3. December, 1949. Page 2. Briarcliff Manor-Scarborough Historical Society.
2. Briarcliff Manor, N.Y., League of Women Voters. October, 1957. Vol. 9, Number 3.

Chapter 19

1. *Guideposts.* June, 1985.
2. Borrok, Ronny. "Foreword." Congregation Sons of

Israel Album. 1981. Briarcliff Manor-Scarborough Historical Society.

3. Baratz, Aubrey. *The History of the Congregation Sons of Israel 1891–1966.* Three pages. 1966.
4. *The National Cyclopaedia of American Biography.* Volume 53, page 495.
5. Gannett Westchester Newspapers. Feb. 13, 1977.
6. Gannett Westchester Newspapers. June 2, 1982.
7. Hamilton, Anne M. "Plans and Priorities: An Interview with the President." *King's Life.* Volume 33, Number 3. Spring, 1986.
8. The King's College Catalog. 1984–1985.
9. The King's College Catalog. 1984–1985.
10. *The Citizen Register.* December 9, 1989.
11. Dinwiddie, Marion, and Florence, interviewed by Bill McClurken and Bob Davis. February 5, 1972. Audiotape.
12. Rosenberg, Harriett. "Full House." Gannett Westchester Newspapers. March 28, 1988.
13. Notebooks of Walter W. Law Briarcliff Manor-Scarorough Historical Society.
14. *A History of All Saints Church Briar Cliff.* December 13, 1954.
15. Dinwiddie tape.

Chapter 20

1. "Briarcliff: A Touch of 1962 Class." *The New York Times.* Sunday, September 25, 1977.
2. Buder, Leonard. "Briarcliff College on the Brink." *The New York Times.* February 6, 1977.
3. Gannett Westchester Newspapers. March 12, 1969.
4. *The Patent Trader.* October 22, 1970.
5. Gannett Westchester Newspapers. October 8, 1970.
6. *The Wall Street Journal.* November 14, 1974. Page 243.
7. "Caryatid" was the title of the college literary magazine, adopted years previously as symbolic of the place in society of Briarcliff women, as female pillars.

Chapter 21

1. "Honor Roll. In Solemn Remembrance of the Men of Briarcliff Manor, New York, Who Died in the Service of Their Country." The Ossining Historical Society. 1989.
2. Ossining Historical Society. Op. cit.

Chapter 22

1. Gannett Westchester Newspapers. January 1, 1988.
2. Gannett Westchester Newspapers. February and March, 1986.

Chapter 23

1. Hergenian, Joyce, "Only 15, But She Got the Village to Act." Gannett Westchester Newspapers. February 26, 1971.
2. Gannett Westchester Newspapers. July 26, 1971.
3. Gannett Westchester Newspapers. February 7, 1985.
4. Urban County News, Division of Housing and Community Development. September, 1984.

Chapter 25

1. Daniels, Lee A., "Blending Old Estate with New Project," *The New York Times,* November 18, 1983.
2. The information about development in this section was culled from several newspaper accounts and reviewed and supplemented by the Village Director of Community Development and his staff.
3. Gannett Westchester Newspapers. January 3, 1989.
4. Published October, 1989, by M. Evans and distributed by Little, Brown & Company.
5. September 24, 1988.
6. Gannett Westchester Newspapers. August 21, 1989.
7. Gannett Westchester Newspapers. January 19, 1990.
8. Report of Recreation Department. December, 1989.
9. Gannett Westchester Newspapers. December 2, 1989.
10. Information submitted by Dr. Warren Landesberg. Briarcliff Manor Rotary Club historian.
11. Gannett Westchester Newspapers. October 7, 1989.

Chapter 26

1. Gerdts, William H. *American Impressionism.* Abbeville Press. New York. 1984.
2. Mogelon, Alex. Catalogue of Myril Adler exhibition of graphics and collages at the Hudson River Museum, Yonkers, N.Y. May-June, 1972.
3. Poirier, Maurice. "Color Coded Mysteries." *ARTnews.* January, 1985.
4. Poirier. Op. cit.
5. Vanderlip, F. A. *From Farmboy to Financier.* Page 223.
6. *The National Cyclopaedia of American Biography.* Volume XXVII, page 467.
7. *The Dictionary of American Biography.* Volume IX, page 231.
8. *The National Cyclopaedia of American Biography.*
9. Baker, Michael A. "Where's Archville? The Archville Fire Department History and Dedication since 1909."
10. Boyer, Peter. "Dissecting the CBS Westmoreland Documentary." *The New York Times.* November 28, 1988.
11. Benjamin, Burton. *Fair Play.* Harper & Row. New York. 1988.
12. *The New York Times,* May 30, 1990.
13. Gannett Westchester Newspapers. March 11, 1961.

People Who Have Served Our Community

Mayors

William DeNyse Nichols	1902–1905	John A. Riegel	1951–1955	Fred H. Kossow	1967–1969
Walter William Law, Jr.	1905–1918	Alexander M. Hunter	1955–1959	Frederick G. Butler	1969–1971
Henry H. Law	1918–1936	Robert C. Plumb	1959–1961	Chester L. Fisher, Jr.	1971–1977
Charles H. Schuman	1936–1949	Howard Holmes	1961–1963	George F. Kennard	1977–1983
J. Henry Ingham	1949–1951	Emile H. Munier	1963–1967	Edward T. Dorsey	1983–1990

Trustees

W.W. Law, Jr.	Peter Olney	Robert E. O'Brien	George F. Kennard
J. Sidney Bayliss	Roger Sherman	Robert Arnold	Mary Roegge
V. Everit Macy	Norton Conway	William F. Olson	William A. Wetzel
Richard F.Stewart	John R. Rode	Richard B. Purdy	Barbara Zinke
William McGowan	Kingslant T. Rood	Albert C. Goudvis	James Biezer
Dr. B.F. Curtis	James M. Bisioly	Frederick G. Butler	Charles Strome
Henry H. Law	Harry A. King	Bryan Houston	Freda Delton
Dr. Dwight Holbrook	Robert C. Plumb	Kenneth L. Holmes	Robert L. Cerrone
William C. Holden	Hollister W. Marquardt	James J. McCaffrey	Kathryn Pacchiana
John H. Simpson	Alexander M. Hunter	Chester L. Fisher, Jr.	Edward Dorsey
Oliver J. Bevier	Walter McPhee	Stephen McQueeny	Martin B. Engelhardt, Jr.
Edward Caterson	Howard Holmes	Jerome H. Low	Patricia Knapp
James L. Selfridge	George Dillon	David De Wahl	William Stewart
Isaac C. Hotaling	Emile H. Munier	Jerome W. Harris	Daniel Zucchi
J. Henry Ingham	Fred H. Kossow	Richard W. Murray	Jerome Morrissy
Norman C. Babcock	Franklin Middleton	Anita P. Miller	

Village Adminstrator/Managers

Max Vogel	1966–1968	N. Michael Markl	1968–1973	Lynn M. McCrum	1973–

Village Clerks

Albert Coddington	1902	Idamae Oakley	1952	Lynn M. McCrum	1976–1981
William H. Coleman	1902–1921	Paul Schuman	1952–1970	Imogene N. Fink	1981–
Alfred H. Pearson	1921–1952	Elizabeth Sarich	1970–1976		

Police Department Chiefs

L.H. Bayley	1906–1907	Arthur W. Johnson, Sr.	1939–1963	Joseph P. McHenry	1966–1984
Edward Cashman	1907–1910	Harry L. Addis	1963–1965	Arthur W. Johnson, Jr.	1984–1990
Allan O. Keator	1910–1939	C. Everett Garvey	1965–1966	Ronald N. Trainham	1990–

Fire Department Chiefs

Fred C. Messinger	1901–1911	LeRoy Buck Johnson	1944–1946	Donald E. Heinze	1970–1972
J.F. Dorherty	1911	William A. Magee	1946–1948	Thomas V. Daggett	1972–1974
Fred C. Messinger	1911–1916	L. John Sestrom	1948–1950	Sidney R. Carter	1974–1976
Henry Vandermark	1916–1918	Everett D.D. Bell	1950–1952	James Gaffney	1976–1978
Charles H. Schuman	1918–1919	Fred H. Kossow	1952–1954	Henry Kaufman	1978–1980
Henry Jordan	1919–1922	George F. Sullivan	1954–1956	David L. Crowley	1980–1981
Fred C. Messinger	1922–1928	William H. Bowers	1956–1958	Robert J. King	1981–1983
Gilbert Johnson	1928–1930	Joseph Y. Leighton	1958–1960	Joseph I. Piazzi	1983–1984
Charles Matthes	1930–1936	Edward R. Fitzgerald	1960–1962	William L. Kowack	1984–1986
Rowland H. Doughty	1936–1939	Walter L. Erickson	1962–1964	James Y. Snedecor	1986–1988
Harold L. Lewis	1939–1941	Vincent J. Pancovic	1964–1966	William Kossow	1988–1990
William W. Bevier	1941–1942	Donald F. Kolb	1966–1968	Lawrence I. Reilly, Jr.	1990–
Paul E. Schuman	1942–1944	John J. Kovach	1968–1970		

Public Works

(In 1941 the Street Commissioner and Water Department officials became part of the Public Works Department.)

John Hotaling	1902–1908	Chester Schoonmaker	1921–1941	James P. DiMarzo	1967–1982
L.H. Bayley	1908–1911	Patrick Manahan	1908–1940	Anthony DeCesaris	1982–1987
James Holden	1911–1913	Irving Manahan	1941–1967	Robert Ferreira	1987–
Arthur Brown	1914–1921				

Postmasters

Briarcliff Manor

John Whitson	Vincent Phelps	Edward Fitzgerald	John O'Hagan
Walter E. Howard	Lillian O'Connor	Raymond Daggett	Dolores H. Moro
Charles H. Whitson			

Scarborough

T. Neidi	George O. Fountain	Betty Erdely	Rose McEachem
C. Parker	George Secor	Joseph Di Gioia	Drew Oliver
Charles Timmons			

Superintendents of Schools

George A. Todd, Jr.	1867–1906	Robert C. Plumb	1919–1922	Forbes B. Morris	1957–1963
Edgar L. Andrews	1906–1910	Arthur W. Silliman	1922	Hollis L. Desoe	1964–1968
Charles C. Hunt	1910–1913	Otto E. Huddle	1922–1945	Gardner P. Dunnan	1969–1974
J.C. Lewis, Jr.	1914–1916	John A. Nicholson	1945–1947	Barry Farnham	1975–1985
Horatio P. Baum	1917–1919	Edward A. Moyer	1947–1957	Carol A. Harrington	1985–1990

Board of Education

Joseph Pierce	Nicholas B. Marden	Jacob Evanshon	Susan Dawkins
George A. Todd, Jr.	Henry O. Letiecq	George S. Dillon	Dr. Barbara Stewart
Mrs. E.C. Carter	Emile Brown	William C. Eadie	Dr. Robert W. Murray
Mrs. R.M. Hersey	Mrs. F.S. Sergenian	Charles E. Rodgers, Jr.	Roy G. Dollard
Mrs. Leon Brown	Mrs. G.O. Evans	Jerome W. Harris	Thomas H. Dunkerton
Andrew B. Vosler	Fritz C. Heynen	Harold A. Mandlebaum	Jean H. Flink
Henry B. Valentine	Theodore B. Malsin	Allan A. Michie	Richard W. Murray
Mrs. Sherman Dean	Ralph Lewis	Betty J. Lee	Peter D. Hofstedt
Mrs. William Kallman	Wilbur H. Ferry	Harry K. O'Gara	Michael A. McNerney
Albert Matthes	Raymond R. Ammarell	Dr. Robert D. Dugan	Joan Austin
Lawrence P. Bengert	Virginia Grinager	Thomas B. Shearman	Kathleen Caltagirone
John O. Logan	William F. Matthes, Jr.	William J. Lamb	Ronald Konove
Edward P. Anderson	Benjamin F. Erlanger	Myra Sobel	Helen Krasnow
Mrs. E.R. Beal	Dudley V.I. Darling	Murray Neitlich	Charles K. Trainor
Robert C. Heim	Virginia B. Wuori	Dr. Gerald M. Shattuck	Justine H. Glassman

Library Directors

Louise Miller	1921–1926	Mrs. William Osborne	1956–1963	Mrs. Bryden M. Dow	1965
Elizabeth Kelly	1926–1928	Mrs. Robert Widenhorn	1963	Bettie Diver	1965–1968
Grace B. Hersey	1928–1956	Helen Barolini	1964–1965	Charles Farkas	1968–

Library Board

Dr. Ronald Hanover	Robert Jordan	Walter Florent	Mary Alenstein
Thelma Carter	Katherine Feeks	Donald Wilde	Herbert Mintzer
Ed Zimmerman	Marion Sader		

Clergy Leaders

Saint Mary's Episcopal

William Creighton	1839–1865	Charles W. Baldwin	1914–1951	Paul F.M. Zahl	1982–1988
Edward N. Mead	1865–1877	Leland B. Henry	1951–1965	Nancy W. Hanna (assistant	
Abraham H. Gesner	1882–1895	Stuart Zabriskie	1965–1969	rector)	1986–1989
Thomas R. Harris	1895–1904	William C. Clague	1969–1981	Hillary Bercovici	1989–
Berry Oakley Baldwin	1904–1914				

All Saints Episcopal

J. Breckenridge Gibson	1869–1878	Thomas Hazzard	1902–1907	George F. Bratt	1935–1948
Abraham H. Gesner	1878–1882	Alleyne C. Howell	1908	Constant W. Southworth	1948–1952
A.F. Tenney	1882–1884	John A. Howell	1908–1914	William E. Arnold	1952–1981
A.M. Sherman	1884–1887	Henry A. Dexter	1914–1931	Miles Omaly (priest in charge)	1982–1983
H.L. Myrick	1887–1900	George Whitmeyer	1931–1935	Steven J. Yagerman	1984–
James Sheerin	1900–1901				

Scarborough Presbyterian

Frank F. Blessing	1892–1900	Edmund M. Wylie	1938–1947	Adam W. Craig	1963–1974
Benjamin T. Marshall	1900–1906	Robert P. Montgomery	1947–1956	Robert W. Hare	1975–
Anthony N. Petersen	1907–1938	Roger A. Huber	1957–1963		

Briarcliff Congregational

Alexander A. MacColl	1897–1907	Stanley U. North	1927–1941	Stuart E. Rapp	1960–1971
Carl H. Elmore	1908–1920	Wayne A. Nicholas	1942–1947	Eugene W. Meyer	1972–1980
John E. Steen	1920–1927	Richard K. Beebe	1947–1959	George B. Higgins	1980–

Saint Theresa's Roman Catholic

James F. Kelly	1926–1946	Msgr. James Roberts	1959–1965	Bernard J. O'Connor	1970–1974
Albert A. Pinckney	1946–1959	Msgr. John Harrington	1965–1970	Robert T. Dunn	1975–

Congregation Sons of Israel
(Founded in Ossining, N.Y. in 1891)

Rabbi Wolenchick	–1920	Rabbi Baum	1943–1944	Rabbi Bernard Gelbart	1954–1973
Rabbi Samuel Lifton	1920–1928	Rabbi Samuel Gopin	1944–1945	Rabbi Philip Schnairson	1973–1975
Rabbi Moses Goldman	1928–1937	Rabbi Mortimer Rubin	1945–1950	Rabbi Elliott Rosen	1975–1979
Rabbi Louis Feder	1937–1942	Rabbi David Prince	1950–1954	Rabbi Daniel J. Isaak	1979–
Rabbi Brown	1942–1943	*(Moved to Briarcliff Manor in 1960)*			

Faith Lutheran Brethren

Everald Strom	1960–1963	John Kilde	1968–1973	Joel R. Egge	1979–1988
Silas Bergstad	1964–1967	Harold Peeders	1973–1977	Steven J. Brue	1988–
(Moved from Scarsdale, N.Y. in 1965)		Robert L. Duncanson	1977–1979		

Briarcliff Manor-Scarborough Historical Society Officers And Trustees 1974–1989

William Sharman	Carroll B. Colby	Barbara Cleveland	Arthur Kover	William Ingram
Margaret Finne	Audrey Sharman	Stanley Goldstein	Harriet Olden	Maureen T. Crowley
Edwin Walton, Jr.	Joyce Pandolfi	Barbara Dollard	Rosemary B. Cook	Barbara Lewis
Marion Sader	Debbie Hunter	Helen Murray	Alice Marxreiter	Siegrun Kane
Joy Ozzello	Steve Broudy	Edwin Payne	Robert McComsey	Marjorie Paddock
Edith Bronson	Marian Smidinger	Mimi Donius	Robert Shaffer	Robert Marville
Stephen McQueeny	Janet Byers	Ann Munier	Anthony Stern	Martin Taylor
Marilyn Olson	Fritz Heynen	Clara Eldridge	Winifred Wolf	William Sorsby
Edwin Scott, Jr.	Eileen Collins	Arthur K. Myers	Elsie Smith	Wanda Callihan
Thomas Shearman	Lila Colby	Sherline Dunkerton	Joan Levanti	Anita Hegarty
Eileen O'Connor Weber	Grace Fisher	Livingston Miller	Allen Gowen	Devora Gronauer
Dick Newman	Herbert Mintzer	William Holden	Thomas Stauffer	Robert Gronauer
C. Donald Schuman	Michael Geraci	Richard Banahan	Ellen Heagle	

Bibliography

A History of All Saints Church Briar Cliff: In Commemoration of its Centenary, December 13, 1954.

Archeology of Eastern North America, Volume 2, Spring, 1974, and Volume 5, Fall, 1977. The Eastern States Archeological Federation.

Bolton, Robert, Jr. *A History of the County of Westchester from its First Settlement to the Present Time*. Alexander S. Gould, New York, 1848.

Baratz, Aubrey. *The History of the Congregation Sons of Israel 1891–1966*, 3 pages. The Congregation Sons of Israel, 1966.

Birmingham, Stephen. *Our Crowd*. Berkley Books, New York, 1967.

Boyle, Robert H. *The Hudson River, A Natural and Unnatural History*. W.W. Norton, New York, 1969.

Brennan, Louis. "Literature Search for a Cultural Resource Survey of the Beechwood Project (former Vanderlip Estate)," for MTS Associates, 2315 Broadway, New York, N.Y. Typescript, 15 pages plus addenda. Ossining, 1981–82.

Briarcliff Manor, A Village Between Two Rivers. The Briarcliff Manor-Scarborough Historical Society. White Plains, New York, 1977.

Briarcliff Manor: Our Village, 1902 to 1952. The Briarcliff Manor-Scarborough Historical Society.

Caesar, Gene. *Incredible Detective, The Biography of William J. Burns*. Prentice-Hall, Inc., Englewood Cliffs, New Jersey, 1968.

Canning, Jeff, and Buxton, Wally. *History of the Tarrytowns*. Harbor Hill Books, Harrison, New York, 1975.

Carmer, Carl. *The Hudson*, Rinehart & Company, Inc., New York 1939.

Crouthamel, James. *James Watson Webb: A Biography*, Wesleyan University Press, New York, 1969.

D'Alvia, Mary Josephine. *The History of the New Croton Dam*. 1976.

Haight, Ada C. *Genealogy of the Washburn Family*. 1937.

Handbook of North American Indians. William C. Sturtevant, general editor, Volume 15, *Northeast*, Bruce G. Trigger, volume editor. Smithsonian Institution, Washington, D.C., 1978.

Henry, The Reverend Leland Boyd, D.D. *St. Mary's Church of Scarborough, New York*. 1962.

Hibbard, Shirley. "An investigation of the Vanderlip 'Preservation' Project at Sparta, New York." 1987. Typescript.

Horne, Philip Field. *A Land of Peace, The Early History of Sparta, A Landing Town on the Hudson*. Ossining, New York, 1976.

Kalm, Peter, *Travels in North America*. The English Version of 1770, revised and edited by Adolph B. Benson, Volume 1, New York. Dover Publications, Inc., 1966.

Keller, Allan. *Life Along the Hudson*. Sleepy Hollow Press, Tarrytown, New York, 1976.

Knapp, Anne Holden. *The History of Scarborough Presbyterian Church*. Typescript, 26 pages. August, 1960.

Lewis, R.W.B. *Edith Wharton, A Biography*. Fromm International Publishing Corporation. New York, 1985.

Lindsley, James Elliott. *This Planted Vine: A Narrative History of the Episcopal Diocese of New York*. Harper & Rowe, New York, 1984.

Many Trails. Catherine Coleman Brawer, editor. The Katonah Gallery, 1983.

Pattison, Robert B. *A History of Briarcliff Manor*. Reprinted from *The Briarcliff Weekly*. Briarcliff Manor, 1939.

Pattison, Robert B. *The History of the Briarcliff Congregational Church*. Briarcliff Manor, New York. 1946.

Robins, Natalie, and Aronson, Steven M.L. *Savage Grace*. Dell Publishing Company, New York, 1985.

Sanchis, Frank E. *American Architecture: Westchester County, New York*. North River Press, Inc., 1977.

Scharf, J. Thomas. *History of Westchester County, New York*. Two volumes, illustrated. L.E. Preston & Company, Philadelphia, Pa., 1886.

Schindler, Elizabeth, editor and designer. *Windows to the Past: Reflections on 150 Years at St. Mary's Church of Scarborough*. Scarborough, New York, 1987.

Sloane, Florence Adele. *Maverick In Mauve: The Diary of a Romantic Age*. Commentary by Louis Auchincloss. Doubleday & Company, Garden City, New York, 1983.

Shonnard, Frederic, and Spooner, W.W. *The History of Westchester County, New York*. The New York History Company, New York, 1900. Also 1974 edition. Harbor Hill Books, Harrison, New York.

Swanson, Susan Cochran, and Fuller, Elizabeth Green. *Westchester County: A Pictorial History*. Donning Company. Norfolk/Virginia Beach, VA. 1982.

The American Railway. Reprinted from the 1897 edition. Reissued 1972 by Benjamin Blom, Inc., New York.

Vanderlip, Frank A., in collaboration with Boyden Sparkes. *From Farmboy to Financier*. D. Appleton Century Company, Incorporated, New York, 1935.

Verplanck, William E., and Collyer, Moses W. *The Sloops of the Hudson*. G.P. Putnam's Sons, New York, 1908.

Watrous, Hilda. "Narcissa Cox Vanderlip." Foundation for Citizen Education, 1982.

Wharton, Edith, and Codman, Ogden, Jr. *The Decoration of Houses*. The Classical American Series in Art and Architecture. W.W. Norton & Company. New York. 1978. Reprint from Scribner's, New York, 1902 edition.

Wilstach, Paul. *Hudson River Landings*. Tudor Publishing Company, New York, 1933.

Wood, James Playsted, *Of Lasting Interest, The Story of the Reader's Digest*. Doubleday & Company, Inc., Garden City, New York, 1967.

Zukowsky, John, and Stimson, Robbe Pierce. *Hudson River Villas*. Rizzoli. New York. 1985.

Illustrations and Credits

Although the majority of the illustrations included in *The Changing Landscape* came from the archives of the Briarcliff Manor-Scarborough Historical Society the author and the Society are deeply grateful to all those members of the community who provided material specifically for this volume. Special thanks are due Dr. Charles C. Daly who painstakingly rephotographed many original prints not available to us and who also took a number of photographs expressly for the book.

The following includes all illustrations listed in the order in which they appear. The abbreviated caption is followed by the source, the photographer's or delineator's name where known, and the page on which it appears. In this list the Briarcliff Manor-Scarborough Historical Society is abbreviated BM-SHS.

Index

Purdy, Cynthia, 195
Purdy, Isaac, 24
Purdy, Randall Breward, 190
Purdy, Richard B., 233
Puritans, the, 7

Quakers, the, 7, 15, 55
Quimby, Langdon, 84
Quincy, Edmund, Jr., 136
Quinn, Mr. and Mrs. Arthur, 140
Quinn, Arthur J., Jr., 140; illus., 140

Racolin, Mr. and Mrs. Alexander, ix, 152, 177, 214, 221, 224, house, 208
Racolin Press, the, 152, 221
Racquet Club, the, 104
Radandt, Friedhelm K., 173, 175
Radice, Arthur, 146
Radice, Mrs. Florence, ix, 146
Randall, Maxine, 162
Rapoport, John, 192
Rapp, Stuart E., 235
Rayburns, the, 76, 78
Reaser, Dr. Matthew H., 73
Reif, Rita, 116
Reilly, Lawrence I., Jr., 208, 233
Reilly, Timothy J., 208
Reiman, Don, 151, 216, 218; illus., 216
Reiman, Ginger (Gwen), ix, 216
Remsen family, 29, 85, house, 85, 87
Remsen, Henry Rutgers, 22, 24, 85, 86
Reynolds, William, 123
Rhinebeck, 116
Rhodes, Josiah, 18
Rhodeses, the, 78
Rice, Virginia, 217
Ricks, Charlotte, ix
Riegel, Mayor John A., 148, 233
Ringling, John, 119
River Front Acting Company, 160
River Gate House, 93
River Road Association, 205
Riverdale, 54, 87
Robert Martin Associates, 194
Roberts, Msgr. James, 235
Robinson, Judge Charles P., 124, 132
Rockas, Dr. Leo, 185, 186
Rockefeller, John D., 91, 98, 112, estate (*Kykuit*), 92, 116
Rockefeller, Nelson, 116
Rockefeller, William, 98, 102, 111–113, 133, land, 79, 91
Rockefeller, Mrs. William, 113
Rockwood, Aspinwall estate, 112
Rockwood Hall, Wm. Rockefeller estate, 111, 112; illus., 112
Rodgers, Charles E., Jr., 191, 192, 234; illus., 192
Rodgers, Charles, III, 192
Rode, John R., 130, 134, 143, 233
Roegge, Mary, 233
Rogers, Fanny E., 178
Rogers, Hubert, 116, 147, 179, estate, 116–117, 194
Rogers, Mrs. Hubert, 116
Rogers, Joseph Warren, 28, 177, house (*Hillside*), 18, 28, 94

Romaine, George E., 37
Romaine, George E., family, 37–38; illus., Mr. and Mrs., 37
Rood, Kingslant T., 233
Rood, Mrs. Kingslant, 130
Roosevelt, Mr. and Mrs. Archibald, 98
Roosevelt, Eleanor, 91, 96, 98, 109
Roosevelt, Franklin D., 40, 98, 109, 122, 136, 193
Roosevelt, President Theodore, 89, 119
Rose, Harold, 179
Rose, Marc, 148
Rosecliff, 1, 196
Rosecliff development, 109, 202–203
Rosemond, Mr. and Mrs. Leland E., 124–125, residence, 147, 206; illus., 125
Rosen, Rabbi Elliot, 235
Rosenthal, Richard, 125
Rotary Club of Briarcliff Manor, 210
Roy Anthony's Marketing Innovation Company, 147, 204
Rubin, Rabbi Mortimer, 167, 235
Rudd, Mark, 185
"Rugs to riches," 36
Russell, Rosalind, 137
Rust, Frances, ix
Ruud, Mrs. Joan, 170
Ryder family, the, 122
Ryder, Jesse, 115
Ryder, Lydia and Edward, land of, 25
Rye, 24, 59

S.S. Carmania, 35
S.S. Luciana, 35
Sader, Marion, 234, 235
Saint Mary's Episcopal Church (St. Mary's Beechwood), 18, 19, 26, 29, 55, 87, 113, 133, 147, 175–177, 179–180, 216, 235; illus., 19, 176, 177
Saint Theresa of the Infant Jesus Catholic Church, 79, 140, 157, 166, 191, 196, 216, 226, 235, school, 157; illus., 79, 165, school, 157
Salvation Army, the, 104
Samson, Charles, property, 177
Sanchis, Frank, 52
Sandnes, Tom, illus., 171
Sarazen, Gene, 40
Sarich, Elizabeth, 233
Savoy Development Corporation, 204
Scalzo, James (The Art Shelf), 152
Scarborough, vii, 5, 7, 11, 16, 18, 23, 24, 25, 26, 28, 29, 38, 39, 41, 43, 44, 47, 48, 50, 52, 54, 58, 62, 65, 84, 87, 89, 90, 91, 92, 94, 96, 97, 98, 101, 102, 116, 119, 120, 129, 130, 131, 134, 136, 137, 139, 140, 152, 161, 169, 170, 176, 177, 193, 195, 202, 207, 211, 216, 217, 218, 220, 221, 223, 225, 226
Scarborough Corners, 16, 31
Scarborough Dock, 54, 62, 106
Scarborough Engine Company, 208
Scarborough House, 204, 205
Scarborough-on-Hudson, N.Y. 10510, address, 101
Scarborough Park, 208
Scarborough Players, 138
Scarborough Post Office, 27, 101, postmaster, 139
Scarborough Presbyterian Church, 16, 50, 52–54, 158, 235; illus., buildings, 51, 53; group outing, 54

Patrons

Andre R. Alterr
(In Memoriam)

Mrs. Vincent Astor

John and Wanda Callihan

Rosemary Bonnett Cook

Jack Michael Ferraro & Marianne Ferraro

Carrie Wallach Garrison

Mr. & Mrs. Robert A. Goldschmidt

Alice and Stanley Goldstein

Mr. & Mrs. Jerrier A. Haddad

Michael and Anita Hegarty

Helen and Arne Hovdesven

David and Siegrun Kane

Carlie and David Krolick

Mr. & Mrs. Robert R. McComsey

Mrs. William J. Melady

Jonathan D. Paddock
(In Memoriam)

Lois Rosenthal

Helen Searle
(In Memoriam)

Dr. Tom G. Stauffer

Mr. & Mrs. Daniel E. Zucchi

Designed by A. L. Morris,
the text of this volume was composed in Bem
and printed by Knowlton & McLeary
in Farmington, Maine
on Mohawk Vellum Text.
The jacket was printed on
Warren's Lustro Offset Enamel Gloss
and the endleaves on Strathmore American Text.
The binding in Holliston Mills Roxite
and James River Graphics Kivar
was executed by New Hampshire Bindery
in Concord, New Hampshire.

THE CHANGING LANDSCAPE

has been published in a first edition

of three thousand copies

of which one hundred

have been numbered and signed

by the author.

This is copy number

and is here signed.